Ellis Henry Roberts

Government Revenue

Ellis Henry Roberts

Government Revenue

ISBN/EAN: 9783744725729

Printed in Europe, USA, Canada, Australia, Japan

Cover: Foto ©Suzi / pixelio.de

More available books at **www.hansebooks.com**

GOVERNMENT REVENUE:

ESPECIALLY

THE AMERICAN SYSTEM.

AN ARGUMENT FOR

INDUSTRIAL FREEDOM, AGAINST THE FALLACIES OF FREE TRADE.

BY

ELLIS H. ROBERTS.

BOSTON:
HOUGHTON, MIFFLIN AND COMPANY.
New York: 11 East Seventeenth Street.
The Riverside Press, Cambridge.
1884.

PREFACE.

At the Commencement of Cornell University, in June, 1883, Hon. Samuel Campbell, of New York Mills, proposed to provide for the delivery of a course of lectures on Political Economy, from the point of view of American legislation. Because in many institutions the instruction runs in free trade lines, but less in Cornell University than in many others, he recommended the statement of the protective policy, and of the logical grounds upon which it rests. Upon his nomination a lecturer was appointed, and in February of 1884, a course of ten lectures was delivered to the two upper classes, with members of the Board of Trustees and of the Faculty, and townspeople, for whose convenience Library Hall in the village was occupied.

The Trustees of Hamilton College, at the Commencement in 1883, extended an invitation for the delivery of the same lectures at that institution. The author consented to give a part of the course there in April and May following.

The substance of these lectures constitutes the present volume. It is the embodiment of studies which run back to the early boyhood of the author, when Henry Clay was in his sunset splendor. These studies were extended at Yale College when President Woolsey drew out from undergraduates criticisms upon the text-books then in use there in Political Economy. Labors on the Ways and Means Committee of the House of Representatives directed further attention to the subject. Subsequent examination and reflection and the perusal of various authors have contributed to deepen the convictions which are here urged, as the teachings of history and of logic, of the application of scientific principles to the experience of nations.

OFFICE OF THE UTICA MORNING HERALD,
    UTICA, N. Y., *March*, 1884.

CONTENTS.

CHAPTER I.

INTRODUCTION.

Our Inquiry relates to getting Money for the Public Treasury. — The American System of Revenue. — Political Economy and its Divisions. — Origin of Government. — Society a Necessity. — Grotius. — Locke. — Rousseau. — Hobbes. — Herbert Spencer. — Theocracy. — Divine Right. — All Men have Equal Rights. — Freedom Fundamental. — Order comes from Conflict. — Constitutions. — *Civitate Dei.* — Restraints of Government. — Plato's Republic. — Utopia of Sir Thomas More. — Solomon's House of Lord Bacon. — Law in its Final Analysis. — Evolution of Nations. — Their Divisions. — A Nation has a Distinct Character and Special Tasks. — Nations must continue to Exist. — Is Political Economy a Science? — The Experience of States with reference to Revenue. — The Best Witnesses. — Laws as uniform as any outside of Pure Mathematics 15

CHAPTER II.

OLD WORLD METHODS.

EGYPT. — Joseph and his Brethren. — Pharaoh's Levy on Grain. — Royal Domain. — The Kings seek Profit out of Commerce. — Own the Mines. — Duties on Manufactures. — Personal Service. — Vast Revenues. — First Export Duty. — Kings and Priests forbidden to use Articles not produced in the Country.
THE HEBREWS. — Royal Domain. — Three Tenths. — Presents. — Tax on Merchants. — Solomon's Importations and Trade. — No Sign of Tax on Industry. — Personal Service. — Spoils of Conquered Enemies.
ASSYRIA. — Imports, Exports, and Revenue in Darkness. — Re-

ceipts from the Satrapies. — Institutes of Manou. — Rates on Cattle, Mines, Grain, Sales. — A Capitation Tax. — Discrimination between Raw Material and Finished Silk. — Kings of Persia forbidden to eat or drink anything produced out of the Country.

PHŒNICIANS. — Tyre and Sidon original Ocean Carriers. — Phœnician Commerce based on Domestic Industry. — Hiram's Exports and Enterprise. — Ezekiel's Description of the Commerce of Tyre. — Carthage; its Trade with Cornwall; its Colonies. — Collects Import Duties. — Taxes on the Provinces. — Manufactures under Royal Direction. — The State the Chief Merchant. — Spanish Mines. — Commercial Treaties with Rome.

GREECE. — Tribute of Allied Cities to Attica. — Public Domain. — Silver Mines. — Revenue from Customs. — Tax on Aliens. — Court Fees. — Peculiar Form of Personal Service. — First Direct Tax in Athens. — Assessment on Slaves. — Surplus Revenue of Athens. — Farmers of the Revenue. — Solon's Classification. — Income Tax. — The Peloponnesian War caused by Commercial Rivalries. — Pericles' Boast of Fostering Industry. — Aristotle favors Encouragement and Restriction of Commerce.

ROME. — Revenue from Land. — Taxes by Classes. — Duties on Imports. — The Register of Augustus. — Tributes from the Colonies. — Augustus adds to the Customs Duties; Tax on Salt; Imposes an Excise; Invents the Tax on Legacies and Successions. — Farmers of the Revenue. — Constantine. — Capitation. — Tax on Occupations. — Gifts to the Emperors. — Justinian's Estimates of Peculation.

CHINA. — Its Revenue Methods parallel with those of Western Nations. — Tax on Land. — Charges on Occupations. — Transit Duties. — Salt Tax. — Imposts on Manufactures. — Import and Export Duties. — Sale of Offices and Degrees. — Adjustment of the Tariff after the Wars with Britain.

ITALIAN REPUBLICS. — Prominence given to Manufactures. — The Basis of their Commerce. — The State spared in Taxation the Earnings of Labor. — Great Revenues of Florence. — Customs Duties in Venice.

GERMANY. — Charles the Fifth continues Old Methods. — Austria. — Prussia. — Tax on Land, Occupations, Income. — Modern Enforcement of Protective Policy. — Bismarck's Avowed Purpose. — Hamburg enters the Zollverein.

FRANCE. — Land Tax. — Royal Domain. — Tithes. — Domains of Cities. — Early Reliance on Customs Duties. — Sully and Colbert. — Income Charges. — Turgot. — *Patentes*. — Farming the Revenue. — Octroi Duties. — The Cobden-Chevalier Treaty. — President Thiers restores Protection. — Conventional and General Schedules in the Tariff.

ENGLAND. — Land Tax. — Tithes for the Crusades. — The Great Charter and Merchants. — Direct Tax on London and the Jews. — First Import Duties in England. — First Fruits of the Church. — Benevolences of Henry the Eighth. — Queen Elizabeth and Commerce; Increases Customs Duties. — The Stuarts and the Revenue. — Farming the Revenue. — Monopolies. — Prohibition of Manufactures in the Colonies. — The Navigation Laws. — Lord Brougham. — Loans. — Prohibition of the Growing of Tobacco. — Stewart's Political Economy. — British Budget for 1882. — Movement in England for Fair Trade. — Demand for Direct Taxation in Lieu of all Duties. — Professor Fawcett.

SPAIN AND THE NETHERLANDS. — Evils of Bad Systems. — John De Witt. — Destructive Charges on Land. — Dependence of the Netherlands on its Colonies. — Movement against Free Trade in Holland.

FARMERS OF THE REVENUE. — Cost of Collecting Government Charges 26

CHAPTER III.

MODERN PRACTICES ABROAD AND AT HOME.

Duties on Exports. — On Imports. — Tax on Land. — Public Domain. — Mines. — Monopolies. — Taxes on Liquors and Tobacco. — Railroads and Telegraphs. — Corporations. — Salt, Sugar, Tea, Coffee. — Incomes. — *Patentes.* — Stamps. — Succession. — Lotteries. — Peculiar Sources of Revenue.

TABLE OF REVENUE OF DIFFERENT NATIONS. — Effort universal to collect some Revenue from Commerce. — All Countries except Two adopt a Protective Policy. — Contrast by Numbers. — The Latest Legislation is Protective.

ORIGIN OF PROTECTION. — Not with Cromwell and Colbert. — Goes back to Egypt and Phœnicia. — Acharnians of Aristophanes. — The Strife between Athena and Poseidon. — Cæsar. — France. — England. — Ruskin: "No Nation dares to abolish its Custom Houses." — Fawcett. — Sidgwick. — Appeal to Authority. — Protection sustained *semper ab omnibus ubique* 66

CHAPTER IV.

AMERICAN METHODS AND RESULTS.

The British Stamp Tax for the Colonies. — Pitt's Distinction between Internal and External Taxes. — Commissioners to collect Import Duties. — The Revolution began our Revenue. — The Power to levy Taxes and regulate Commerce conceded to the National Government. — The Architects of the Union Experts in Matters of Revenue — The Second Statute a Tariff. — The Precedent for our Fiscal Legislation. — Madison in advance of Hamilton. — Hamilton's First Report as Secretary of the Treasury. — Tariffs of 1790 and 1791. — Hamilton's Report on Manufactures. — Legislation before 1812. — Report of Gallatin, Secretary of the Treasury. — Internal Taxes of 1791. — Resistance to Law. — Internal Taxes repealed under Jefferson. — Hostile to the Genius of a Free People. — The Public Lands. — The War of 1812. — Fluctuations in Imports. — Secretary Dallas and the Tariff of 1816. — The Debate. — Clay, Webster, Calhoun. — Tariff of 1824. — Convention of 1827. — Debate and Legislation in 1828. — Nullification. — The Clay Compromise. — Fiscal Acts of Thirty Years. — Internal Taxes again. — Effect of the Reductions of Duties under the Compromise. — Election of 1840. — Tariff of 1842. — Report of Robert J. Walker. — Free Trade Acts of 1846 and of 1857. — From Nullification to Secession. — Gold driven from the Country. — The Morrill Tariff. — Increments and Reductions. — Repeal of the Moiety Laws. — Act of the Tariff Commission. — Internal Taxes a Third Time. — Vast Revenues collected in 1866. — Four Periods in our Revenue Legislation. — The Influence of Slavery. — The Southern Confederacy makes the only Attempt to embody in Fundamental Law a Prohibition of Duties to foster Industry. — Limits of the Four Periods by Events and by Time. — Rates of Duties. — The Free List. — National, State, and Local Imposts 82

CHAPTER V.

THE INCIDENCE OF IMPOSTS.

Why are Charges paid to Governments ? — Upon whom do they finally fall ? — *Droits*. — Duties. — National Life. — Charges adjusted to Services; to Sacrifices. — Voluntary Offerings. —

Direct and Indirect Taxes. — Incidence of the Land Tax. — Taxes on Personal Property. — Imposts on Trades and Occupations. — Stamps. — The Poll Tax. — Articles of First Necessity. — Whisky and Tobacco. — Imposts become a Business Risk. — The Stamp upon Matches. — Cigars. — Effects of Imposts on Consumption. — Sugar. — Tea. — Coffee. — Salt in France and England. — Incidence of Customs Duties like that of Internal Taxes. — Duties become an Element of Cost. — Effect of Supply and Demand. — After the Treaty of Ghent British Manufacturers sold in this Country below Cost. — They sought to control our Markets. — British Surplus of Books and Merchandise. — Silks. — Railroad Supplies. — Bessemer Rails. — Undervaluations prove that Foreign Producers pay heavily to enter our Markets. — Growth of American Silk Manufacture. — Fall in Prices. — The Law of Incidence. — Imposts relative to Earnings and Capital. — The Friction of Imposts. — Cost of Collection. — Imposts should not be a Terror. — Should be adjusted to accord Largest Measure of Freedom in Property, Labor, and Home 132

CHAPTER VI.

FREEDOM OF PRODUCTION.

Imposts obstruct Commerce. — They obstruct Production. — The Statesman must aim First at Freedom for Production, not for Trade. — Quesnay: Agriculture the Only Source of Wealth. — The Mercantile Theory. — Locke. — Adam Smith. — Agriculture, Manufactures, Commerce. — Production different from Transportation and Exchange. — How to build a State. — Distribution and Consumption. — Freedom renders Labor Fruitful. — Burke: "The Revenue is the State." — Labor before Exchange. — Domestic Industry Stable. — Commerce Fitful. — Homes. — Henry C. Carey: Diversity of Industry. — Increase of Production. — New Industries offer Fresh Prizes. — Alleged Overproduction. — Sidgwick: "Society is always in a Condition of Underproduction." — Agriculture and Manufactures. — Statistics of J. R. Dodge, of the Agricultural Department. — The Tariff and Production. — Pig Iron. — Manufactures in 1850 and Subsequent Decades. — Mining Industries. — Wealth *per capita*. — Gladstone: the American Republic "the Wealthiest of all the Nations." — Testimony of Bismarck. — Carlyle. — The Tax-gatherers should touch

Production at the fewest Points. — Duties on Imposts limited to the Frontier. — Leave all the Rest of the Country untouched. — No Inquisition 165

CHAPTER VII.

COMMERCE BROADER THAN BARTER.

Shall a Revenue System protect Production or Commerce in Largest Measure ? — The Balance of Trade no Mystery. — The Individual who buys more than he sells tends to Bankruptcy. — Commerce confers Value. — A Nation's Trade only the Sum of that of its Individuals. — Capital, Earnings, Debt. — The American War Loans. — Say. — Mill. — Blanqui. — Coin and Bullion. — The School of Free Trade. — The Attitude of the Nations. — Buckle. — Broad Humanity. — Profits of Commerce. — Balance against Britain. — Margin of Gains. — The Carrying Trade. — British Capital Abroad. — The World's Banker. — France. — American Commerce. — Immigration. — British Exports and Imports. — Exports and Imports of the United States. — Comparative Growth since 1865. — Admission of Sir Thomas Brassey. — "MacMillan's Magazine." — Mr. Gladstone's Prediction of the Commercial Supremacy of the United States. — No Reason to change our Policy. — British System does not even promote Commerce . 203

CHAPTER VIII.

FALLACIES ABOUT MARKETS.

The Place to sell and the Place to buy. — Commerce Complex and Continuous. — Creating Foreign Markets. — The Trade with Brazil. — The Trade with China. — Great Britain and the United States. — The Home and the Foreign Market. — McCulloch's Fallacy. — Two Deposits. — The Whole Apple, or only a Part. — Markets and Government Charges. — Revenue collected at Home. — Aggregate of Taxation. — Shall Labor or Trade support Markets ? — Britain and its Revenue System. — Mr. Gladstone's Statement about Manufactures. — Sir Eardley Wilmot. — "Nineteenth Century." — Raw Materials. — Wool. — Germany. — Protected Industries. — Boots and Shoes. — Our own Markets the Best for us 235

CONTENTS.

CHAPTER IX.

DUTIES, WAGES, AND PRICES.

Many Causes of the Material Development of the United States. — Condition of American Labor. — Benefits of High Wages. — Happiness in the United States. — Industrial Activity and Progress. — Robert P. Porter on Wages. — John Bright on English Wages. — A Cotton Mill in Bolton, England, compared with a Cotton Mill in the State of New York. — A Woolen Mill in Scotland and one in New York. — The Consular Reports. — Report of the Peabody Trust in London. — "Chambers' Journal." — Ratio of Capital, Labor, and Imposts. — Testimony before the Tariff Commission. — Logic of Immigration. — Savings Banks. — Railroad Charges. — Expenses of Government. — Prices of Commodities. — New York and Liverpool Markets. — Details. — Summary. — Cost of Living. — Figures from Consul-General Merritt. — The Charity Organization in England. — Classes of Expenses. — Living in the State of New York. — How Wages are expended. — Retail Prices in the Country. — Clothing from One Tenth to One Fifth of Expenses of a Family. — Purchasing Power of Money tends to Equilibrium. — Efficiency of Labor. — Example in Cotton. — Wages in Britain and on the Continent. — British Production. — American Results. — A Revenue Policy which will strike down Wages cannot be tolerated 264

CHAPTER X.

ALTERNATIVES OF PROTECTION.

Sciences of Administration. — Political Economy an Applied Science. — Cairnes' Classification. — A Professor before the Tariff Commission. — Senior. — The Teachings of Experience. — Political Economy Everybody's Business. — If not by Protective Duties, how shall Government be supported ? — The British System and the American System. — Appeal for Fair Trade in England. — The Cobden Club. — Demand to abolish all Customs and Excise. — Financial Reform Association. — Direct Taxation asked for. — Opposition here to any Tariff at all. — British Taxes burden Labor. — American Imposts fall on Wealth and Waste. — Duties should be adjusted to protect American Industry at Fair Prices. — The Equation of Wages.

— Cotton. — Iron. — Stability the First Need. — German Action. — Exaggeration. — The Chancellor and the Army. — Lasker. — Three Schools of Political Economy. — Incidental Protection: repudiated by John C. Calhoun. — Legislation must affect Production. — Should be Deliberate and Intelligent. — Duties should be Adequate. — Free Trade and Labor. — Free Trade compels Specializing. — We must provide for Growth of Population. — Free Production enlists Idle Capital and Labor. — Enlarges Competition. — Patents give Monopolies. — Complaints of British Workmen. — Complaint in London "Quarterly" on behalf of Property and Land. — London "Spectator" on Free Trade. — The Choice between the American and the British System 308

CHAPTER XI.

THE RIVALRIES OF COMMERCE.

The Protective System interferes with Commerce, but asserts Industrial Freedom. — The War of 1812 and the Rebellion hurt our Carrying Trade. — The Price of British Commerce. — John Bright on Wars waged by Britain. — Professor Seeley's Expansion of England. — The Spanish War and English Foreign Trade. — Three Centuries of Conflict. — Pitt. — Carlyle. — £100,000,000 spent in Thirty Years in Avoidable Wars. — Turkey and Egypt. — Greater Britain. — Trade of the Colonies. — Protection of Colonies against the Home Country. — The Home Country collects Duties on the Tea of India. — Imports and Exports of Britain, Germany, France, the United States. — Turkey and Egypt a Part of the British Possessions in Fact. — The Colonial Trade not Foreign Commerce. — Duration of Nations. — War and Commerce. — State Interference in Britain. — George J. Goschen. — Herbert Spencer. — Freedom at Home 341

CHAPTER XII.

CONCLUSION.

Fallacy of Free Trade. — Fact of Freedom of Industry. — State Interference most Beneficent when exerted in Behalf of Industry. — Freedom most Fruitful in Production. — Free Will most Active in the United States. — Low Wages the Bequest of Ancient Serfdom. — They increase with Population. — They advance with Liberty. — Extent of Territory does not compel High Wages. — Destruction of Caste. — Soldiers. — Clergymen. — Lawyers. — Doctors. — Salaries and Earnings. — Science and Industry. — Pay of Skilled Mechanics. — Rewards of Production. — Advantages of such Rewards. — Professor Seeley's Declaration. — Our Continental Position. — Our Diversified Production will develop Commerce. — Our Flag will return to the Ocean to stay. — Mr. Gladstone's Prediction of our Commercial Supremacy the Echo of our Home Industries . . 365

GOVERNMENT REVENUE.

CHAPTER I.

INTRODUCTION.

Our Inquiry relates to getting Money for the Public Treasury. — The American System of Revenue. — Political Economy and its Divisions. — Origin of Government. — Society a Necessity. — Grotius. — Locke. — Rousseau. — Hobbes. — Herbert Spencer. — Theocracy. — Divine Right. — All Men have Equal Rights. — Freedom Fundamental. — Order comes from Conflict. — Constitutions. — *Civitate Dei.* — Restraints of Government. — Plato's Republic. — Utopia of Sir Thomas More. — Solomon's House of Lord Bacon. — Law in its Final Analysis. — Evolution of Nations. — Their Divisions. — A Nation has a Distinct Character and Special Tasks. — Nations must continue to Exist. — Is Political Economy a Science ? — The Experience of States with reference to Revenue. — The Best Witnesses. — Laws as uniform as any outside of Pure Mathematics.

OUR theme carries us into the field of political economy, that "science of wealth," so wide in its scope, so varied in its branches. I shall ask you to study broadly and deeply the subject of revenue, especially the getting of money for the public treasury. The cognate topic of spending the public moneys will well repay consideration; but just now our inquiry relates to filling the treasury, and not to emptying it. We are to find out about the income of states. Our studies are for a practical purpose: we are not simply to seek what is curious and attractive, but we are to learn what men have done in order to judge what we ought to do. So we are to enter the domain of history, and to apply to its records the light of analysis and of criticism. The theme is very broad, and we shall render it more definite, and on many accounts more instructive, if we try to limit it by directing our investigations to whatever illustrates and establishes the American system of revenue, as it has been and as it ought to be.

Political economy treats of the principles of production, of exchange, and of revenue. The details of production belong to several departments, — to the trades and special industries, to the arts of agriculture and mechanism. The details of exchange divide themselves into the various branches of traffic, — into banking and currency, into transportation and the wide reach of mercantile enterprise, and the multiform mysteries of commerce. The problems of revenue will bring us immediately upon the relations of government to the people. We shall need to speak of production and exchange only as they relate to the income of states.

The origin of government, and of the ideas fundamental to it, have been the theme of much curious theory. If we assume the existence of man, no great mystery attends the beginning of states. For we find order existing everywhere in nature. With the lowest forms of life, system appears. The grasses grow with the regularity of an army with banners. The forests stand arrayed like a multitude of warriors, or scattered like scouts on duty. The flight of birds may have suggested the Greek phalanx and the battle lines of other peoples. Even amid birds of prey a system is apparent in their excursions and their life together. The excellence of the organization of the beavers and the bees is the text of constant study for the naturalist. When mankind gathered in families, and later in tribes, organization sprang out of the exigencies of the situation. Government in its last analysis is little more than the family or the tribe organized. Add to the swarm of bees, to the flock of sheep, to the herd of cattle, to the den of lions, intelligence and a moral sense, and the result is government.

Society is as absolutely a mathematical necessity as the presence of numbers can create, when men find themselves together. That society may be barbarous or civil, and many grades may be discovered in the history of the race, but in its crude form it is as natural a development as the association of the lower orders of existence.

Grotius is the father of the theory that a social compact is the basis of the state. But when man is possessed of sufficient intelligence to frame such a compact, government must already be in existence. The organization essential to agree upon terms of living in a state, is already an inchoate state. Locke did little more than vary the expression of Grotius. Rousseau's social contract is at bottom identical. Hobbes' suggestion, that government is a refuge from a condition of war natural to man, has been explained to rest upon a like basis. His thought was probably the radical and imperative necessity for government, in the nature of man, and thus did not accept the idea of compact. Herbert Spencer conceives a stock company for protection. But that again presupposes the organization which can frame the company.[1]

Historically no social contract has ever been cited, and investigation does not justify any such assumption. On the contrary the early peoples all start from a theocracy in some form. To the Hebrews God spake directly, and bore rule over their commonwealth. Gods were the original rulers of the Eastern as well as the Western states. The monarchical derivation is from on high. Sovereigns never weary of resting their title upon divine right.

The radical principle is that society is the normal condition of man; and that the state, rude it may be, but real, must coexist with it. Where two or three are gathered together, society already has been established, and some form of rule has grown out of necessity. In such society and such a state, all men must have equal rights. They must be as free within that political element as the fish is in the water, as

---

[1] See on this point of social contract Hearn's *Aryan Household*, p. 10.

the bird in the air, as the wild beast in his lair. Thus freedom is no outgrowth of convention; it is the absolute source of all rule, and it springs from divine right in as complete a sense as any human condition can claim to rely upon divine title.[1]

Since thus government is a necessity for mankind, each individual becomes an integral part of it, in the analysis of history, and a vital part. His claim to a place in it is as complete as his right to breathe the air or walk the earth. He owes nothing to any monarch, and derives no share of his rights from the state. For convenience, privileges and obligations, rights and duties, are defined by laws and constitutions; but these all rest on the original manhood of the individual, and on the reason and moral sense which are its chief constituents. Personal liberty is

---

[1] This is the doctrine of the Declaration of Independence. It was most vigorously maintained by James Otis in a paper published in July, 1764. One of its paragraphs is in these words:—

"Government is founded not on force, as was the theory of Hobbes; nor on compact, as was the theory of Locke and of the revolution of 1688; nor on property, as was asserted by Harrington. It springs from the necessities of our nature, and has an everlasting foundation in the unchangeable will of God. Man came into the world and into society at the same instant. There must exist in every earthly society a supreme sovereign, from whose final decision there can be no appeal but directly to Heaven. This supreme power is originally and ultimately in the people; and the people never did in fact freely, nor can rightfully, make an unlimited renunciation of this divine right. Kingcraft and priestcraft are a trick to gull the vulgar. The happiness of mankind demands that this grand and ancient alliance should be broken off forever."— Quoted by Bancroft, *History of U. S.*, vol. iii. p. 80.

not the creature of any political organization; but every government owes its entire claim to life to the necessity which is fundamental to our humanity. Every member of the state holds precisely the same relations to it as his fellow. Age, sex, health, strength, intellect, confer no additional rights under the government. The rights attach to the individual, and not to his conditions. If the state steps in to define its members, it may restrict its privileges, may establish classes, *by force;* but no power exists in reason other than that of the mass of persons who act together for political convenience. They may say that for certain purposes, mature age or the distinction of sex shall be the standard of participation in council and action; and the sword-bearer thus becomes the citizen and the legislator. But absolute equality of rights and of responsibilities, limited only by natural abilities, is none the less the logical demand of the very foundations of all government.

Order does not come without conflict in any field of nature. Among men as among beasts the sway of the strongest is the beginning of authority. Intelligence and morality have a constant struggle with force. Their effort for mastery is the great tragedy of the ages. By it are determined forms of government. After the sway of brute violence comes that of intelligent strength. Then follow gropings for systems and constitutions, and for the full embodiment in statutes of the original right of every member of the state to a voice in its councils and a share in all its blessings.

The culmination of such a progress inspired the dream of the great theologian, who portrays the saints in heaven in no loose disorder, but in *Civitate Dei*, the "Commonwealth of God." To him the citizen was the consummation of the highest ideal.

While social relations must continue, it is not quite certain that the restraints of government must not grow more and more mild and less and less tangible and visible as the human race attains higher degrees of elevation in moral and intellectual character.

The practical statesman is compelled to acknowledge that the greatest minds of the race have agreed in attributing to the state the most intimate and direct control over the individual and his family, over his education, his industry, and his life. The Republic of Plato, the Utopia of Sir Thomas More, the Solomon's House of Lord Bacon are the utterances of the most pronounced communism. But experience has not adopted the theories of these brilliant and consistent dreamers. Common sense has not accepted their philosophy.

On the contrary the tendency of modern statesmanship has been away from the paternal theory, from the demand that the government shall do everything for the subject, and to the broader ground that the individual attains the best development for himself as a unit and as a part of the aggregate through the largest measure of freedom. Government involves restraint. Law may be consistent with the highest liberty, for law is not necessarily compulsion; it is only the expression of the conditions essential to peace and order in the state. The law of the stars and the universe is the record of their courses. In the final analysis law may become the expression of the conduct of the true man. If ever all men become true, penalties will disappear, and the restraints of government will fade away.

While government is a natural development, the sphere within which it acts cannot extend over the globe. There must be divisions. On the family, tribes grew up, then races. Nations were evolved by leaders, or natural lines, rivers and mountains and oceans. The differentiation of language helped to intensify the separations. Nations attained to individuality. They learned the need of self-defense, of independent care, of separate lines of action, of special developments. The man is most useful to the family who is well balanced and self-reliant and industrious; the family is most an ornament to the state when it develops all that is best within itself, and seeks to raise itself and all its members to the highest usefulness and culture. That state again is nearest to the ideal standard which employs all of its energies, which builds up every one of its own resources, which adds everything possible for it to add to the sum of human wealth and power and progress.

The town or parish, the county, the state, are elements of the nation. The specific sphere of each may vary for local convenience. To the outside world the nation is the representative of sovereignty, whether in the republic of the United States, the empire of Britain or Germany, the kingdom of Italy, or the Asiatic governments of China and Japan.

Nations are the great facts of history. They are distinct and they must be recognized. They must continue to stand, so long as various interests and diverse tongues divide men. They have sprung out of the necessities and the conveniences of peoples, as well as out of the strifes and ambitions of rulers. Who can expose the influences which have created nationalities and overthrown them; which have separated and again united races and segments of peoples? Such organizations have had their tasks; they have been and are factors in the movements of humanity. They have been the agents in the triumphs of civilization, and sometimes in its decay. The nation is a vital energy as distinct and separate as an individual. It has its sphere of action, its work to do, its trials, and its difficulties. It has its lines of thought and influence, at particular intervals; as Athens had under Pericles, as Rome had under Julius Cæsar, as England had under Elizabeth; as Germany has now under William and Bismarck; as Britain has to-day under Victoria and Gladstone. Especially has the United States in these days its own position to maintain, its task to perform, its high purpose to subserve. You will find that the man who is most true to his own manhood is the most devoted champion of humanity in its broadest reach. That nation which does its own work most thoroughly, which trains its own citizens to the most complete usefulness and ripest development, serves the whole world most effectually, and adds the most to the achievements and the happiness of mankind.

Philosophy has had its master-minds, who have worked out a glowing period for humanity. They have conceived of various forms of government. They have dealt with problems too profound to be worked out in daily life. They have attained to calmer heights than it can be hoped that men can climb on earth. Not one of them has ever believed that nations will cease to be. Poet and thinker are content to draw fields of perfection, where conflict shall never be heard. They portray a day after

"The nations' airy navies grappling in the central blue,"

when disputes shall be settled —

"In the Parliament of man, the Federation of the world."[1]

Nations must stand to work out the vast aims of civilization. We must accept them as hardly less essential than individual men.

The question whether political economy is a science at all, or whether it is simply an art or even a simple device, or a certain cunning, has long been discussed. The same question has arisen over the whole matter of state-craft, of politics in its broadest sense. At this time we will not enter into that

[1] *Locksley Hall.*

particular discussion. We will inquire into the experience of states with reference to revenue, and try to discover what the long centuries have found by actual tests, and what has been the sum of theory in its effect upon action. Incidentally we will learn what some of the leading teachers have had to say upon this matter; but the first and probably the best witnesses whom we can summon will be the nations that have led mankind along the path of progress. They may inform us that government revenue can be adjusted according to laws as well determined as those of any science outside of pure mathematics. That must be our conclusion, if it shall appear that the experience of mankind points with marvelous uniformity in the same lines of theory and of practice.

CHAPTER II.

OLD WORLD METHODS.

EGYPT.— Joseph and his Brethren. — Pharaoh's Levy on Grain. — Royal Domain. — The Kings seek Profit out of Commerce. — Own the Mines. — Duties on Manufactures. — Personal Service. — Vast Revenues. — First Export Duty. — Kings and Priests forbidden to use Articles not produced in the Country.

THE HEBREWS. — Royal Domain. — Three Tenths. — Presents. — Tax on Merchants. — Solomon's Importations and Trade. — No Sign of Tax on Industry. — Personal Service. — Spoils of Conquered Enemies.

ASSYRIA. — Imports, Exports, and Revenue in Darkness. — Receipts from the Satrapies. — Institutes of Manou. — Rates on Cattle, Mines, Grain, Sales. — A Capitation Tax. — Discrimination between Raw Material and Finished Silk. — Kings of Persia forbidden to eat or drink anything produced out of the Country.

PHŒNICIANS.— Tyre and Sidon original Ocean Carriers. — Phœnician Commerce based on Domestic Industry. — Hiram's Exports and Enterprise. — Ezekiel's Description of the Commerce of Tyre. — Carthage; its Trade with Cornwall; its Colonies. — Collects Import Duties. — Taxes on the Provinces. — Manufactures under Royal Direction. — The State the Chief Merchant. — Spanish Mines. — Commercial Treaties with Rome.

GREECE. — Tribute of Allied Cities to Attica. — Public Domain. — Silver Mines. — Revenue from Customs. — Tax on Aliens. — Court Fees. — Peculiar Form of Personal Service. — First Direct Tax in Athens. — Assessment on Slaves. — Surplus Revenue of Athens. — Farmers of the Revenue. — Solon's Classification. — Income Tax. — The Peloponnesian War caused by Commercial Rivalries. — Pericles' Boast of Fostering Industry. — Aristotle favors Encouragement and Restriction of Commerce.

Rome. — Revenue from Land. — Taxes by Classes. — Duties on Imports. — The Register of Augustus. — Tributes from the Colonies. — Augustus adds to the Customs Duties; Tax on Salt; Imposes an Excise; Invents the Tax on Legacies and Successions. — Farmers of the Revenue. — Constantine. — Capitation. — Tax on Occupations. — Gifts to the Emperors. — Justinian's Estimates of Peculation.

China. — Its Revenue Methods parallel with those of Western Nations. — Tax on Land. — Charges on Occupations. — Transit Duties. — Salt Tax. — Imposts on Manufactures. — Import and Export Duties. — Sale of Offices and Degrees. — Adjustment of the Tariff after the Wars with Britain.

Italian Republics. — Prominence given to Manufactures. — The Basis of their Commerce. — The State spared in Taxation the Earnings of Labor. — Great Revenues of Florence. — Customs Duties in Venice.

Germany. — Charles the Fifth continues Old Methods. — Austria. — Prussia. — Tax on Land, Occupations, Income. — Modern Enforcement of Protective Policy. — Bismarck's Avowed Purpose. — Hamburg enters the Zollverein.

France. — Land Tax. — Royal Domain. — Tithes. — Domains of Cities. — Early Reliance on Customs Duties. — Sully and Colbert. — Income Charges. — Turgot. — *Patentes*. — Farming the Revenue. — Octroi Duties. — The Cobden-Chevalier Treaty. — President Thiers restores Protection. — Conventional and General Schedules in the Tariff.

England. — Land Tax. — Tithes for the Crusades. — The Great Charter and Merchants. — Direct Tax on London and the Jews. — First Import Duties in England. — First Fruits of the Church. — Benevolences of Henry the Eighth. — Queen Elizabeth and Commerce; Increases Customs Duties. — The Stuarts and the Revenue. — Farming the Revenue. — Monopolies. — Prohibition of Manufactures in the Colonies. — The Navigation Laws. — Lord Brougham. — Loans. — Prohibition of the Growing of Tobacco. — Stewart's Political Economy. — British Budget for 1882. — Movement in England for Fair Trade. — Demand for Direct Taxation in Lieu of all Duties. — Professor Fawcett.

Spain and the Netherlands. — Evils of Bad Systems. — John

De Witt. — Destructive Charges on Land. — Dependence of the Netherlands on its Colonies. — Movement against Free Trade in Holland.

FARMERS OF THE REVENUE. — Cost of Collecting Government Charges.

EGYPT.

THE story of Joseph and his brethren presents, with the exception of the spoils of war, the first instance of the collection of public revenue. In the years of plenty, Pharaoh gathered one fifth of the grain in kind; in modern phrase, he levied a tax on land of twenty per cent. of the gross product. Other records prove that much of the soil of Egypt was royal domain, and the only other owners were the priests and warrior classes. From these assessments were made.[1] Joseph's brethren went down to Egypt, as Abraham had gone before them, because that country had long been the granary of the Mediterranean nations. From the royal granaries the Hebrews were supplied. The king was in this way seeking profit out of commerce. He took his tribute also from all merchants who entered his land. The Pharaohs held the mines in their own possession; it appears that they worked them on commission. Proof exists that they levied dues on linen, and doubtless also on other kinds of manufactures. Not only in the case of slaves, but of Egyptians as well, the monarch claimed mastery over the persons and labor of all but the priests and warriors. The complaints of the Hebrews before the exodus exhibit the hardships of the demands. Even with the modern

---

[1] Wilkinson's *Ancient Egypt.*

additions to our knowledge, it is difficult to understand how, with a population never so great as that of the State of New York to-day, Egypt built its pyramids and temples and tombs which overwhelm our estimates of wealth and material forces. When the pyramids were built, that land waged no foreign wars. Afterwards vast treasure was won by conquest from subject nations, but the military array which overran other lands must have been in the first instance established by Egypt itself. The domestic revenue must have been in all ages very great. It came in the largest measure from the soil, especially in the valley of the Nile, from royal domains, and from a share of the products of other cultivators. Commerce contributed its full share, by traffic in the name of the ruler, by charges on traders, and the first example of an export duty is traced to that ancient land.[1] In addition, every industry and all kinds of property were held subject to the royal demands, and the personal labor of all the inhabitants outside of the temples and the army was liable to the calls of the government for cultivation of the royal domain, and for the construction of the vast works which yet testify of the wealth and power of all the dynasties.

Egypt was greater than its kings or priests; for both were forbidden to use any article not produced in the country. The development of all classes of production was thus persistently fostered.[2]

[1] Sinclair.
[2] *History of Political Economy* by Mesnil-Marigny, vol. i. p. 263.

THE HEBREWS.

The Hebrew methods rested upon the soil as the beginning of the revenue. Under the kings the royal domains, the cornfields, vineyards, and pastures were extensive, and received frequent increase by confiscations on slight pretexts of rebellion or other offenses. Large flocks were the property of the rulers. In addition the government collected a tenth of the grain and fruits of the vine and of the flocks, besides the two tenths devoted to the priests and the sacrifices. In the earlier days, as often now in the East, all visitors were expected to make a present of value to the king, and the proceeds from this source were considerable and regular. The tax on merchants passing through the country, as well as on those entering for purposes of trade, was enforced often with rigor. Solomon illustrates the practice of other kings by his ventures in importing gold and silver, ivory, and oriental birds and animals. His ships sailed to Ophir and probably to China, and his caravans must have penetrated far eastern lands. The spices of Arabia poured their perfume into the palaces from every merchant's chest, Tyrian purple and blue decked Hebrew princesses, and the glass of Sidon served for ornament and reflected their beauty; Babylon and Nineveh must have paid their tribute before Assyria achieved its conquest. Except in the nature of the gifts which the kings received, no testimony is afforded that the mechanical industries of the country were taxed. But the kings possessed broad power of extorting personal labor from Hebrews as well as foreigners sojourning in the land. As the Hebrews spoiled the Canaanites on their return from Egypt, so they continued at all times to derive large resources from their conquered enemies, until in their decline they were compelled to pay spoils to their conquerors.

ASSYRIA.

Assyria, like Egypt, must have extorted heavy taxes from its people, for its monuments bear witness of its greatness. But Rawlinson can after all of his investigations only tell us that its imports, exports, and revenue are involved in almost total darkness. The central authority derived a large revenue in money and produce from all the satrapies. These undoubtedly came first of all from the land and its products, and next from trade in all of its forms. By the institutes of Manou in India a tax of one fifteenth was levied on the net revenue of cattle, and mines of gold and silver; one sixth, one eighth, or one twelfth, according to circumstances, on the quantity of grain; one sixth on sales generally, and to adjust this charge a minute statement was required of the cost, the transportation, and the buyer; on the sales of immovables, the tax was one twentieth.[1] Traces of a capitation tax are found.[2] Heavier duties were levied on silk fabrics than on the raw

[1] Marigny.   [2] De Parieu.

material, for the encouragement of the weaver and dyer. With all his power, the king of Persia was forbidden to eat or drink anything produced out of the country. In emergency in India one fourth of the property of the subjects could be taken by law. It was by the strong hand of despotism that treasure was collected to equip the armies of Darius and Cyrus, and to send the fleet of Xerxes to Salamis.

THE PHŒNICIANS.

Out of the mystery surrounding the people who gave letters to the Western nations, the splendors of Phœnician commerce illumine all seas and all lands to far eastern Asia and the British Isles. Tyre and Sidon, and their greater daughter Carthage, were the original ocean carriers, and the leaders in the mastery of commerce. Hiram was the pioneer of Solomon in both the Eastern and the Western trade. Carthage risked voyages on the Atlantic, and created traffic more varied than any other nation of its own day. Phœnician commerce had for a basis domestic products and diversified industry. Cedars from Lebanon and wheat for food and pure oil were sent to the king of Jerusalem, and cunning work in brass and fabrics beautiful in purple and fine in blue, demonstrated the skill of Hiram and his workmen. Modern enterprise can justify no more gorgeous description than Ezekiel portrays of the commerce of Tyre, with its sails of broidered work. Much of this traffic was transacted for the profit of the ruler; it was Hiram himself who furnished Solomon with the cedar of Lebanon and with implements of brass, and who joined him in ventures to Tarshish and to Ophir. So Carthage in its extensive commerce maintained monopolies from which the state drew large profits. It was on account of the state that the mines of Spain were worked, and that tin was brought from far-off Cornwall. By no government, ancient or modern, has a greater share of the world's trade ever been concentrated. It was for the sake of commerce that Phœnician and afterwards Carthagenian colonies were established really as trading factories. Upon commerce conducted by private persons heavy import duties were collected. In addition, taxes were levied on the provinces and cities subject to Carthage, from the provinces in kind, and from the cities in money. These were the sources of revenue for the Phœnician cities; the domestic manufactures were under royal direction; to foreign commerce Phœnician energy devoted itself, and the state was the chief merchant. Except as personal service is implied no other taxes upon the citizens of the capital are indicated. In the provinces it is plain that some assessments were made upon the products of the soil.

From its commerce, "very glorious in the midst of the seas," Tyre derived vast resources; and Carthage obtained from its Spanish mines alone the moneys necessary for carrying on its second great war with Rome. During the intense rivalries with its enemy and final conqueror, Carthage framed with it two commercial treaties, forerunners of methods boastfully claimed for our own times.

GREECE.

At the culmination of Greek power, when Attica held the hegemony and Pericles was rendering Athens the glory of the confederation, the revenue of the state came in chief measure from the tribute of the allied cities. Grote estimates three fifths from that source. Attica held for itself landed property in city and country, pastures and woods and olive-groves, and the silver mines at Laurium contributed steadily to its treasures.[1] The other states owned public domain, and some of them transferred the title, and not simply the income, to the head of the confederation. Athens, with its wide commerce, derived revenue from customs, as in less degree did other states of the peninsula. Export duties were regularly collected. Resident aliens paid a tax on persons as well as for license to trade. The court fees were large, and more than sufficient to cover the

---

[1] Aristophanes, in his *Wasps*, gives this summary:—

"Count lightly, not with calculi,
But on the fingers, what a sum of tribute
Comes to us from the cities, and besides,
The many hundredths, Prytanean pledges,
The metals, markets, harbors, salaries,
And sale of public confiscations.
From these we draw nearly two thousand talents."
(Wheelwright's Translation, lines 709-715.)

costs of the suits. Personal service took a peculiar form, owing to the intensity of Athenian patriotism. The chief citizens fitted out ships and manned them at their own cost; they undertook the support and direction of the choruses in the theatre, and of the public games, the entertainment of foreign guests, and the celebrations of a religious and official nature. These were the only charges paid by the Athenians for a long time; and it is cited as a notable exception that in the disasters of the fourth year of the Peloponnesian War they were for the first time forced to pay a direct tax.[1] Owners of slaves were assessed according to their number, and harbor and market dues were collected. Athens stands out as the only ancient state which was accustomed to gather a surplus of revenue in times of peace in preparation for war; and especially under Pericles this practice was maintained. To attack Syracuse Athens had three thousand talents, or three million four hundred and fifty thousand dollars, in its treasury; and when Chios revolted, a third as much had been saved to defend Piræus from a hostile fleet. The mines, the lands, and the customs were intrusted to farmers of the revenue, and not to officers of the government.[2]

The classification of citizens by Solon according to their annual income does not appear to have been for purposes of taxation; it was the basis of political power. Yet it has historical significance in financial legislation, as a prophecy of levying government

[1] Grote. [2] Curtius.

charges by classes, and especially of the income tax, which has been attributed as a discovery to other law-makers.

Commercial rivalries were the cause of some of the greatest of Greek wars. The Athenians excluded the Megarians from their markets; and Sparta by trying to force an unwelcome trade upon them brought on the Peloponnesian War. After the defeat of Ægos-Potamos, Corinth demanded that its commercial rival, Athens, should be destroyed; but Sparta refused its assent to the cruel proposition. No people ever made greater efforts to provide for production at home. Pericles in his famous speech boasts of giving employment to all at Athens, and his successors in the government were themselves tradesmen and mechanics, as Aristophanes shows in his comedies. Xenophon complains that in order to control their trade craftsmen kept their processes secret. Aristotle, in his "Rhetoric," insists that commerce must, according to circumstances, submit to many restrictions and receive encouragements. Obviously his plan is a protective system.

ROME.

The land was the original dependence of Rome for its revenues. The state claimed at the outset much of the soil, and as colonies were planted the territory became public property. As early as Servius Tullius the citizens were divided into six classes and these into centuries, first for military purposes, and yet according to wealth. Taxes came to be apportioned to these classes, and thus they partook of the nature both of capitation and income charges. Duties were levied upon imports from a remote period. Gibbon pathetically remarks: "History has never, perhaps, suffered a greater or more irreparable injury than in the loss of the curious register bequeathed by Augustus to the Senate, in which that experienced prince so accurately balanced the revenues and expenses of the Roman empire."[1] That register would show the monstrous tributes collected from the provinces through the oppressions of the proconsuls, when Asia paid as much as twenty-one million dollars a year, Egypt more than eleven million dollars, and Carthage a war indemnity of twenty million dollars to be paid within fifty years out of its ruins. Guizot and Wenck estimate the annual tributes in the time of Augustus at not less than two hundred million dollars.[2] That sum, when money was worth perhaps eight times what it is now, ought to have sufficed for all the expenditures of the empire. But it was one of the first tasks of that emperor to add to the customs duties which Julius Cæsar had restored from ancient practice,[3] and to extend the system; the duties ranged from an eighth to a fortieth of the value of the commodity. The excise dates from the time of Augustus; it was always a low rate, but it covered all sales of real or

---

[1] Gibbon's *Decline and Fall*, vol. i. p. 187.
[2] Vol. i. p. 189.   [3] Merivale, vol. iii. p. 545.

personal property, even to the small items of the retailer for daily use. Augustus seems to have been the inventor of the tax on legacies and successions; it was to be five per cent. on all inheritances exceeding a certain value to any others than the nearest of kin on the father's side. The farmers of the revenue were the objects of frequent complaints, and of occasional efforts by statutes to restrict their exactions.

Constantine attempted to apply a more arbitrary and direct method of taxation. His commissioners extorted a share in the produce of the land in kind, and the historian testifies that the agriculture of the provinces was insensibly ruined.[1] The assessment partook of the substance of a land tax with the forms of a capitation. Thus a sum was apportioned to a particular province and divided by its population, so that each head was reckoned at such a price. The common standard of the impositions in Gaul was about forty-five dollars a head, which Gibbon calculates at four times the average of French taxes in his day. To avoid the utter ruin of the poorer classes which such a rate would produce, several such persons were included in the assessable head. On the very poor a poll tax was levied. The device of a tax upon occupations comes to us from Rome, and it included all vocations, down to the petty retailer, and even to those whose trade is not mentioned to polite ears. Mines and quarries, salt, fisheries, and for-

[1] Gibbon, vol. ii. p. 144.

ests were subject to special charges, and tolls were collected on post-roads and bridges.[1] Gifts to the monarch, which began as honors at a triumph, soon became a recognized charge from cities and provinces on any festive or notable occasion. Rome itself was expected to make a present to the emperor at such periods of the sum of three hundred and twenty thousand dollars. Justinian testifies that in Egypt the taxes payable in money, which ought to equal those payable in grain, were frequently reduced to nothing, through the weakness or crime of the prefect. As the total amount derived from Egypt was about six million dollars a year, the peculations or losses appear to have reached about one half of that sum. Perhaps we see more plainly in Roman history than in other chapters of the life of nations the extortions and wrongs committed by rulers and farmers of the revenue. Yet under similar systems like experiences were probable elsewhere; and the complaints of the Roman provinces and the crimes of the Roman officers are, it may be, the type of those which other subject countries suffered from, and from which our own times are practically free in all lands.

CHINA.

One of the curious phases of the history of revenue systems is that the Chinese methods have been in so many respects parallel with those of the Western nations. Like needs have developed like devices,

[1] Merivale, vol. iii. p. 543.

and similar evils have followed from similar causes. China has from a period beyond the beginnings of history maintained a tax on land, payable even yet about one half in kind; the rate for soil under cultivation varies from one fifth to one third of the gross product.[1] All buildings pay a ground-rent to the government.[2] Taxes answering to the French *patentes* are collected on stores, markets, and corporations, but keepers of small shops and persons who practice the liberal arts are exempt.[3] Transit duties on all trade produce, next to the land tax, the largest share of the revenue.[4] In the rural districts the land bears by far the most of the burdens. Salt pays a separate tax; there have been imposts on certain manufactures, as porcelain, silk, and varnish. Foreign commerce is charged with both export and import duties. The sale of offices and degrees is a regular source of income to the government.

Official returns show that foreign commerce paid in recent years from five to six times more than domestic trade in the way of revenue to China.[5] At all times difficulty has arisen in the collection, particularly of the internal taxes, and violence has been used to enforce the government charges.[6]

After both wars with Britain and its allies, the

---

[1] De Paricu, from the *Moniteur*, vol. i. p. 221.
[2] Williams' *Middle Kingdom*, vol. i. p. 739.
[3] De Parieu, vol. i. p. 290.
[4] Williams' *Middle Kingdom*, vol. i. p. 444.
[5] Williams' *Middle Kingdom*, vol. ii. p. 404.
[6] Williams' *Middle Kingdom*, vol. i. p. 498.

adjustment of the tariff was the first demand of the conquerors. They recognized the protective policy of the Chinese while seeking to force foreign commerce upon them. The story of the introduction of opium is pathetically narrated by Professor S. Wells Williams, in his "Middle Kingdom." "The trade in opium was legalized at a lower rate than was paid on tea and silk entering England," and the "moral sense of a people was broken down." The policy by which British commerce, and in fact nearly always the commerce of all peoples, has been extended, can be read in the recent history of China. France is to-day repeating in Tonquin the application of similar methods.

ITALIAN REPUBLICS.

The Italian republics of the Middle Ages afford curious fields for economic study. They gave a prominence to production and to commerce such as has never been surpassed. In some of them it was necessary to work at some trade or pursue some art, to be a citizen and to aspire to a place in the government. The manufacture of silk and of wool conferred a certain nobility. They sought to make that with which they could command foreign commerce. Venice was chief among them, and Florence alone competed with it for mastery. At Venice it was that cotton was fabricated in fine and attractive forms; its silk was lustrous in beauty and precious in value; its linen rivaled the products of old Tyre, and its dyes equaled the Eastern splendors; its arms had the fame of those of Damascus and Cordova; its furniture was the adornment of palaces; its glass and gold devices and its laces have not yet lost their place in mechanical annals; and its leather approached the delicacy of art. Venetian workmen were forbidden by grave penalties to transfer their skill to other lands.[1] Thus Venice was able to gather in the most precious commodities of the East and of all lands. Its commerce was for that age world-wide. The Venetians grew rich, and their prosperity attracted the rivalry of all Europe, until foreign and intestine strifes brought ruin.[2]

[1] Blanqui, p. 202.

[2] "I have prepared," says the Doge Moncenigo, "a statement of the products of our [Venetian] commerce:—

	Ducats.
Every week there comes to us from Milan seventeen or eighteen thousand ducats, which makes per year	900,000
From Monza, a thousand per week, and per year	52,000
From Como, two thousand per week, and per year	104,000
From Alessandria, one thousand per week, and per year	52,000
From Tortono and Novara, two thousand per week, and per year	104,000
From Pavia, two thousand per week, and per year	104,000
From Cremona, two thousand per week, and per year	104,000
From Bergamo, fifteen hundred per week, and per year	78,000
From Palermo, two thousand per week, and per year	104,000
From Piacenza, one thousand per week, and per year	52,000
	1,654,000

In all the splendor of these Italian republics one rule prevailed: the state rarely touched by taxation the earnings or savings of labor. Florence, in 1338, drew more than one half of her revenue

"What evidently establishes the truth of this result is the acknowledgment of all the bankers, who declare that every year the Milanese has to pay us sixteen hundred thousand ducats. Do you find this a pretty fine garden which Venice is enjoying, without its occasioning her any expense?

	Ducats.
Tortona and Novara use per year six thousand pieces of cloth, which, at fifteen ducats a piece, make . .	90,000
Pavia, 3,000 pieces	45,000
Milan, 4,000 pieces of fine cloth at thirty ducats . . .	120,000
Como, 12,000 pieces at fifteen ducats	180,000
Monza, 6,000 pieces at fifteen ducats	90,000
Brescia, 5,000 pieces at fifteen ducats	75,000
Bergamo, 10,000 pieces at seven ducats	70,000
Cremona, 140,000 pieces of fustian at four and one quarter ducats	70,000
Parma, 4,000 pieces of cloth at fifteen ducats . . .	60,000

"In all 94,000 pieces; and the import and export duties, at simply one ducat per piece, bring us 200,000 ducats.

"We have a trade with Lombardy estimated at 28,000,000 ducats.

"Do you think Venice has there a pretty fine garden?

	Ducats.
Then come the hemps for the sum of	100,000
The Lombards buy of you every year 5,000 pounds of cotton for	250,000
Twenty thousand quintals of thread (or, perhaps, of spun cotton), at fifteen or twenty ducats per hundred	30,000
Two million pounds of Catalogne wool at sixty ducats per one thousand	120,000
As many from France	120,000
Cloths of silk and gold for	250,000
Three thousand lots of pepper at one hundred ducats per lot	300,000

directly from commerce, and the internal taxes were little more than nominal.[1] The days of Florentine splendor can be traced almost absolutely by

	Ducats.
Four hundred loads of cinnamon at one hundred and sixty ducats per load	64,000
Two hundred thousand pounds of ginger at forty ducats a thousand	8,000
Sugars taxed from two or three to fifteen ducats per hundred	95,000
Other commodities for sewing and embroidery . . .	30,000
Four thousand thousands of dye woods at thirty ducats a thousand	120,000
Grains and plants for tinctures	50,000
Soaps	250,000
Slaves	30,000
Total	1,817,000

"I do not count the product of the sale of salt. Acknowledge that such a commerce is a fine estate. Consider how many vessels the movement of all this merchandise keeps employed, either in carrying it to Lombardy or in going for it to Syria, Romania, Catalogne, Flanders, Cyprus, Sicily, and all parts of the world. Venice makes two and a half or three per cent. on the freight. See how many people live from this movement: brokers, workmen, sailors, thousands of families, and finally the merchants, whose profit does not amount to less than 600,000 ducats.

"That is what your garden produces. Have you a mind to destroy it? No, indeed. Well, you must defend it against whoever may come to attack it." — Daru's *History of Venice*, vol. ii. p. 293–314.

[1] Revenues of the city and republic of Florence, from 1336 to 1338, in gold florins of the weight of seventy-two grammes, at twenty-four carats: —

	Florins.
Port duties, or import and export duties on merchandise and provisions, farmed out by the year at . . .	90,200
Import on the sale of wines at retail, one third of the value	59,300

the productions of cloth, and when that industry was at its height, the revenues of that little state

	Florins.
Estimo, or land tax on the country places	30,100
Tax on salt sold at forty sols a bushel to the bourgeois and twenty sols to the peasant	14,450
Revenue from the property of rebels, exiled and condemned	7,000
Tax on lenders and usurers	3,000
Dues from nobles invested with territorial possessions	2,000
Tax from contracts (inscriptions like mortgages)	11,000
Tax on butcheries of the city	15,000
Tax on butcheries of the country	4,400
Tax for rents	4,050
Tax on flour and mills	4,250
Imposts on citizens appointed podestas in a foreign country	3,500
Tax on indictments	1,400
Profit on the coinage of gold pieces	2,300
Profit on the coinage of copper pieces	1,500
Rent of lands of the corporation and tolls	1,600
Tax on cattle dealers in the city	2,150
Tax on the verification of weights and measures	600
Street sweepings and rents of the deposits of Orto San-Michele	750
Tax on country rents	550
Tax on country tradesmen	2,000
Fines and sentences from which payment is obtained	20,000
Defaults of soldiers (for exemption from military duty)	7,000
Tax on doors and houses in Florence	5,550
Tax on fruit women and old clothes women	450
Permission to carry arms, at twenty sols per head	1,300
Tax on sergeants	100
Tax on woods floated on the Arno	100
Tax on the examiners of guaranties given to the corporation	200
Share of the state in duties collected by the art-consuls	300

were greater than those of England under Elizabeth.

Venice controlled her commerce with practical absoluteness. The state claimed the exclusive right to its own ports and to the gulf which surrounds them. The ships and their owners and sailors must be Venetian, and no foreign merchant could be even received on a Venetian vessel. The customs duties fell twice as heavily on foreigners as on natives of Venice. Blanqui tells us [1] that "as national manufactures acquired importance, the government departed from the liberal policy it had hitherto pursued, and the manufacturers obtained an absolute prohibition of such foreign merchandise as they produced." The truth is, that as Venetian mechanism was developed, its importance was promptly recognized, and commerce grew up around and upon it. The splendors of these Italian republics are the charm of the Middle Ages. They reached out their arms with marvelous grasp, considering their population and their extent. They became the successors of Macedon and Rome, as well as of Tyre and Sidon; they overran the East with their arms as well as

	Florins.
Tax on citizens who reside in the country	1,000
Tax on possessions in the country	
Tax on battles without weapons	
Tax on Firenzuola	
Tax on mills and fishing	
The total exceeds	300,000

(Sismondi, *History of the Italian Republics*, vol. iv. p. 166.)

[1] Page 200.

their arts and their commerce. They were strong while they pursued the works of peace, and based their power on production and the commerce which was developed by it. They fell by causes outside of their industrial policy. Their systems of revenue favored industry on the soil to a degree never elsewhere surpassed, and they relied upon commerce for the revenues of the states to an extent equal to that of any policy ever introduced in any land.

GERMAN STATES.

Blanqui, a Frenchman opposed to the whole current of French financial legislation, discovers in the accession of Charles the Fifth a change in the course of political economy in Europe.[1] No other writer has discovered any such radical difference in the spirit of government in any of its branches at that era. Charles the Fifth devoted himself to conquest, but in that respect he followed examples much older than his age. He devoted himself to the aggrandizement of his own country, of Spain, and of Germany. In this policy he copied the examples of every ruler of strong character from the beginnings of history. He maintained for Germany and Spain the system of developing internal industry, and of imposing charges upon foreign commerce, as had been done by every ruler known to human annals. Julius Cæsar certainly applied customs duties to purposes of protection, and Charles the Fifth only carried out the

[1] Chap. xxi.

lessons of revenue systems which the experience of other lands had impressed upon his country and his time. When the empire fell apart, each separate state held to the traditions and the practices which had prevailed.

In the chief German states, in early days, the financial systems were very complex. A land tax has existed in some form in all of them from the beginning of history. The charges on commerce were collected by the several petty princes with circumstances of much rigor. Austria had a tariff which often varied, and covered merchandise of every sort. Its internal taxes were manifold and vexatious. Prussia pursued the same policy. Both of these leading governments have collected, from a very remote period, taxes on persons, on industries, on movable wealth, on food, and on beverages. The burden of military service has been heavy in Germany in all times. It will be hard to find in financial systems any charge which has not been tried on the Rhine and the Danube. The diverse methods for reaching occupations and personal property in Prussia and Austria, before the middle of this century, leave scarcely any room for new devices. The personal tax in Prussia, graduated according to income, has involved all of the annoyances which have been alleged in Britain against the income tax. In that country, a class tax is collected from 5,115,555 persons, and even from those whose income is as low as $105 and not above $750 a year;

but the technical income tax comes from 163,024 persons, who report $750 a year or more. There, as elsewhere, prosecutions are numerous for these taxes, and last year no less than 1,556,507 executions were issued for non-payment of the class imposts. Just now, the sharpest discussion is in progress in Prussia over these taxes.[1] These personal charges, according to a prominent French author and statesman,[2] are endured in countries inhabited by the pure Germanic race or its principal branches, while among the Neo-Latin peoples they have but a small number of isolated applications, temporary or from pressing necessity.

In the present generation, and especially within the past decade, Germany has revived with increasing force the protective policy which has been traditional in all of its states. In the adjustment between Austria and Hungary in 1877, the finances presented one of the points of difficulty.[3] Hungary, buying little coffee or petroleum, assented to heavy duties upon them, and the Austrian manufactures were protected by high duties. Again, in 1882, the Austrians increased their customs duties, for purposes of protection. In the Northern German states the tariff has occasioned prolonged discussion and various partisan combinations. Bismarck has asserted the policy of protection with all the vigor of Colbert and Cromwell. Since 1878 he has insisted with un-

---

[1] *Saturday Review.*   [2] De Parieu.
[3] Muller's *History*, p. 591.

flinching determination on collecting such duties as will develop German production. He states that the measure which he has carried through and made the law of the empire was prompted by "the necessity not alone of assisting individual branches of industry by special protective duties, but still more to secure to native industry in all branches an advantage over foreign industry in the home market," with a view also to extend the exportation of native goods.[1] The great chancellor has endeavored to win the support of the extreme radicals by measures entirely independent of his protective policy, and he has not been sustained by the elections in those measures, although the emperor has taken his part. But the protective features which he has embodied in such vigor in legislation have won for him the favor of the land-owners, whose burdens he has mitigated, and of the industrial classes, whose earnings he has increased.

Hamburg was long a free city, and sought commerce by every device. It has been one of the points at which trade has been more nearly exempt from all charges than in any large country. But that city has in 1882 asked to be admitted into the German Zollverein, and to collect the protective duties which are a part of the purposes of that union. The city passes into the general German methods; meanwhile a spot is reserved in which a free port will be maintained. But Hamburg chooses to look

[1] Muller's *History*, p. 644.

to the manufactures of Germany for its trade and for the basis of its commerce, and thus becomes a strong example of the progress of protection.

FRANCE.

France, in spite of the allegation of De Parieu, is a conspicuous illustration that systems of revenue do not depend at all upon race. For there the whole field can be closely studied from domestic experience. The land tax has prevailed from the establishment of the nation. Charlemagne relied upon the products and rents of the royal domain for his revenue.[1] Tithes were early collected, and Philip Augustus ordered such an impost for the third crusade. Since 1376 customs have brought money into the treasury. In various provinces the rates and policy have been different, and cities like Lyons as late as the sixteenth century maintained their own douane. Not until 1790 were the divergent systems of customs merged into a uniform tariff. Export duties have figured in French methods. Whether by separate provinces or for the nation customs duties have been a chief reliance for revenue in France, since in 1576 Jean Bodin, who was at the head of the financial administration, asserted the principle of moderate restriction of commerce for protective purposes, in his work "De la Republique."

Under Louis XIV a capitation tax was collected from twenty-two classes of persons. Sully and Col-

---

[1] See his *Capitularies*, Blanqui, p. 114.

bert abolished many oppressive charges, and the latter raised the customs to render them more strongly protective.[1] In 1710 ten per cent. was levied on incomes of every kind, whether from land, or from movable property, or from industrial or professional occupations. Interrupted at intervals the tenth was collected from land as well as from other sources until 1749, when the twentieth took the place of the tenth. But this rate has been doubled and under stress tripled ; so that the charge upon land has been at times as high as thirty per cent. In 1830, Dupin[2] states the tax on land sold was so heavy as to absorb two years' income. Turgot tried to concentrate all taxes into a single impost on the net product of the soil.[3] In 1791 the law of "*pa-*

---

[1] Colbert's aim in revising the customs was to make them a means of protection for national manufactures, in the place of a simple finaucial resource, as they formerly were. Most articles of foreign manufacture had duties imposed upon them, so as to secure to similar French merchandise the home market. At the same time Colbert spared neither sacrifices nor encouragement to give activity to the manufacturing spirit in our country. He caused the most skillful workmen of every kind to come from abroad ; and he subjected manufacturers to a severe discipline, that they should not lose their vigilance, relying on the tariffs.

He had himself summed up in a few words his system in the memorial he presented to the king : "To reduce export duties on provisions and manufactures of the kingdom ; to diminish import duties on everything which is of use in manufactures ; and to repel the products of foreign manufactures, by raising the duties."— *History of Political Economy*, by J. A. Blanqui, pp. 283–4.

[2] *Forces Productive*, vol. i. p. 130.

[3] Blanqui, p. 373.

tentes," which is in many respects peculiar, became a fixed part of the financial scheme of France. These *patentes* are charges upon vocations according to an arbitrary classification, raised nominally on the presumed importance and profit, on location relative to city and country, on rent, and number of persons or machines employed. The list is curious, and the complexity of the system renders it costly and onerous. Taxes on food, on consumption in the broadest sense, have been long the rule in France. It was, says De Parieu, in spite of the Roman example, the true fatherland of the tax on salt, which it still insists upon collecting. It was the country in which farming the revenue attained the greatest importance. To France alone can we look for the toleration of separate custom houses at the entrance of over fourteen hundred of its communes; for the octroi duties involve that consequence. These are an inheritance coming down from 1323, when they were collected for the benefit of the state; afterwards they were divided between the state and the communes, and have latterly been conceded wholly to local objects. They are collected from beverages, edibles, fuel, forage, and certain raw materials in chief part. The rates are often monstrous, and were (1866) on coal in Paris three dollars and sixty cents a ton, and this was more than the cost of that article at other points. Varying from a few centimes *per capita* in some localities they amount to five dollars *per capita* in Marseilles, and to eight dollars *per capita* in Paris. The cost of collecting them rises to twelve per cent. in some communes, and for the whole country averaged a few years ago ten per cent.[1] The tobacco monopoly is maintained in France in all its rigor.

The estimate is made that counting taxation and conscription, the French workingmen, taking the average of them, pay one fifth of all their earnings to the government.

Among the many evils which the third Napoleon brought upon France was the partial overthrow of the policy of protecting the national industries. He was overreached by Cobden in a commercial treaty when M. Chevalier introduced the fallacies of the free trade school. Not a little of the popular repulsion which after Sedan rendered the empire impossible grew out of the depression of industry and trade. President Thiers,[2] with marvelous reconstructive power, followed the negotiations for peace and the organization of the republic by a brave return to the policy under which France had prospered, and which all of her strong statesmen, whether royalist or republican, and not least the first Napoleon, deemed vital to her prosperity. That protective policy is maintained by the republic, and during the past year President Grévy has refused to renew the reciprocity treaty with Britain.[3] Out of this policy France has

---

[1] De Parieu, vol. iv.

[2] Muller's *Political History of Recent Times*, p. 475.

[3] *Annual Register*, 1882.

surprised Europe by paying $200,000,000 of its debt, and reducing its taxes by $60,000,000 a year.

A peculiarity of the French tariff is that two schedules exist, one styled conventional and the other general. The former applies to countries, like Germany and Britain, with which commercial treaties are maintained; and the other is enforced against the rest of the world, and bears with severity on some American products. In some instances the rates under treaties are higher than under the general schedules, but the rule is the reverse, and notably in the case of important commodities. It is under this system that complaint has arisen over the practical prohibition of American pork.[1]

ENGLAND.

The Danegeld tells of the origin of the land tax in England. It has existed in all parts of Britain from the beginning of our knowledge of any public in-

---

[1] Some of these differences are: —

	Conventional Tariff.	General Tariff.
See Schedule of Beverages.	Francs.	Francs.
Wines, per hectoliter	3.50	4.50
Alcohol and brandy, per hectoliter	15.00	30.00
In schedule "Yarns and threads:"		
Cotton yarn, according to fineness, per 100 kilos.	15.00 to 300.00	18.50 to 372.00
Woolen yarn, per 100 kilos.	10.00 to 100.00	31.00 to 124.00
In schedule "Tissues:"		
Cotton, unbleached (according to weight), per 100 kilos.	50.00 to 300.00	62.00 to 625.00
Woolen, per 100 kilos.	(a)	75.00 to 620.00
In schedule "Animals:"		
Live oxen, each	2.60	15.00
Hogs, each	.30	3.00

a 10 per cent. ad valorem.

come. The Conqueror had a revenue of only two million dollars, and the kings of the Houses of York and Lancaster only about a half a million dollars a year. To raise these sums levies were made without form of law by royal prescript under the Normans, and special extortions were excused by some exigency of the ruler. Stephen imposed no regular taxes, but seized what he wanted. Before the time of Henry II, the land bore the largest share of the taxes, but tithes were levied for the crusades near the close of his reign,[1] and thereafter personal property was burdened from a thirtieth to a seventh, and in the case of the Jews even to a fourth. A clause in the great charter forbids more than the ancient customs on merchants entering or leaving the realm. This prohibition points to the practice of the kings of collecting money as license, or as continuous tax, at their pleasure, perhaps as a guaranty for personal protection, upon all strangers, and this came soon to be a charge upon traffic, by whomsoever conducted. Henry III required from London, and from the Jews, direct payments into his coffers. Edward I was sovereign when a tenth was collected from grain and from animals for the crown; and to him also were granted, the first time in England, duties on imports. The poll tax dates from Richard II, and it was levied on all persons, male and female, above the age of fifteen years. Henry VII sent out commissioners to collect a sixteenth of every man's sub-

---

[1] Green's *History of the English People*, vol. i. p. 322.

stance, and took it in money, plate, or jewels. Henry VIII, with the help of Cardinal Wolsey, found in the church rich mines to work, and appropriated the first fruits and tenths to himself. Doubtless, whenever princes wanted funds, they resorted to loans to get them; but Henry VIII took four shillings in the pound from the clergy, and three shillings from the laity, under this pretext; and his benevolences, pretended voluntary contributions, exasperated his subjects.

Queen Elizabeth took ventures for the crown in the commercial enterprises which marked her reign. With Raleigh, and with Drake, with daring navigators who carried English greed into remote seas, she enlisted capital, and looked for her share of the returns.[1] She evidently followed the example of Solomon, and serves as a brilliant example of the almost uniform policy of drawing from commerce in some shape the largest practicable addition to the royal revenues. She understood the subject, for she had probably read Sir Walter Raleigh's Essay on Trade, in which he advocates measures for favoring English manufactures and controlling foreign commerce. In 1590 she increased the customs charges from £14,000 to £50,000 a year, taking from that source by so much larger a share of her revenue.[2]

The Stuarts brought not a little of their trouble upon themselves by their extortions in taxes, and by

[1] Cunningham's *Growth of English Industry and Commerce*, p. 306.
[2] Hume, vol. iv. p. 218.

the attempt to get them by proclamation, without vote of Parliament. To Charles I his first Parliament conceded $6,000,000 a year, from customs, excise, crown lands, and hearth money;[1] but he sought more by illegal means, and sold state lands, set up monopolies, drew subsidies, and reduced extortion to a system. Ship money aroused John Hampden. The resistance to the farmers of the revenue was a reversal of ancient practice, for Elizabeth had a struggle over them, and only yielded in part near the close of her reign. As early as 1329 the Bardi of Florence paid twenty pounds a day, Sundays excepted, for the revenue. Under Elizabeth the rent was £14,000 to £50,000 a year upon total receipts never so large as £500,000.[2] Both James and Charles made the worst of the monopolies, which were extended to cover many articles of prime necessity, such as salt and soap, coal, starch, pepper, alum. In 1671 English taxes were taken out of farm, and subjected to the control of commissioners, and they have remained so ever since.

The British system has for three centuries been directed to building up commerce. For commerce, adventurers were sent over every ocean. For commerce, colonies were planted. For commerce, the eighteenth century was made a century of warfare in the New World, and for the prize of India. In 1750 the British Parliament enacted: "From and after the 24th day of June, 1750, no mill or other

---

[1] Hallam, chap. xv. [2] Hume, vol. iv. p. 216.

engine for slitting or rolling bar-iron, or any plaiting forge to work with a tilt-hammer, or any furnace for making of steel, shall be erected, or, after erection, continued in any of his Majesty's colonies in America." [1] This was the spirit in which even Chatham treated the colonies, when he sought to prevent them from making even a hob-nail. It has been the traditional temper of Britain towards other countries. It is the expression of the strong purpose to hold control of the world's manufactures for the sake of supremacy in commerce.

This purpose to monopolize the trade of America brought on the Revolution, by unjust taxes and the crushing out of local industries. The same purpose inspired the navigation laws, the manifold grievances which were designed to cripple our commerce and to obstruct our industrial independence. They drove our republic into the War of 1812, in which, while we failed to extort in treaties the recognition of our claims, we nevertheless asserted our nationality, and compelled respect for our power, our courage, and our growing vitality. British statesmen and traders learned that a new competitor had appeared, if not yet to challenge foreign commerce, at least to be master in its own markets. Then began the war on our industries by indirection, of which Lord Brougham gave the sinister proclamation. He said: "It was well worth while to incur a loss on the first exportation, in order by the glut to stifle in the cradle those

[1] Act 3 George II, c. 29, sec. 9.

rising manufactures in the United States which the war has forced into existence." The same policy was maintained towards Ireland with deadly effect.

At the close of the Napoleonic wars the British revenue came from customs, excise, stamps, land, and assessed taxes on property, income, including pensions and salaries, lottery profits, besides heavy loans, which had become a regular dependence in Britain as well as in France, and in all Europe.

The customs were levied with an immediate view to develop internal industries, and to enable them to compete with the products of other countries. Up to 1846, in considerable part to 1859, the British policy was more rigidly protective than that of any other land.

A feature of the British statutes which exhibits their stern adaptation to their end is the prohibition of the growing of tobacco. By an act passed August 23, 1831, no tobacco can be grown anywhere in the United Kingdom, "except in the physic garden of the universities, or of a private physician," and then only in very limited quantities.

Stewart's "Political Economy," which List well described as an expression of British experience, insists that the only way to promote industry is by positive action, and not simply by permission and protection. No government ever did more than England for three centuries to develop home manufactures, and to crush out competition.

The British Budget for 1882 shows that £19,300,000 was raised from customs, £27,230,000 from excise, £11,145,000 from stamps, £2,775,000 from land tax, etc., £11,662,000 from income tax, £7,150,000 from the post-office, £1,650,000 from telegraphs, £380,000 from crown lands, £1,180,000 from interest on advances, and £4,725,000 from miscellaneous sources. This is a total of £87,197,000. To this must be added the collections for local purposes, as poor rates, school tax, police, roads, and the like, £61,174,480, making a grand total of £148,371,480, or in dollars, $741,857,400, to a total population of 35,262,762.

Customs duties are now collected in Great Britain on cocoa, coffee, chicory, tea, tobacco, wine, beer, and ale; and duties to countervail the excise charges are collected on spirits and strong waters, chloroform, chloral hydrate, collodion, ether, ethyl, naphtha, soap, and varnish.

The British system does not now rest without assault. A movement for fair trade, with duties to protect home industry, has secured a foothold in Parliament, and maintains a popular organization. The answer of the government to a proposition for duties of ten per cent. on foreign manufactures was given by Mr. Chamberlain, that the British people would thus be compelled to pay forty million pounds more for their food. The British colonies cannot produce the amount of food required in the home islands, and cannot buy the manufactures necessary to pay for the needed food. Even more threatening to the British financial system is a sentiment which finds advocates in "the Financial Reform association," which, through elaborate publications, insists upon the substitution of direct taxation "in lieu of the present unequal, complicated, and expensively-collected duties upon commodities."[1] Especially does this association demand that the land tax shall be readjusted. Our discussion in the United States on topics of revenue arouses no more bitterness than these proposals excite in Britain, and certainly does not threaten any such sharp divisions of our people into distinct classes.

Professor Fawcett's elaborate argument against protective duties for retaliation against the United States, in his work on "Free Trade and Protection," is evidence of the growing tendency in England to question the wisdom of the present policy of revenue.

SPAIN AND THE NETHERLANDS.

Ancient Spain and the Netherlands add little to the theories or facts of revenue except bad administration and excessive rates. Both maintained a colonial policy for the extension of their commerce, and they tried to maintain trade by heavy duties. In Spain the internal charges became so onerous that McCulloch attributes to them a greater loss than was caused by the exclusion of the Moors, and he traces

---

[1] See in *Financial Reform Almanack* for 1883, catalogue of thirty-seven tracts.

to taxes the decay of the country. Spain did not abandon farmers of the revenue until 1849. In Holland in 1750 the land tax bore so ruinously upon property that owners sought to be relieved by abandoning their lands to the state. But this privilege was formally denied to them by edict of 1751. In 1790 the tax greatly reduced was yet from eight to nine per cent. of the gross produce. John De Witt, in 1746, had boasted of the wealth of the Netherlands, and declared it was " because its trade and all exchanges were left unfettered, unimpeded, unlegislated upon; and that by this free trade the Netherlands became both the most peopled and the richest country on the earth." Five years later some of its land would not meet the taxes upon it. The people who could contest with Britain for the possession of the New World as well as for the mastery of the Orient fell behind their neighbors, and soon ceased to be accounted even a secondary power. Their bankers still compete with other money-lenders; but trade has fallen to a low ebb, and except as the nation derives a revenue from the remnants of its colonies, as from Java especially, the Netherlands can hardly claim to rank among the producers of the world. The student of finance must be struck with the fact that this nation, so boastful of the freedom of its trade, as a government concerned in agriculture, enforces a seventh of the labor of the colonists for public profit, and seeks more than a third of its revenue from colonial products raised by the government and handled by its agents.

No recent manifestation has been more suggestive than the movement in Holland for the return to the protective policy. The Chamber of Commerce of Helmond protests against the system of revenue which prevails, as destructive to commerce as well as to production. Wages have been reduced to the minimum, and yet Belgium competes successfully with the Dutch on their own soil. The American consul at Amsterdam, in a report to our state department, declares that the mechanics and artisans very generally enlist in this movement, and join in demanding unrestricted trade with the Dutch colonies, and the adjustment of the tariff to protect home industries against foreign competition. The experience of the Netherlands justifies this protest against its revenue system, and furnishes strong arguments promising the success of the advocates of a protective policy.

COLLECTING THE REVENUE.

Farmers of the revenue have always aggravated the burdens of taxation. French authorities declare that under Henry IV individuals paid a hundred and fifty million francs, while the treasury received only thirty million. Under Louis XIV. half the money paid by the nation failed to reach the government. In the United Provinces, in the last century, almost half the gross taxes went to pay for administration and collection.[1] Rau, a German author,

---

[1] De Parieu.

testifies that in Rhenish Bavaria, at one time, 247,081 florins were paid for getting 101,017 for the treasury. These are illustrations of rates which were the rule in the era of abuses under all governments; but, without robbery, costs have often exceeded the income. For thirty years before 1763, the remittances of revenue from the American colonies averaged only £1,900, and the expenses for officers were £7,000 a year. With improved methods, rates have been very high. France still pays fifteen per cent. and upwards for gathering in its customs, and its octroi cost the communes an average of ten per cent. These figures seem very large in Britain and the United States, for the British customs have not for years involved expenses above five per cent. In the United States the internal revenue has been assessed and collected for 3.63 per cent., as in 1880, with the rate increasing by the diminution in the sum collected. The cost of customs is now 3.7 per cent.

CHAPTER III.

MODERN PRACTICES ABROAD AND AT HOME.

Duties on Exports. — On Imports. — Tax on Land. — Public Domain. — Mines. — Monopolies. — Taxes on Liquors and Tobacco. — Railroads and Telegraphs. — Corporations. — Salt, Sugar, Tea, Coffee. — Incomes. — *Patentes*. — Stamps. — Succession. — Lotteries. — Peculiar Sources of Revenue.

TABLE OF REVENUE OF DIFFERENT NATIONS. — Effort universal to collect some Revenue from Commerce. — All Countries except Two adopt a Protective Policy. — Contrast by Numbers. — The Latest Legislation is Protective.

ORIGIN OF PROTECTION. — Not with Cromwell and Colbert. — Goes Back to Egypt and Phœnicia. — Acharnians of Aristophanes. — The Strife between Athena and Poseidon. — Cæsar. — France. — England. — Ruskin : "No Nation dares to abolish its Custom Houses." — Fawcett. — Sidgwick. — Appeal to Authority. — Protection sustained *semper ab omnibus ubique*.

TURNING now from individual nations, let us group modern countries by the classes of imposts which they collect. We shall find that no example exists of a failure to derive a considerable share of revenue from commerce. China includes exports in its schedules of duties; so do Brazil and Guatemala. New Zealand collects an export charge on gold. Every nation which has any system of revenue at all imposes duties on imports. Under the combination of the Zollverein the German states make collections of customs and divide the proceeds on the basis of the population of the several states included in the alliance. Mexico still maintains custom houses on the borders of its several states.

A tax on land is also one of the uniform dependences of modern governments. Russia, before the emancipation of its serfs, levied no tax on the soil, doubtless owing to the tenure under which it was held. In the United States, with three brief exceptions, all due to war necessities, the national government has made no charges upon the land, but has allotted that sphere to the states, and all of them, except Pennsylvania and New Jersey, rely chiefly upon it. In Europe and the Asiatic countries, the yearly revenues come in large part from the land. A public domain still as in ancient times affords returns in many nations either by sale or lease. In this republic our public lands have not yet ceased to pour their millions into the treasury. In Belgium, Colombia, and Japan, a special tax is levied on mines; and Greece continues, as in the time of the glory of Athens, to receive contributions from the silver mines at Laurium.

Monopolies on certain articles are yet maintained. France still permits tobacco to be sold only under this restraint. Austria-Hungary draws profit from the concession of monopolies on salt and tobacco. Italy, Spain, Roumania, Costa Rica, Honduras, Nicaragua, and the Dutch West Indies also employ the same methods for getting money.

Fermented and distilled liquors and tobacco are

common objects of special taxation, by licenses, by stamps on the packages, or by tax on the manufacture, or by two or all of these plans combined.

Comparatively new as railroads and telegraphs are, they have been very generally chosen as sources of revenue. In England the telegraph is monopolized by the government. In Belgium and France the railroads are commonly, as in Russia, in great part owned by the state. In these countries and in Germany, guaranties are given by the state of a part or all of the capital, and everywhere governments seek by tax or from a share in the profits to get income from railway traffic and from telegraphing. In Pennsylvania especially, in New Jersey, and latterly in New York, such corporations are assessed separately. This uniformity of imposition of taxes upon such interests indicates the deliberate aim of securing funds for public use from domestic trade through the instruments upon which it relies most for active and prompt movement.

Salt and sugar, with tea and coffee, are subjected to heavy charges in many lands; the first in France and India, the second in most European and American states, tea and coffee notably in Great Britain. The levying of taxes on consumption of articles of prime necessity is a principle in the Old World.

The tax on incomes with which Americans were familiar during the rebellion, is levied in Great Britain, Prussia, and Sweden, with rate increasing on large incomes, and with exceptions in favor of those falling below a fixed standard. The *patentes* of France are charges upon occupations; Belgium, Prussia, Bavaria, Austria-Hungary, also collect imposts upon trades. Stamps upon certain papers or on various commodities are required in Great Britain, some German states, Sweden, and Portugal. Taxes on the succession of property are maintained in Britain, Prussia, and Denmark, and in some American states.

Lotteries pay fees to Austria-Hungary, Prussia, Italy, the Netherlands, Spain, and Brazil, and in this country to Louisiana and Kentucky.

Of peculiar sources of revenue, Germany and Sweden derive money from state banks; and Germany from a state printing-office; Servia has a capitation tax graded according to rank, occupation, and income, with a distinction between married and unmarried persons; India gets profit from opium, and raises quinine on government account; and Peru before its unfortunate complications with Chili, relied largely on the sale of guano.

The two free cities have been traders and not producers, and their systems of revenue have been adapted to their position. Hamburg before entering the Zollverein got $6,500,000 a year from its domains, from lotteries, from stamps and like charges, and from official fees. Bremen requires $2,500,000 annually, and picks it up, one third from public property, one third from direct taxes, and the remainder from indirect imposts. Perhaps Gibraltar deserves

AMERICAN SYSTEM OF REVENUE.

	Customs.	Land Tax.	Property and Direct Taxes.a	Domain and Other State Property.	Excise.b	Stamps and Fees.	Post Office and Telegraphs.	Railways.	Special and Indirect Taxes.	State Lottery.	Miscellaneous.
Austria-Hungary	6.68	10.90	9.82	—	19.69	10.92	5.15	—	18.58c	4.54	9.28
Belgium	7.23	8.30	11.73	.68	10.82	11.30	—	42.70	2.06	—	5.18
Bavaria	4.68	6.61	4.30	14.03	—	—	.01	45.52d	24.80	—	.56
Denmark	48.10e	—	18.30	2.36	—	7.95	5.43	6.28	3.24	—	13.76
France	10.22	7.65	13.29	12.07	—	9.00	3.48	—	31.61	—	10.73
Germany	31.66	—	—	.44	23.92f	3.21	3.48	2.06	18.94g	—	16.56
Great Britain	22.46	3.17	11.59	11.27	31.74	14.25	10.06	—	—	—	6.25
Greece	32.42	2.38	17.30	2.11	2.20	9.89	3.65h	—	13.00	5.62	8.06
Italy	11.12	14.66	14.93	1.58	15.71	.59	3.81	5.30	22.76	.40	3.79
Netherlands	4.89	10.04	13.52	4.65	36.53	—	4.94	1.99	21.85i	—	4.74
Norway	42.47	—	.53	.80	13.70	3.21	5.60	8.84	—	—	21.60
Portugal	34.19	15.12	9.50	14.26	—	10.37	2.48	3.53	17.09	.43	6.72
Prussia	2.03k	7.31	3.64	5.65	—	—	—	39.82	4.69l	—	2.63
Russia	14.60	—	17.06	8.08	—	—	3.48	—	37.36	—	21.84
Spain	14.74	—	29.50	6.50	20.88	28.30m	6.25	10.50	21.00	—	2.77
Sweden	33.64	8.18	5.01	.35	—	3.67	37.28	.05	15.74	—	5.36
Switzerland	37.72	—	—	—	—	—	—	—	—	—	8.66
Turkey	12.14	30.44	14.47	.69	—	12.13	1.34	25.08	13.72	—	18.20
Egypt	17.38	51.85	2.16	—	15.74	5.85	.04	1.41	1.57	—	1.96
Japan	3.89	64.26	—	.64	—	—	—	—	3.28	—	4.87
Canada	62.40	—	—	.61	18.03	.91	4.56	9.31	.39	—	3.62
Mexico	49.15	—	10.70	—	13.63	14.76	4.95	—	—	2.95	3.92
Argentine Confederation	15.44	3.10	4.57	4.57	—	4.40	2.93	3.69	—	—	5.97
Brazil	67.78	—	—	—	—	—	—	—	26.17	—	6.04

to be mentioned as a free port, but its trade is very trifling.

A different classification will still farther enable us to judge of the relations of different revenue systems. Comparisons are difficult from the variations in the statements which are published, and the fact that in many countries local taxes are collected which do not appear in the national budgets. The figures analyzed on page 70 are those of the British Statesman's Year-Book for 1883, corrected and extended from the Almanach De Gotha for the same year, from official publications, and other sources. The table states the percentages of the total revenue received in the various countries from the different classes of imposts.

a. The income tax where it is collected, as in Britain and Prussia, is stated with the property and direct taxes.

b. France includes excise in its report of indirect taxes.

c. The salt and tobacco monopoly are included in this statement from Austria-Hungary.

d. The figures for railways in Bavaria include also mines.

e. In Denmark the returns on customs include the tax on beet sugar.

f. In Germany the excise includes salt and tobacco with beverages. In the Netherlands the report includes divers articles.

g. Germany receives contributions from the states, included here with other receipts.

h. Greece puts receipts from the mint with those from the post-office.

i. The Netherlands include here the receipts from stamps.

k. The customs reported for Prussia are its share from the imperial treasury.

l. Prussia thus reports the produce of its furnaces and forges.

m. Spain reports excise and stamps and fees together.

Enforced military service must be accounted a form of taxation, and it may become the most burdensome. In European countries it is now one of the causes of most grievous complaint. One out of twenty-eight of the population of the seven great powers is a soldier, and must be supported by the other bread-winners. One seventh of the people of France, it is estimated, is required for the army, either to fill its ranks, or to support it. In the United States during the rebellion, the draft and the excessive bounties afforded illustrations of this practice. But the subject belongs more strictly to other branches of political science than to that of revenue.

The imposts of which we have been speaking are those of the state, of the general government. The provinces, the counties, the communes, and the cities have in the Old World, as the commonwealths and the chief local divisions have with us, their distinct treasuries. In the Old World the taxes for these minor organizations are generally assimilated to those of the state. They as a rule fall upon the same objects. The French octroi are a conspicuous exception. But the local systems outside of France introduce no principles which are not applied in the imposts of the general governments.

Since there are local as well as state taxes, to use our American phrases, in addition to those of the general government, comparisons are difficult. But local and state taxes fall upon land and articles of prime necessity, in other lands as well as in the

United States, as the general rule. Our tables show that the effort is universal to throw some considerable part of the charges of the central government upon foreign commerce.

TESTIMONY OF THE NATIONS.

All economists agree that the only countries which levy imposts for the support of government with a view to favor commerce in the first degree are Great Britain and the Netherlands. These are examples of free trade.

The revenue systems of all the Asiatic countries are protective, and in Europe, France, Austria, Northern Germany, Russia, Italy, Spain, and Switzerland are systematically and increasingly devoted to the policy of levying charges, with the purpose of favoring home production.

While Great Britain maintains a free trade policy at home, her colonies, except New South Wales, insist for themselves on rigid protection. The West Indies, as the "Westminster Review"[1] complains, violate the rules of free trade by collecting, as in Jamaica, thirty per cent. of the revenue from imported food. Canada, by her national policy adopted in 1880, prefers home production to commerce. In Australasia the colony of Victoria is a sturdy champion of protection. New South Wales is quoted for free trade, but it presents the striking example of a state in which no direct tax is collected. The chief part

[1] October, 1883.

of the revenue is derived from public lands, either by sale or rent, and nearly one fourth of its revenue comes from customs. New Zealand secures its revenue chiefly from customs, and from land sales. The same is the case with Queensland and South Australia. Western Australia adds to these sources certain licenses. Even India until 1882 protected itself by restrictive duties against British cottons.

While the commercial policy of revenue is maintained by Great Britain and the Netherlands, with an aggregate population of less than 40,000,000, the industrial system is enforced by all the other Western nations, with a population of not less than 340,-000,000. With this majority of eight times the numbers of the minority are arrayed, in at least equal degree, the intelligence and progress of mankind. The eastern nations are quite solid on the side of the industrial system, not excluding until 1882 even British India.

The latest examples of revenue legislation unbiased by vested interests, and in the face of the fullest discussions, are to be found in Germany in its unification, in the several British colonies, and in Japan in introducing Western methods. In all of these instances, without obligations pleading for a particular policy, the system which has been adopted has been strongly and even rigidly protective.

All of the changes in revenue policy which have been most recently adopted in Europe have been in favor of a protective system.

Austria and North Germany have within a few years extended and invigorated their protective policy. The French Republic has with continued discussion stood firmly by the principle of Colbert and of the periods of French glory. Russia develops its vast resources by close adherence to a protective system, and in 1882 added ten per cent. to its customs duties. Even Britain wavers. In India the government control is absolute, and the purpose to control all industry and all trade for British advantage is at the bottom of the entire administration and possession. The Australasian colonies are following the example of the United States in financial policy as well as in other respects, with practical defiance of English teaching and of English desires.

ORIGIN OF A PROTECTIVE POLICY.

The credit of establishing the principle of protection has been assigned to Cromwell and to Colbert. Our investigation has corrected any such misapprehension. No revenue system existed in the olden times in which one chief purpose was not to build up the country at the cost of foreigners. Hiram and Solomon conducted commerce for the profit of their governments, as Egypt had before them sought to draw wealth from outside peoples. The policy of Carthage was conspicuous for its protective character. It destroyed the ships of competitors who sought to get metals to build up competing industries. In Persia, as the records show, royalty itself was confined to the use of home-made articles. The Philistines compelled the Jews to put out the fires of their forges,[1] so that they might not become independent, just as, nearly eighteen hundred years later, England required the American colonies to do. Athens was distinctively protective in its policy.

The first of the plays of Aristophanes which has come down to us is devoted to a satire of the Acharnians, who, as the dramatist suggests, because they burned charcoal, were not ready to have free trade forced upon them by war. The anxiety of the Megarians to smuggle in their commodities, whether short mantles or little pigs, finds its counterpart in those who to-day try to place the world under tribute to their arms and their diplomacy. Dikaiopolis, who is ready to peddle out peace and to sacrifice everything for free trade for himself, proves at least that when Athens was greatest it was the master of its own markets and the protector of its own industries.

Aristophanes represents Dikaiopolis buying peace for himself against the wishes and policy of Athens, and this is the proclamation which he makes: —

> These are the limits of my market-place, —
> 'T is lawful here for all Peloponnesians
> To traffic, all Megarians and Bœotians,
> Trading with me, but not for Lamachos.[2]

[1] 1 Sam. xiii. 19.
[2] This is the burden of the play, lines 719–722: —

> ὅροι μὲν ἀγορᾶς εἰσιν οἵδε τῆς ἐμῆς.
> ἐνταῦθ' ἀγοράζειν πᾶσι Πελοποννησίοις
> ἔξεστι καὶ Μεγαρεῦσι καὶ Βοιωτίοις
> ἐφ' ᾧτε πωλεῖν πρὸς ἐμέ, Λαμάχῳ δὲ μή.

PRACTICES ABROAD AND AT HOME. 77

Throughout his plays this comic poet makes fun of his country for putting tanners, lamp-makers, and other artisans into the chief places, for the successors of Pericles were chosen from such trades. Athens exalted the mechanic arts as well as those of painting, sculpture, and literature; and the satirist proves the policy of the city in the era of its greatness by his elaborate ridicule of it.

Lamachos and Dikaiopolis stand for the opposite policies of trade. Lamachos is prompt to fight always to protect the home market against the Megarians and Peloponnesians. Dikaiopolis insists on a free market, which he proposes to secure by making a separate peace for himself. The rollicking spirit in which their strife is depicted is the essence of the play. The persistence with which free trade is aimed at, but funnily enough only for the negotiator himself, illustrates the current of economic history. Here, in lines 623–625, we read:—

> ἐγὼ δὲ κηρύττω γε Πελοποννησίοις
> ἅπασι καὶ Μεγαρεῦσι καὶ Βοιωτίοις
> πωλεῖν ἀγοράζειν πρὸς ἐμὲ, Λαμάχῳ δὲ μή.

Long before the great satirist, and at the beginning of Athens, the struggle between industry and commerce began, and on the rocky height above the city was erected the temple which proclaimed the triumph of production. The legend recites how Athena and Poseidon strove for the mastery of land and people. With her olive-tree and her industrial arts Athena drove Poseidon to the caves of the sea, and the statue of gold and ivory which shone from the Parthenon across the midland sea testified to the achievements of art and industry. The world has not learned to build a structure of more beauty and grandeur than that white temple on the hill, which even yet looks down on Pnyx and Agora, on Phalerum and Salamis. At its side the Greeks built their edifice to Wingless Victory. From them comes the wise lesson of the dependence of commerce on domestic development, and from them it is for us to learn how to lay even more firmly the foundations of a victory which shall never flee away.

Julius and Augustus Cæsar restored the protective policy which had originally prevailed in Rome, but had been interrupted in the corrupt and weak days. Gibbon testifies that "the rate of the customs under Augustus varied from one eighth to one fortieth part of the value of the commodity; and we have the right to suppose that the variation was directed by the unalterable maxims of policy; that a higher duty was fixed on the articles of luxury than on those of necessity, and that the productions raised or manufactured by the labor of the subjects of the empire were treated with more indulgence than was shown to the pernicious, or at least the unpopular, commerce of Arabia and India."[1]

The world-wide struggles of the eighteenth century were for the markets of the nations. First France and England fought for the possession of

---

[1] *Decline and Fall*, vol. i. p. 190.

America and of India. Then England had to meet Spain and Holland in battle for the same prize of the world's trade. Cromwell and Colbert are only the types of England and France, and of their consistent policy.

When Holland failed by war to maintain the mastery of commerce, the attempt was made to win foreign trade by relieving it of charges which had previously been collected from it. But Britain held to its stern protective policy, and step by step, through all the influences which its government could exert, it sought to draw commerce to its ports, and even more especially to secure foreign markets for its commodities. From a very early day various writers advocated free trade, as in 1739, an essay on the "Decline of Foreign Trade" boldly proposed "that all sorts of merchandise be imported and exported at all times without paying any customs or fees."[1] But until 1846 the arguments of the farmers and manufacturers outweighed the appeal of mere commerce.

Blanqui, with all his audacity, moans that "the prohibitory system," for so he styles the policy of the civilized world, outside of two countries, "has infected all Europe."[2] Mr. Ruskin admits that "no nation dares to abolish its custom houses." The infection has been the result of the experience of all the centuries. In the course of revolutions nations have been found to dare anything which promised

[1] Cunningham's *English Industry and Commerce*, p. 374.
[2] Page 526.

greatness and prosperity, but not one has yet dared in any madness or exaltation to abolish its custom houses. The lesson is as eloquent as all the ages can render it, that every government, with two exceptions within recent days, has relied in large part upon charges upon commerce for its revenue, and with a direct purpose to encourage its own laborers and to enlarge production upon its own soil. That is the declaration of the common sense of mankind.

Professor Fawcett, one of the foremost advocates of the British system, declares with something of pathos, that "not only in countries where protection has been long established is there a disinclination to follow the example set by England, but even in new countries, such as Australia, there is constantly displayed an eagerness to introduce protection in one or other of its various forms." Sidgwick [1] declares that "free trade has recently been called in question by an apparently growing party of practical men." This is abundantly true. It is the way in which the prediction of Cobden that England could convert the world to free trade is answered. It is the sturdy adherence of mankind to methods which their sense and their experience approve.

Under due restrictions, the appeal to authority has just weight. Considering the extent of time covered by our investigations, and the array of nations which by their constant practice bear their testimony, demonstrating that the opinion of the world has found

[1] Page 6.

expression in legislation, we insist that upon no point has authority stood so firmly as for a protective system of revenue, — for a revenue system which charges commerce avowedly and vigorously with some share of the burdens of government. Doubters and critics have arisen as they have assailed Christianity.

But no axiom of morals, no doctrine of any creed, hardly any fact in science outside of pure mathematics, has ever been so uniformly sustained by the teachings and practice, certainly not by such a consent of legislation, of mankind in all ages. Whatever strength can be derived from the approval of mankind, from general acceptance, *semper ab omnibus ubique*, belongs to a revenue system which protects home industry by levying imposts upon commerce.

CHAPTER IV.

AMERICAN METHODS AND RESULTS.

The British Stamp Tax for the Colonies. — Pitt's Distinction between Internal and External Taxes. — Commissioners to collect Import Duties. — The Revolution began our Revenue. — The Power to levy Taxes and regulate Commerce conceded to the National Government. — The Architects of the Union Experts in Matters of Revenue. — The Second Statute a Tariff. — The Precedent for our Fiscal Legislation. — Madison in advance of Hamilton. — Hamilton's First Report as Secretary of the Treasury. — Tariffs of 1790 and 1791. — Hamilton's Report on Manufactures. — Legislation before 1812. — Report of Gallatin, Secretary of the Treasury. — Internal Taxes of 1791. — Resistance to Law. — Internal Taxes repealed under Jefferson. — Hostile to the Genius of a Free People. — The Public Lands. — The War of 1812. — Fluctuations in Imports. — Secretary Dallas and the Tariff of 1816. — The Debate. — Clay, Webster, Calhoun. — Tariff of 1824. — Convention of 1827. — Debate and Legislation in 1828. — Nullification. — The Clay Compromise. — Fiscal Acts of Thirty Years. — Internal Taxes again. — Effect of the Reductions of Duties under the Compromise. — Election of 1840. — Tariff of 1842. — Report of Robert J. Walker. — Free Trade Acts of 1846 and of 1857. — From Nullification to Secession. — Gold driven from the Country. — The Morrill Tariff. — Increments and Reductions. — Repeal of the Moiety Laws. — Act of the Tariff Commission. — Internal Taxes a Third Time. — Vast Revenues collected in 1866. — Four Periods in our Revenue Legislation. — The Influence of Slavery. — The Southern Confederacy makes the only Attempt to embody in Fundamental Law a Prohibition of Duties to foster Industry. — Limits of the Four Periods by Events and by Time. — Rates of Duties. — The Free List. — National, State, and Local Imposts.

THE chronicles of American revenue begin with the attempt of the British Parliament to collect a stamp tax in the colonies. It was natural for the home authorities to seek to get back some of the money which the settlements on this side of the Atlantic were costing. Pitt, in his remarkable response to Grenville, drew a sharp line between internal and external taxes, and clearly intimated that customs duties might be collected in the colonies without offense. Franklin, as agent for Pennsylvania, gave expression to like suggestions. At all events, in the beginning the colonists based their opposition wholly on the nature of the tax which was imposed. But the repeal of the stamp tax was followed by the billeting of troops on Boston and New York, and friction was continued and grew more intense. The appointment of commissioners to collect import duties found the spirit of liberty aroused, and the protest, "No taxation without representation," was the foundation of union. In fact, owing to distance and to slowness of communication representation for the colonies in the British Parliament was impracticable. The demands of the colonists were, therefore, that Britain should not impose any taxes upon them, but that any contribution to the general government should be conceded by the colonial legislatures upon request from the ministers in London. Radical principles were declared in high places in those days. Pitt insisted in Parliament that taxation was no part of the governing power, but that moneys must be conceded by the people. The colonists perhaps made no distinction between kinds of taxes; they felt the movements of independence, and the grievance of the stamp tax brought their spirit of freedom into action. Another kind of burden at that time might have served as well for organizing the tendency to separation. As a matter of fact the corner-stone of American Union was laid in revenue.

Trouble enough there was during the days of the confederation to raise moneys for carrying on the struggle. The impracticability of relying upon separate states for a national fund was demonstrated. When the constitution was framed this was one of the radical difficulties, and, with the methods of supervising commerce, presented grave obstacles to the formation of a republic. The concessions were made, and the power to levy taxes and to regulate commerce became fundamental with the national government.

The architects of the Union had been trained in a hard school of revenue. To them it was true, as Frederick List said later: "The best book on political economy in this new country is the volume of life." They were familiar with all the discussions with the mother country. They had experienced the trials of the confederation. They had known all the opposition to national systems of taxation and of commerce. They were no novices in the principles and the practical application of methods for raising revenue, and developing trade and industry. Whether as students of history or as subjects of the rough discipline of establishing a new government, they were as well equipped for pronouncing upon the questions involved as any like number of statesmen whom the world has ever seen gathered in one place.

THE FIRST AMERICAN TARIFF.

They began prudently, and with a clear understanding of the purposes which they had in view and of the measures which were necessary for attaining them. The second statute which Congress enacted, and which Washington signed, declared in a preamble, that it was " necessary for the support of the government, for the discharge of the debt of the United States, and the encouragement and protection of manufactures, that duties be laid." This was the beginning of American legislation on the revenue. It expresses the principles which have grown into the American system. No one among the leaders of our politics during the first three quarters of a century failed to accept the doctrine,[1] although several have given utterance also to the belief that a tariff ought not to seek to protect domestic industry. We may find such contradictions in the career of many of our statesmen. Our legislation does not show such variations. Until we reach the tariff of 1846 the statutes are a succession of imposts prompted by the spirit which enacted the original American tariff.

[1] In Greeley's Essays on Political Economy, he gives an abstract of the opinions of early American statesmen on the tariff.

The charge has been put forth that American revenue legislation is complex and confusing. No other branch of our statutes shows less of blundering, less of tendency to change, less of crude and ill-meant work. There is no mystery about our tariffs, save that which comes from the variety of our commerce, the diversity of our industries, and the vast sums of money which our continental growth and our foreign wars and the great civil strife have entailed.

When the national government began its career the treasury was empty, and borrowing had been carried quite as far as was prudent. Congress had no more pressing obligation than to provide means for supporting the new institutions. The plain duty was to lay the foundations of a system of revenue which could grow with the nation. Experience and reason had taught the necessity of adequate receipts from sure resources. The Continental Congress had proposed customs duties, and all of the states except New York had assented to their collection. On the basis of that scheme, Mr. Madison, who as one of the framers and chief champions of the constitution understood the tasks which confronted Congress in the very early days of the session, set to work to provide a revenue. He was ready for broader action than was even his associate in the "Federalist."[1]

[1] In his special message of February 20, 1815, "laying before Congress copies of the treaty of peace and amity between the United States and his Britannic majesty," Mr. Madison urges:—

"But there is no subject that can enter with greater force and merit into the deliberations of Congress than a consideration of the means

Hamilton was not prepared for fixing specific duties and enumerating articles, but Madison deemed to preserve and promote the manufactures which have sprung into existence and attained an unparalleled maturity throughout the United States during the period of the European wars. *This source of national independence and wealth I anxiously recommend, therefore, to the prompt and constant guardianship of Congress."*

In a letter dated "Montpelier, October 10, 1827," and addressed to the Lynchburg *Virginian*, Mr. Madison declares that the doctrine of protection " had been entertained and acted on from the commencement of the Constitution of the United States by the several branches of every administration under it," and that "the power of Congress, in its enlarged sense," was " a primary and known object in forming the constitution."

Writing September 18, 1828, to Joseph C. Cabell, Mr. Madison, who had been claimed as sympathizing with the South Carolina hostility to the new tariff, said: —

" That the encouragement of manufactures was an object of the power to regulate trade is proved by the use made of the power for that object in the first session of the first Congress under the constitution, when, among the members present, there were so many who had been members of the federal convention which framed the constitution, and of the state conventions which ratified it; each of these classes consisting also of members who had opposed and who had espoused the constitution in its actual form. It does not appear from the printed proceedings of Congress on that occasion that the power was denied by any of them. And it may be remarked that members from Virginia, in particular, as well of the anti-federal as the federal party, the names then distinguishing those who had opposed and those who had approved the constitution, did not hesitate to propose duties, and to suggest even prohibitions in favor of several articles of her production. By one a duty was proposed on mineral coal in favor of the Virginia coal pits; by another a duty on hemp was proposed to encourage the growth of that article; and by a third a prohibition even of foreign beef was suggested as a measure of sound policy.

" A further evidence in support of the constitutional power to protect and foster manufactures by regulations of trade, an evidence that it wise to begin in that way, and Congress agreed with him. The original law prescribed certain specific duties, with enumeration of merchandise, in addition to *ad valorem* charges, with drawbacks on articles exported within a year. At the same time a discrimination of ten per cent. was allowed on goods brought in by American vessels. This act of July 4, 1789, — for it was passed on the thirteenth anniversary of our national independence, — consists of less than three pages of the law books. The highest *ad valorem* rate was fifteen per cent. on carriages; the specific rates are adjusted at ten cents a gallon on Jamaica spirits, eighteen cents on wine, six to fifteen cents a pound on tea, and at like standards; while the rate on all unenumerated articles was five per cent. with a short free list.

The duties charged on American ships entering the ports of the country were established at six cents per ton, while foreign owners were required to pay fifty cents a ton. When the vessels were owned partly in the United States and partly abroad, the rates were thirty cents a ton. This first tariff went into effect on the first of August, 1789.

ought of itself to settle the question, is the uniform and practical sanction given to the power by the general government for nearly forty years, with a concurrence or acquiescence of every state government throughout the same period; and, it may be added, through all the vicissitudes of party which marked the period. No novel construction, however ingeniously devised, or however respectable and patriotic its patrons, can withstand the weight of such authorities, or the unbroken current of so prolonged and universal a practice."

In a second letter to Mr. Cabell, October 30, 1828, Mr. Madison advocated the exercise of this power.

The treasury was formally organized as a department September 2, 1789, and Alexander Hamilton was the first secretary. His first report dealt with the debt which was pressing, and the means to pay the annual interest as well as the current demands of the government. He wanted in all $2,839,163. He argued that this sum might be derived from the existing duties on imports and tonnage, increased, as could well be done. He classed the articles which were enumerated as all of them in reality luxuries. Under this inspiration the tariff of 1790 was enacted, which made an average increase in duties of two and one half per cent. The imports for the year ending September 30, 1790, were, at duties of five per cent., $13,778,510; at seven and a half per cent., $960,138; at ten per cent., $644,326; and at fifteen per cent., $5,429. But it must be remembered that especially in the United States money was worth a great deal in those days of poverty, and the imports and the rates of duties are to be measured in that light. The duties on distilled spirits were modified according to proof, by act of March 3, 1791, and carried up to forty cents a gallon.

HAMILTON'S REPORT ON MANUFACTURES.

These acts were prophecies of the famous report of Alexander Hamilton on manufactures, communicated to Congress December 5, 1791, and still a classic on topics connected with the production and the finances of our country. He dwelt on the disadvantages surrounding our foreign trade by reason of the restrictive regulations of Britain, which were "abridging the vent of our agricultural produce," and on the wisdom of seeking at home for an indemnification for these external disadvantages, "as well as an occasion of resources favorable to national independence and safety." He insisted that the national government had the power to encourage learning, manufactures, agriculture, and commerce. He presented import duties as a proper means of encouraging manufactures, and suggested also bounties, premiums, exemption of raw materials from duty, drawbacks, the incitement to inventions, with the development of means of communication. His review of the existing industries is elaborate and instructive. The building up of American manufactures he declared would increase immigration, and would establish a steady demand for the produce of the soil in domestic markets.

Congress and the nation accepted the report of Hamilton as proclaiming the true American policy. The statutes were framed in accordance with his teachings. The revolutionary period coming down to the War of 1812 is little more than the expansion and enforcement of the tariffs of Madison and Hamilton. The books contain in all fifteen statutes bearing upon duties, and they cover thirty-six pages.[1]

---

[1] These statutes are : —

Act of July 4, 1789, less than three pages, fixing duties.

August 10, 1790, two and a half pages, repealing the former, and changing duties.

The average duties collected in 1791 were on all importations 15.34 per cent. They fell to 11.54 per cent. in 1792. They became 19.99 per cent. in 1798. They reached 30.67 per cent. in 1802 on importations which were decreasing. Falling again, they mounted to 37.22 per cent. in 1809.

The development of our manufactures within this interval of twenty-three years justified the legislation which aimed at that result. In his report of April 17, 1810, Albert Gallatin, then Secretary of the Treasury, estimated their annual product at $120,000,000.

March 2, 1791, explanatory of duties on chintzes and colored calicoes, one third page.

March 3, 1791, relative to duties on spirits, foreign and domestic, fifteen and one fourth pages.

May 2, 1792, modifying duties on wines and spirits, and beer; also altering certain other duties, one and one fourth page; and general provisions bringing the statute to five pages.

June 5, 1794, concerning duties on spirits, stills, wines, and teas, three pages.

June 7, 1794, enlarging the dutiable list, one and three fourths of a page.

Act January 29, 1795, to remedy difficulties in ascertaining certain duties, three pages.

March 3, 1797, relative to sugar, tea, velvet, plain cotton goods, and cocoa, to raise money to apply on the principal of the debt, one page.

July 8, 1797, for an additional duty on salt, three fourths of a page.

May 13, 1800, adding to the duties on sugar and wines, one page.

March 3, 1804, relative to drawbacks, one half page.

March 27, 1804, for imposing more specific duties on certain articles, one and three fourths of a page.

March 3, 1807, repealing the duties on salt, one half page.

March 4, 1808, to allow old copper, saltpetre, and sulphur to come in free, half a page.

On the classes of merchandise which it was the design to develop the duties were not extreme. On both iron and leather, the rates were gradually brought up to seventeen and a half per cent. On calicoes they were the same, and had been advanced by the same steps from the original five per cent. which had been collected from them as unenumerated articles. Wool raw was kept free, and its manufactures had been rated at fifteen per cent. before the beginning of the war. Salt had been placed at ten cents a bushel by the first tariff, and raised to twenty cents in 1797, but it had been put on the free list in 1807. Sugar was the object of considerable discussion, beginning with one cent a pound for brown, and advancing up to two and a half cents, while refined started at three cents a pound and before the war was nine cents a pound.

INTERNAL TAXES.

As early as March, 1791, Congress resorted to internal taxes, and they at once aroused opposition. In the succeeding year, Secretary Hamilton was ordered to present a report on the subject. He tried to meet the objections that the system was offensive to liberty, injurious to morals, and involved heavy penalties and frequent litigation. The taxes fell especially upon spirits, but the term excise was popularly taken to cover the principle of internal taxation. The resistance to the law became flagrant, and drew in persons of prominence. In Pennsylvania, Albert Gallatin was an officer at a meeting to denounce the system. He published a sketch of the finances in 1796, to expose the weakness of the methods of excise adopted. But the country and the courts, which were appealed to on the plea that the law was unconstitutional, sustained Congress. The policy was extended. Carriages, sales at auction, vellum, and paper used for legal documents, sugar refined within the United States, and snuff, were included in the scheme of taxation. But the treasury wanted still more money. Two plans were suggested: first, to extend these internal taxes; and second, to impose direct taxes, apportioned among the States. Oliver Wolcott, Hamilton's successor at the head of the Treasury, insisted that "a direct taxation, as odd as it may seem, is essentially necessary to induce a people to love their government." A statute was enacted to levy direct taxes. But with the coming in of Jefferson's administration all internal taxation was abolished. The prejudice against the army of officers, who numbered three hundred and fifty-three in all, and the friction and penalties, which aroused constant hostility, were the incitement to this action. John Randolph, as chairman of the Ways and Means Committee, charged that it had cost a fifth of the income to assess and collect these taxes; in fact, the cost was less than one ninth. But the vexation and oppression, the hostility to the genius of a free people, and the multiplication of officers, were assigned as reasons for abolishing the whole system, and they were accepted as abundantly adequate. Never since, except under the stress of war, has the nation resorted to either direct or other internal taxes.[1]

THE PUBLIC LANDS.

But the public lands afforded an additional argument for the abolition of internal imposts. They had begun in 1796 to bring money into the treasury by sales, and in 1811 the sum had reached the magnitude, then unparalleled, of $1,040,237. By 1807, Secretary Gallatin reported that the government had a surplus of over three million dollars unappropriated. The debt had become manageable. The embargo act soon cut down the receipts from customs and tonnage, and a deficiency began to appear in 1809. The country was drifting into conflict with Great Britain. The first chapter in our national finances had been written, and the second was to begin.

THE WAR OF 1812.

On the first of July, 1812, to prepare for the conflict which had been formally declared on the 18th of June, the duties were all doubled, and the increase of one hundred per cent. was to continue for a year after the conclusion of peace. The struggle was one of commerce and of rights at sea. Great Britain had never secured real peace with our country, had never accepted as real our national independence. Grounds

---

[1] The repeal was carried upon a report by John Randolph, April 2, 1802.

of difference had been left open, and the rivalries of trade were suffered to keep alive animosities on both sides. Certainly in the steps which led to hostilities the commercial elements were prominent. The desire of Congress in doubling the duties was to place heavy charges upon every article which might in any form reach our shores from British manufacturers. Our own industries were already varied and extensive. The purpose of becoming independent of our great rival, and of all other nations, had taken definite form. The erection of factories and furnaces was not simply a business enterprise; it had been lifted up into a patriotic duty.

The importations had aggregated $138,500,000 in 1808. They fell to $22,005,000 in 1813, and to $12,965,000 in 1814. The duties on commodities valued at $77,030,000 had averaged 13.07 per cent. in the fiscal year 1812, nearly the whole of which antedated hostilities. The average rates attained in 1813 the extreme altitude of 69.03 per cent. This is by far the highest average ever attained in our customs. In 1814 the duties fell to 46.79 per cent. By the Treaty of Ghent peace was declared on the 17th of February, 1815, and on the 3d of March discriminating duties were abolished in the case of nations which had abolished like discriminations against us. The importations amounted to $113,041,274, more than a hundred million dollars more than in the twelve months immediately preceding. The duties fell to the low average of 6.84 per cent., a minimum which is unprecedented in our records. The statute-books will prove that these fluctuations were due, not to legislation, but to the vagaries of commerce upon an identical basis; for the war duties would not cease, by their terms, until the 17th of February, 1816, and they were in fact continued by act of Congress until the 30th of June of that year, and then prolonged at an increase of forty-two per cent. instead of one hundred per cent. over the duties before July 1, 1812. But neither of these extensions went into effect, for the revision of 1816 was completed by the 27th of April of that year.

THE TARIFF OF 1816.

Some writers are accustomed to speak of this measure as a free trade tariff. It does not deserve that title. The report of Alexander J. Dallas, Secretary of the Treasury, was the incentive to the act, and laid down the principles upon which it was framed and adopted. He marked out three classes of manufactures, according to the degree in which they were produced in this country. In the first class he placed articles of which a full supply could be produced here; in the second class he arranged those which could be produced here only in part; and the third class included commodities which were only slightly grown or made in this country, or not at all. For these he applied the principle of protection by system. For the first class he would secure the home market, and rely on home competition to keep down prices; for this class he suggested the standard of thirty-five per cent. as the rate of duty, as a rule, with exceptions down to twenty per cent. The second class included iron and its products, and cotton and wool. For iron he favored a rate of twenty per cent.; for woolen twenty-eight per cent.; and for cotton thirty-three and one third per cent. The third class was to be placed at such charges as would bring in the best revenue. The bill was reported by Mr. Lowndes, of South Carolina, and was finally adopted with the rates on cotton and woolen fixed at twenty-five per cent., to be reduced to twenty per cent. after three years. The debate on the measure was notable for the persons engaged in it, and for the strength of the arguments presented. The treasury wanted $17,000,000 for its budget. Henry Clay proposed to impose duties of thirty-three and one third per cent. on manufactured cottons. Daniel Webster was willing to concede thirty per cent. for two years, twenty-five per cent. for two years, and afterwards twenty per cent. Mr. Webster had constituents engaged in importing India cotton, and he feared their business would be destroyed, as indeed it was, by the development of American production which followed these rates. Subsequent events rendered the speech of John C. Calhoun the most notable of the debate. Declaring that he had no interest except in the cultivation of the soil, he considered the subject as one connected with the security of the country. So long as we depend on foreign markets, our agriculture as well as our commerce can be destroyed by war. "When our manufactures are grown to a certain perfection," his words are, "as they soon will be under the fostering care of the government, the farmer will find a ready market for his surplus produce; and, what is almost of equal consequence, a certain and cheap supply for all his wants. His prosperity will diffuse itself to every class in the community, and instead of that languor of industry and individual distress now incident to a state of war and suspended commerce, the wealth and vigor of the community will not be materially impeded." He showed how thus taxes could be raised and loans negotiated. Mr. Ingham, of Pennsylvania, declared that the aim was to support the agriculture, manufactures, and commerce of the country; the revenue was only an incidental consideration. The cotton-growers were discovering the value of their staple, and desired to establish a home market for it. Manufactures had grown with great rapidity during the war, and Congress was not willing to invite the competition of hatred intent on crushing out dangerous rivals, seeking, in the words of Lord Brougham, " to stifle those rising manufactures which the war had forced into existence, contrary to the natural course of things."

The average rate of duties on all importations was in 1816, 27.94 per cent.; they were raised to 32.90 in 1817, but by a large increase in importations, making the total $121,750,000 in 1818, the average of duties fell to 16.78 per cent. The number of articles charged with specific duties was largely increased. The application of the rule fixing a minimum value on certain commodities still farther operated in the same direction.

The American people had, during the war, practically lived upon their own productions. The expansion of industries was large enough to supply their entire markets. When peace came, foreign competition rushed in like a flood. The duties on iron were raised in 1818, and the rates on wine were reduced in 1819.

TARIFFS OF 1824 AND 1828.

The country was urging on Congress a general revision of the schedules, and in 1824 a bill was reported dealing with two classes of commodities. On silks, linens, cutlery, and spices new rates were proposed, and for iron, hemp, glass, lead, and wool and its products, an advance in the duties was recommended. James Buchanan appeared as the advocate of the iron industries; he declared that in his own state manufacturers and their laborers had been thrown out of employment, and the neighboring farmer was without a market. Henry Clay made a strong appeal for what he then named the American system of protecting home industry, to cure the distress which he portrayed. He relied upon the example of England to justify the measure, and argued that only by this policy could we hope to compete with that great rival. Daniel Webster had been in private life for some years, and in 1820 had questioned, in a speech in Faneuil Hall, the right of the national government to carry the principle of protection beyond the incidental results which might ensue from revenue duties. He was now again in Congress. He denied the prevalence of industrial distress in the country, and sneered at an American policy which was derived from foreign example. He insisted that the manufacturers had always been protected, and the question now was simply whether certain rates should be increased. He was opposed to the immoderate use of the power of protection. He turned to the iron rates, and said that in Sweden, from which transportation cost only as much as for fifty miles of land travel, men could be found to work at seven cents a day. The question is whether we shall employ them for this labor, and let our own people earn five or six times as much in some other occupation, or seek to compete with these wages, and make up for the difference by a tax on consumers. But the act went upon the statute-books, with duties on cotton cloth at thirty per cent., on woolen manufactures thirty and thirty-three and a third per cent., and on iron manufactures from three to five cents a pound, and on bars $1.50 a hundred-weight. The average rates on all importations were raised to 47.72 per cent. in 1825, and to 50.94 in 1827; on the dutiable articles the rates averaged 50.54 in 1825 and 53.76 in 1827.

In 1827 a convention of manufacturers and others

interested was held at Harrisburg to devise methods for a revision and increase of the tariff. The presidential election was impending, and General Jackson wrote a letter in favor of a "judicious tariff," thus setting the example of dodging the question, which candidates and conventions have been apt to follow. Congress was, on political matters, in accord with the party which elected General Jackson to the presidency. The demand for an increase of duties could not be resisted. A bill was reported by Mr. Mallary, of Vermont, who advocated the principle of protection, and especially showed that on the class of commodities in large part produced in this country duties are not a tax on the consumer. Silas Wright appeared as the advocate of high rates on raw wool, and of a general policy not fully up to the demands of the Harrisburg convention. Mr. McDuffie, of South Carolina, opposed the whole policy. Upon this measure Daniel Webster first took ground for protection. He repelled the charge that New England had forced the policy on the nation, and insisted that the Eastern states had simply accepted the settled policy of the government, and had fixed, to accommodate it, their own pursuits and their own industry. The act of 1828 was the most elaborate tariff which, up to that time, had been enacted. The debate upon it has been pronounced the ablest in our annals upon the general subject. The effect of this act was to carry the average rates of duties on total importations as high as 57.33 per cent., and on dutiable articles 61.69 per cent.

NULLIFICATION. — COMPROMISE.

Already the South Carolina delegation had held a meeting in Washington to concert measures against the tariff legislation. Meetings in South Carolina had denounced the act of 1824 as an act of despotism. The disposition to treat customs duties levied under the established policy of the government as sectional, and as injurious to the South and its interests, was carefully fostered by the extreme leaders, who sought to magnify the power of slavery.

The national debt was undergoing reduction; the treasury was getting rich; it was wise to reduce the collections from the people. Henry Clay, in May, 1830, introduced a resolution for the immediate abolition of all duties on articles not coming into competition with similar articles made or produced in the United States, except those on wines and silks, which ought to be reduced. Mr. Hayne, of South Carolina, moved an amendment for the reduction of all duties, and after fair notice, for the ultimate equalization of all rates. The discussion which followed was elaborate and spirited. Charges on tea, coffee, salt, and molasses were reduced, but no general action was taken until 1832.

On the 9th of January, 1832, Mr. Clay renewed his resolution for a reduction of duties on non-competing articles. President Jackson also recommended a revision of the tariff. There was no lack of plans. Mr. McDuffie, from the Committee on Ways and

Means, demanded the change of all rates to a standard of simple revenue. Two members of his committee brought in a minority report for the maintenance of the existing system, with the abolition of duties not involving the protection of home industry. John Quincy Adams, from the Committee on Manufactures, sustained the same principle in an able paper, with a bill for carrying out the plan.[1] Mr. McDuffie, and Mr. Bell, of Tennessee, led the debate for the Southern interests, and drew the sectional lines very closely, seeking to arouse prejudice against New England. The legislation of the nation found competent defenders, and the sectional argument was met by Mr. Burges, of Rhode Island, who talked plainly of the effect of slavery in preventing the establishment of manufactures at the South. Amendments were offered by Mr. McDuffie to make the duty on cotton and iron twelve and one half per cent., as

[1] In his report made from the Committee on Manufactures on the 22d of May, 1832, John Quincy Adams said: "Under that system of policy the nation has risen from a depth of weakness, imbecility, and distress to an eminence of prosperity unexampled in the annals of the world. It was by counter legislation to the regulations of foreign nations that the first operations of the government of the United States were felt by the people; felt in the encouragement and protection given to their commerce; felt in the fulfillment of the public engagements to the creditors of the nation; felt in the gradual discharge of the debt of gratitude due to the warriors of the Revolution; felt in the rapid increase of our population, in the constantly and profitably occupied industry of the people, in the consideration and respect of foreign nations for our character, in the comfort and well-being and happiness of the community; felt in every nerve and sinew, in every vein and artery, of the body politic."

he said, "for the purpose of unveiling the monster;" and Mr. Burges retorted that it was a monster which had stopped the importation of Indian cotton, and created a vast market for the cottons of the South. Mr. McDuffie's amendments were rejected, and the bill was passed.

This act was the immediate pretext for the nullification attitude of South Carolina. Mr. Calhoun had in 1831 published his plea that each state has the right to judge for itself whether or not the constitution is invaded by Congress or the national government, and to protect itself from any consequences of such violation. The state legislature had called a convention to consider the action of Congress, and this body began its sessions on the 19th of November, 1832. The tariff law of 1828 and its amendment of 1832 were declared null and void, and proclamation was made that if the government of the United States should in any way attempt to enforce the tariff laws by means of its army or navy, then "South Carolina will no longer consider herself a member of the federal Union." General Jackson's proclamation of appeal and warning, and of pledge to use the full power of the Union to put down resistance to the laws, was dated December 11th. The force bill was passed in February. But the hour for civil war had not struck. Both parties were watching the efforts at compromise in progress in Washington. Mr. Clay was the leader in the movement, and his plan was embodied in his bill introduced February 12th, a measure aiming at a gradual reduction of duties while preserving the protective system. Mr. Calhoun was in favor of the object sought by the bill. Mr. Webster opposed any plan which rejected the rule of discrimination, or took away from Congress the discretion to exercise all its constitutional powers for reasonable protection to American industry.

But Mr. Clay's compromise was enacted by strong majorities in both houses. Its provisions, besides additions to the free list, were that, beginning January 1, 1834, on all duties exceeding twenty per cent. on value a reduction should be made of one tenth; after two years a further reduction of one tenth should be made, and then at intervals of two years three like reductions should follow; and with the first of January, 1843, no duty in excess of twenty per cent. should be collected. The South had won its first great victory, which invited it on to the struggle which destroyed slavery. The Congress of the United States had legislated under threats, and had abandoned the policy which had been established deliberately and after exhaustive arguments, and after forty years of experience. While, however, the duties were thus diminished, the protective system was maintained in all of the relations of the imposts to each other.

From the War of 1812 to the compromise with nullification, a period of twenty-one years, the statutes bearing upon customs duties number eighteen; four of them are important; altogether, they occupy nearly thirty-nine pages of the law books.[1] The leg-

[1] The acts of this period are: —

July 1, 1812, imposing an additional duty of one hundred per cent. on rates existing, the increase to continue until one year after the conclusion of peace, three lines.

February 25, 1813, imposing a duty on iron wire, one fourth page.

July 29, 1813, laying a duty on imported salt, with provisions about fisheries, three pages.

March 3, 1815, abolishing discriminating duties in case of nations which have abolished discriminations against the United States, one fourth of a page.

February 5, 1816, continuing the war duties of the act of 1812 until June 30, 1816, and thereafter imposing forty-two per cent. in addition to the rates previous to July 1, 1812, two thirds of a page.

April 27, 1816, general revision, four and three fourths pages.

April 30, 1816, about drawbacks, two and one fourth pages.

April 20, 1818, methods of administration, five pages.

March 3, 1819, two acts, one relating to discriminating duties, one fourth of a page; the other to regulate duties on certain wines, seven eighths of a page.

May 22, 1824, revision of duties, four pages.

February 11, 1825, remitting duties on books and maps for the library of Congress, seven lines.

May 19, 1828, altering certain duties, four and one fourth pages.

May 24, 1828, relative to discriminating duties, three fourths of a page.

May 20, 1830, reducing the imposts on coffee, tea, and cocoa, three fourths of a page.

May 29, 1830, two acts, one to reduce the duty on molasses, and allow a drawback on spirits from foreign material; also an act to reduce the duty on salt; both less than half a page.

July 3, 1832, in the act to carry out the convention with France, a section of seven lines relative to the duties on wines, and an act concerning tonnage on Spanish vessels, one half of a page.

July 14, 1832, revision, six and one half pages.

March 2, 1833, to modify the Clay act of 1832 and all other acts,

islation bears the marks of the chief statesmen of this century in our land. It carried the imposts to the highest rates known to our fiscal annals. Under it our manufactures attained an annual product of at least $450,000,000. The check by nullification was keenly felt, but the vast resources of the nation, with the impetus which had been given, carried forward production in many branches.

1832 TO 1842.

The Clay compromise was a sort of compact between the nation on the one side and the states which chose South Carolina as their representative on the other; between Clay and Calhoun, and the ideas for which they respectively stood. Duties which had averaged 44.23 per cent. on the total importations, and 47.38 on the dutiable commodities in 1831, were carried down in 1834 to 21.83 on the total, and to 40.19 on dutiable goods. In 1837 they were as low as 16.05 per cent. on total importations, and 29.18 on dutiable articles. In 1842, the rates on dutiable commodities had reached the average of 25.81 per cent. Appeal had been taken to the people against the tariff, and in the remarkable revolution of 1840 no other question of policy was so prominent as that of a restoration in some degree of the rates of duty on competing commodities. Very slight modifications had been made in the tariff by acts of July, 1836, and of September 11, 1841.

compromise, two pages. Also to explain and amend act of 1832, one and one half page.

INTERNAL TAXES A SECOND TIME.

Under stress of the war with Great Britain, resort was tried a second time to both internal and direct taxes. Gallatin, as Secretary of the Treasury, asked for $5,000,000 from internal taxes, and $3,000,000 from direct taxes. Congress in special session, in 1813, conceded $5,000,000 from the former source only, but in 1814 yielded the other also. The statutes authorizing the levies were repealed in 1817, when Secretary Crawford reported a full treasury, and the prospect of a continued surplus.

TARIFF OF 1842.

Millard Fillmore reported a bill, which was passed on the 30th of August, 1842. In the Senate the measure received the support of Silas Wright, then a democratic senator from New York, and without his vote a majority could not have been obtained. The act stopped further reduction of rates under the compromise, and made a general revision with increase of rates.[1] The average was raised to 30.50 per cent. on the total importations, and to 36.88 per cent. on dutiable commodities on the business of 1844.

---

[1] In this debate, Mr. Calhoun used this notable language: "It follows that all duties not laid strictly for revenue are purely protective, whether called incidental or not; and hence the distinction taken by the senator from Arkansas immediately on my left [Mr. Sevier] between incidental and accidental protection is not less true and philosophical than striking. The latter is the only protection compatible with the principles on which duties for revenue are laid."

The report from the Committee on Manufactures, presented in March, 1842, insisted upon specific duties as the surest safeguard against frauds, and advocated a general standard of thirty per cent., with a discrimination according to circumstances. The committee declared that every branch of industry was paralyzed, and that an excess of importations was one of the causes. A minority report was also presented, and the debate was long and elaborate. It will repay study.

ROBERT J. WALKER'S REPORT.

Robert J. Walker of Mississippi, whom President Polk had designated as Secretary of the Treasury, in a report dated December 3, 1845, embodied the arguments against protective duties. The agitation for the repeal of the corn laws was at its height in England. Mr. Walker caught the spirit of that agitation, and used not a few of the points made by its leaders. His report is a document which deserves close consideration as a part of the history of our revenue, particularly as it was the inspiration of the tariff of 1846. His position was that all duties should be levied solely for income for the government, and the maximum rates be imposed on luxuries. He insisted that all duties should vary with value, and that all specific charges should be abolished. Care should be taken that all should operate as equally as possible throughout the Union. Without proclaiming a horizontal scale, Mr. Walker advocated twenty per cent. as the standard from which the largest revenue could be collected. He denied that protection enhances the wages of labor, and he denounced the existing tariff as discriminating in favor of manufactures and against agriculture, and urged that if foreign nations cannot sell us their manufactures they must pay for agricultural products bought here in specie, and as they cannot do that, they will cease to buy.

In Congress discussion turned in some part on the relative usefulness of specific duties and rates varying with value. The belief that Britain would take much more of our farm products on account of the repeal of the corn laws was urged as a reason for lower charges on manufactures such as that country would send. Mr. Evans, of Maine, urged in objection the notable fluctuations in revenue which occurred under the compromise. From $22,750,000 in 1830, the receipts ranged up to $30,250,000 and down to $21,500,000, and in the fourth year to $14,750,000. In 1836 the revenue from customs was $26,000,000, and in 1837 just one half that sum. Such fluctuations affecting trade and production were ruinous to commerce, manufactures, monetary interests, in short to every interest of the country, and to all financial operations of the government. Mr. Webster was the ablest champion of the minority in this debate. He charged that the bill taxed the poor man and the laborer; it was not a bill for employment; it was a bill for the relief of the highest and most luxurious classes, imposing onerous duties on the great industrial classes, and taking away the means of living from labor everywhere throughout the land. Mr. McDuffie declared that the great effect by reducing the duties on cotton manufactures would be to cut down the enormous and unjust profits of large capitalists from twenty and forty per cent. to eight or ten per cent. The duties on raw materials to which Mr. Webster had taken exception, he alleged, would be unquestionably favorable to nineteen twentieths of the people of the United States, to the entire valley of the Mississippi, the West, the Southwest, and the South and the Middle States.

FREE TRADE TARIFFS OF 1846 AND 1857.

The Senate was equally divided on the passage of the bill, although Mr. Jarnagin, Whig, of Tennessee, sustained the measure, and it was carried finally by the casting vote of Vice-President Dallas. He stated that " the struggle to exert without abatement the constitutional power of taxation, in such a manner as to protect by high duties on imports many of the productions of our own soil and labor from competition from other countries, had endured for more than thirty years." He claimed that the policy was meant to be temporary, and that a majority of the people had pronounced against it. The act became a law on the 30th of August, 1846. It consisted of nine schedules, designated by letters of the alphabet. In schedule A were placed spirits at a duty of one hundred per cent. Schedule B contained at forty per cent. spices, tobacco, wines, and preserved fruits and meats. Schedule C was long and rated at thirty per cent. carpets, cotton, linen, silk and wool, glass and leather, sugar, and iron, with minor classes. Other schedules fixed rates at twenty-five, at twenty, at fifteen, at ten, and at five per cent. respectively, with a free list. Under this tariff the average duties were on total importations 27.70 per cent. in 1847, and they fell to 21.68 per cent. in 1856.

In 1857 another reduction of duties was made. By the act of March 3, 1857, from twenty to twenty-five per cent. was taken off from most of the imposts, and the free list was greatly enlarged. In debating this measure, Mr. Granger, of New York, declared that three times Congress had resorted to an increase of duties to remedy financial distress in the land. In 1824 the tariff brought relief, and the effect was so obvious and gratifying that the higher tariff of 1828 was enacted, and for ten years the country was blessed with a prosperity never before equaled. By the sliding scale of Mr. Clay's compromise the country found itself without funds and without credit, and production was greatly checked. The tariff of 1842 justified the expectations of its most sanguine friends. In an evil hour a change was made. Protection, he insisted, was vastly more important than revenue, but both could be secured at once. Mr. Boyce, of South Carolina, objected to the tariff of 1846 that it had too many schedules, occasioning perplexity and confusion. Mr. Morrill, of Vermont, favored the reduction of the sum collected and of the surplus in the treasury, and maintained that the wise policy was protection, moderate but certain. Mr. Covode, of Pennsylvania, objected to the measure because it discriminated against American manufactures. The tariff of 1857 preceded by a few months the great commercial and industrial revulsion of the same year.

By that tariff, the average duties were carried down to 15.43 per cent. on the total importations and 19.56 per cent. on dutiable commodities on the commerce of 1859. These rates had not been paralleled in the experience of the republic, except in the troubles attending the difficulties preceding and immediately following the War of 1812. With those exceptions the average of duties had not been so low since 1797 as they were in 1859.

The influences which led to secession were those which enacted the tariffs of 1846 and 1857. The demands of the extreme South and the hostility to the producing interests of the North were inspired by devotion to slavery. The desire to avoid conflict induced many patriots to yield to the claims and arguments of Southern leaders, like Walker, who spoke for Mississippi, McDuffie, who stood for South Carolina, McKay, who was one of the brightest sons of North Carolina, Lewis, who ably represented Alabama, and the strong men whom Virginia and other Southern states chose to legislate for them.

The period between nullification and secession covers twenty-eight years. The statutes bearing on duties number only five, but they were radical in their nature; and the contrast between the tariff of 1842 and those of 1846 and 1857 is striking, as it was keenly felt by all the interests of the country. The law books devote thirty-three pages to the legislation relating to duties within this interval.[1]

If the purpose had been deliberate to drive gold out of the country, it could not have been more effectually carried out than by the tariffs of 1846 and 1857. The importations became unhealthy in magnitude, and the balance of trade was continually against us. The consequence was when the rebellion became flagrant, the nation was poor in its coffers, and the people were lacking in gold. The financial tasks were greatly magnified when the great struggle was forced upon the government. If the policy of the nation had not been changed in 1846, no one can now question that the United States would have been in much better condition to meet the strain and pressure which were requisite for preserving the Union.

[1] These acts are as follows:—

July 4, 1836, abolishing discrimination against Portugal and reducing duties on wines, one half of a page.

September 11, 1841, levying twenty per cent. on certain articles then free, and fixing the free list, two and one half pages.

August 30, 1842, general revision, nineteen pages.

July 30, 1846, to reduce the duties on imports, seven and one fourth pages.

March 3, 1857, reducing the duties on imports, three and three fourths pages.

THE MORRILL TARIFF.

The bill which has become well known as the Morrill tariff, and which, with increments and changes, has stood for over twenty years, was introduced by Hon. Justin S. Morrill, of Vermont, on the 12th of March, 1860, and passed the House of Representatives in May of that year. In the House the bill was supported in chief by John Sherman, of Ohio, with Mr. Morrill; Thaddeus Stevens, of Pennsylvania, was also prominent in the discussion. The opposition was represented by Mr. Barksdale, of Mississippi, Vallandigham, of Ohio, Phelps, of Missouri, and others. The poverty of the treasury and the excessive importations threatening American production were urged on the one side; while on the other, the question of method was raised, and in some cases simple obstruction seemed to be the object. The principles underlying import duties were considered with large breadth and great vigor. The Senate refused to act upon the measure in that session; and at the next session, as the Committee on Finance was so constructed as to fail to represent the majority of the body, a special committee was appointed with instructions to report the bill back within a week. Secession was rampant when, on the first of February, Mr. Simmons, of Rhode Island, brought up the bill, and advocated its passage in an exhaustive speech. Senator Hunter, of Virginia, led the opposition. He admitted that additional revenue was needed, but he wanted to raise the lower duties then collected by a certain percentage and to reduce the free list. Only after conference between the two houses did the bill pass. Mr. Morrill estimated that it would produce $65,-000,000 a year; Mr. Sherman agreed that in times of prosperity that expectation would be justified, but for a year or two the receipts could not be so much. He explained that the taxable lists contained no article not contained in previous tariffs.

A general increase was made in rates, and many duties were changed to specific sums from rates varying with value. Iron in bars was changed from twenty-four per cent. to $15 a ton; window-glass from fifteen per cent. to a charge of from one to five cents a square foot; woolen manufactures from twenty-four per cent. to twelve cents a pound, and twenty-five per cent. on value. Cottons were changed from nineteen per cent. to specific prices on the square yard with ten per cent. added. Copper, which had been free, was subjected to an impost of two cents a pound. On woolens generally with specific rates an additional charge by value was made to compensate for the duty levied on raw wool.

Seven states had proclaimed ordinances of secession before this act was passed, and the demands of the national government at once began to increase with a rapidity calculated to paralyze weak minds. The special session of Congress, which assembled on the fourth of July, 1861, had no more important task than to provide money for the national treasury.

Mr. Stevens, from the Committee on Ways and Means, however, announced that no general revision of the tariff would be undertaken. By an act which bears date August 5, 1861, the rates were advanced, and tea and coffee, with some other commodities, were subjected to duty. The like process of general increase was carried still farther by the act of December 24, 1861. The aim was the same in the statute of July 14, 1862. By joint resolution of April 29, 1864, all duties, except upon white paper, were increased fifty per cent. for sixty days. On the 30th of June, 1864, a permanent increase was provided for. Mr. Morrill in explaining the bill declared that its primary object was to increase the revenue, and at the same time to shelter and nurse our domestic products, from which at that time we were drawing much the largest receipts into the treasury. March 3, 1865, another bill was passed to adjust the duties on imports to the internal taxes which had been augmented. On the 28th of July, a law of four pages was found to be necessary for corrections and adjustment of imposts. March 2, 1867, the imposts on wool were increased.

At this point the war revenues culminated. The process of decided reduction was begun by the act of July 14, 1870. Under that statute the rates on teas, which had been twenty-five cents a pound, were made fifteen cents; coffee, which had been five cents, was made three cents; pig-iron, which had been rated at $9 a ton, was carried down to $7. Spices were generally reduced. Other imposts were changed in a like spirit. The estimated decrease in duties was $29,000,000 a year, from the operation of this law. Tea and coffee were placed on the free list May 1, 1872. On the first of June, 1872, another act was passed still further cutting down the war imposts. It was reported by Mr. Dawes, of Massachusetts, and one of its provisions was to strike off ten per cent. from the rates collected on most of the commodities, and to put others into the free list. The effect of the acts of May and June, 1872, was estimated to be the reduction of the receipts from customs to the extent of $44,374,721 a year.

The business reaction which produced the panic of 1873, and the consequent falling off in government receipts, in addition to the estimated results of legislation, led to the restoration of this ten per cent., March 3, 1873. No important changes in duties occurred until the appointment of the tariff commission, May 15, 1882, and its report leading to the act of March 3, 1883.

In this period of the civil war, extending already for twenty-seven years, if we run back to the tariff of 1857, the demands of the treasury have reached a magnitude unparalleled in this country, and seldom equaled in any land. The legislation has been adequate to those gigantic drafts. The statutes number forty-one, but most of them are brief and of little significance. Seven laws were of vital consequence, first in bringing in money, and then in reducing the surplus revenue. The total space in the books devoted to the statutes bearing on duties within this period is one hundred and forty-three pages, but the important acts cover less than one half of this matter.[1]

[1] The following is the index: —

March 2, 1861, Morrill tariff, to provide for outstanding treasury notes, to authorize a loan, and to regulate and fix the duties on imports, twenty pages.

August 5, 1861, to provide increased revenue from imports, etc.; the tariff sections occupy nearly three pages.

December 24, 1861, to increase the duties on tea, coffee, and sugar, one half of a page.

July 14, 1862, increasing temporarily the duties on imports, seventeen and one half pages.

March 3, 1863, modifying duties, one page.

June 30, 1864, to increase duties, sixteen pages.

March 3, 1865, amendments, two and one half pages.

March 14, 1866, extending time for goods in warehouse, one half of a page.

March 29, 1866, to amend the duties on wool, one eighth of a page.

May 16, 1866, imposing a duty on live animals, nine lines.

July 28, 1866, to protect the revenue, four pages.

March 2, 1867, to provide increased revenue from imported wool, three pages.

March 25, 1867, levying duties on umbrellas and springs, one eighth of a page.

March 26, 1867, admitting certain works of art free, one half of a page.

July 23, 1868, admitting certain statuary free, seven lines.

February 19, 1869, admitting certain machinery free for repair only, one eighth of a page.

February 24, 1869, regulating duties on copper, one half of a page.

July 14, 1870, in the act reducing internal taxes, ten pages are devoted to the tariff.

REPEAL OF THE MOIETY LAWS.

In the process of mitigating the national burdens, the correction of severe methods attracted much at-

December 22, 1870, amending the preceding concerning imposts on sugar, one half of a page.

January 30, 1871, of bonded warehouses, one fourth of a page.

February 10, 1871, to prevent smuggling, one page.

March 5, 1872, admitting certain works of art free, one eighth of a page.

April 5, 1872, admitting goods for relief of sufferers by Chicago fire free, one half of a page.

May 1, 1872, making tea and coffee free, nine lines.

June 6, 1872, to reduce imposts, eight pages.

June 10, 1872, to refund certain duties, one eighth of a page.

February 14, 1873, to refund certain differential duties, one half of a page.

March 1, 1873, to carry into effect the treaty of Washington, one and three fourths page.

March 3, 1873, brief amendments, one page.

May 9, 1874, relative to imported fruits, one fourth of a page.

June 3, 1874, extending time for benefits of refunding acts, one fourth of a page.

June 18, 1874, admitting free articles for the Centennial Exhibition, one fourth of a page.

June 22, 1874, to repeal moieties, six pages.

February 8, 1875, to amend existing customs duties, two and one fourth pages.

March 3, 1875, to protect the sinking fund, one and two thirds page.

March 3, 1875, to restrict refunding of duties, one page.

August 15, 1876, to carry into effect Hawaiian treaty, one half of a page.

July 20, 1876, imposing penalties for selling without paying duties articles from the Centennial Exhibition, one half of a page.

July 1, 1879, making quinine free, five lines.

tention. The moiety system, by which customs officers were rewarded by one half of the moneys recovered for service as informers as well as witnesses and judges, was as old as the government. The statute which repealed it accepted and applied the doctrine of personal rights and of opposition to arbitrary measures under the forms of law, and proved that duties on imposts can be collected without inquisition and without despotic methods.

ACT OF THE TARIFF COMMISSION.

The chairman of the Finance Committee in the Senate estimated that the changes made by the act, based on the report of the Tariff Commission, would reduce the receipts from customs by $45,000,000 annually. They have for the half of the fiscal year actually shown a diminution indicating less than $20,000,000 a year. The new tariff establishes fifteen schedules besides the free list, and under these schedules are classified commodities by their material and nature. This statute was also intended to take $34,790,334 from the internal revenue; but, owing to the increase in the distillation of spirits, the net diminution will prove to be only about $24,500,000.

June 14, 1880, relative to duties on hoop iron, three fourths of a page.

May 4, 1882, concerning discriminating duties beyond the Cape of Good Hope, one eighth of a page.

March 3, 1883, in the act to reduce internal taxation, and for other purposes, thirty-six pages relate to duties. Act of the Tariff Commission.

The law is probably the most elaborate and detailed tariff ever enacted, and with certain provisions relative to modes of procedure, occupies forty-one pages. It is quite as fair to say that we collect our duties from fifteen well-defined classes, as to exaggerate difficulties by counting three or four thousand articles.

INTERNAL TAXES A THIRD TIME.

In the stress of the struggle for the nation's life, resort was had, as twice before, to direct taxes. The act was passed June 7, 1862. The attempt to get money from this source utterly failed, and it was the only failure in all the plans adopted for sustaining the treasury. The single tax levied was only in part collected, when further collections under it were postponed until 1865, and the law was repealed in 1867. The experience in internal taxation generally was very different. By act of July, 1862, afterwards expanded, the bravest assessments were made upon every vocation and all classes of personal property, and individuals and trades and occupations were pursued into all their privacies to get money for the treasury. Every mode of taxation known to men was adopted, except the French octroi, government monopolies in necessaries of life, and public lotteries. The gradual disappearance of all these burdens has been one of the best evidences of the prudence of our legislation.

OUR LARGEST REVENUES.

The largest sum ever collected by the United States as revenue was $519,949,564.38 in 1866. Of this sum, $179,046,651.58 was from customs. From internal revenue was collected $309,226,813.42; from direct taxes, $1,974,754.12; from the public lands, $665,031.03; and from various miscellaneous sources, $29,036,314.23.

At this time our internal revenue system was something monstrous. In that year, of the sum produced from this system, 10.7 per cent. came from spirits. Tobacco furnished 5.3 per cent.; fermented liquors only 1.6 per cent.; banks and bankers paid 1.1 per cent.; from adhesive stamps we collected 4.8 per cent.; manufactures paid no less than 40.9 per cent. of the total sum; from the gross receipts of certain occupations, including advertisements, canals, and railroads, insurance and telegraph companies, we derived 3.6 per cent.; from sales designated the proceeds were 1.2 per cent.; from special taxes on certain classes of business we collected 4.5 per cent.; incomes paid the large share of 23.4 per cent; legacies and successions and various minor matters made up about two per cent.

The taxes on manufactures, with a few exceptions, were abolished in 1868; the taxes on incomes, on gross receipts, sales, and special classes of business, in 1871. So, in 1873, the total receipts from internal revenue had fallen to $114,075,456.08, and of this sum, 45.6 per cent. came from spirits, 30.1 per cent. from tobacco, 8.1 per cent. from fermented liquors, 3.3 per cent. from banks and bankers, 6.7 per cent. from adhesive stamps, and 5.5 per cent. from arrears of assessments on taxes repealed.

Now, at the end of ten years, the internal revenue has been reduced to four classes; to wit, on banks, spirits, fermented liquors, and tobacco, with special taxes on dealers in these articles.

FOUR PERIODS OF REVENUE METHODS.

The history of our tariffs and general financial policy divides itself into the four periods which we have been considering. The first period extends from the Revolution to the War of 1812, and is adorned by such names as those of Madison and Hamilton. The second period extends from the War of 1812 to the compromise with nullification. In this interval the leading names are those of Clay and Webster and Calhoun. The third period is that from nullification to secession. We have hardly yet learned to rank any statesmen with the senatorial triumvirate. Millard Fillmore reported the tariff of 1842; Robert J. Walker was the author of the policy of the tariffs of 1846 and 1857. The fourth period covers the civil war and the return to peace. The Morrill tariff still stands, after manifold changes, as the monument of the ability and shrewdness of its author; and John Sherman, in each of the houses of Congress and in the treasury, is connected with much of our financial legislation and administration.

Our studies have shown us that the extreme pro-slavery influence in Congress was, in 1832 and again in 1846, that which assailed the traditional policy of the republic in its revenue system. When, in 1861, the South attempted to set up a separate confederacy, it embodied in its constitution the same hostility to domestic manufactures which the leaders of secession had before manifested in their action in the Union. The Southern Confederacy attained the distinction of being the only political body which ever inserted in its fundamental law the doctrine of free trade as it is understood to-day. In the constitution of the Confederate States, article 1, section 8, is embalmed in the ruin of the Confederacy this clause: "Nor shall any duties or taxes on importations from foreign nations be laid to promote or foster any branch of industry." That provision stands, or rather has fallen, unique in political history. Neither the Old World nor the New has ever produced its parallel.

Memory is assisted by recalling the divisions of time. From the organization of the national government under the Constitution to the War of 1812, the interval is twenty-three years. From the beginning of that war to the compromise of Mr. Clay is an interval of twenty-one years. From that compromise to the rebellion the space is twenty-eight years. We have already lived twenty-three years in the fourth period, reckoning from 1861. Up to the close of the second period the policy of the government had been steady and pronounced in favor of levying imposts with the declared purpose of encouraging home industry. Clay's compromise marks the surrender to the dictation of slavery in financial legislation by great reductions of duties, but the principle of protection was still maintained. In the third period, the strife between the building up of manufactures on the soil and bidding for foreign commerce was fought bitterly and with varying success. The tariff of 1842 was designed to restore the traditions of the fathers. Walker's report was the proclamation of a new spirit, and it dominated until the sectional demands grew too arrogant, the Southern states seceded, and appeal was taken to arms to determine what shall be the nature of the civilization which is to control this continent. Principles of revenue were involved, if they were not radical elements in the quarrel.

Except in the tariffs of 1846 and 1857, the principle of protection has been distinctly recognized and applied in the whole course of our revenue statutes, and the abolition of the internal and direct taxes in the instances in which they were enacted was also prompted by the same purpose. Therefore, it is true to say that, with the exception of the interval from 1846 to 1861, fifteen years, our laws have steadily applied and enforced the protective principle; the scales stand at eighty years of the industrial system against fifteen years of the system of favors for commerce.

RATES OF DUTIES.

On total importations the rates have been:—

Under the Tariff of	Lowest.	Highest.
1790	11.54 per cent. in 1792.	30.67 per cent. in 1802.
1804	14.07 per cent. in 1810.	37.22 per cent. in 1807.
1812	6.84 per cent. in 1815.	69.03 per cent. in 1813.
1816	16.78 per cent. in 1818.	47.72 per cent. in 1824.
1824	44.74 per cent. in 1828.	50.94 per cent. in 1827.
1828	44.23 per cent. in 1832.	50.73 per cent. in 1830.
1832	28.99 per cent. in 1833.	- - -
1833	17.37 per cent. in 1841.	21.83 per cent. in 1834.
1842	20.13 per cent. in 1842.	30.50 per cent. in 1844.
1846	19.09 per cent. in 1856.	43.49 per cent. in 1848.
1857	14.21 per cent. in 1861.	17.32 per cent. in 1858.
1861	26.08 per cent. in 1862.	46.55 per cent. in 1869.

The rate has not exceeded thirty per cent. since 1876 on total importations. Since 1821, when, on dutiable articles, the rate was 30.99, the lowest rate on such articles was in 1861, 18.84. Except that year the lowest was in 1859, 19.56, and the highest in 1830, 61.69. Since 1861 the lowest rate on dutiable commodities was in 1873, 38.14, and the highest in 1869, 48.69 per cent.

Under the tariff of the Commission the rates are 42.08 on dutiable goods.

The highest average rate of duties ever collected by the United States was in 1813, after the opening of the war with Great Britain, and that rate was 69.03 per cent. The lowest average rate was in 1815, at the close of that war, 6.84 per cent., when the importations were multiplied nearly nine times in a single year. These great changes occurred by the variations in commerce without the modification of a single letter in the statutes.

The average duties on total importations have never exceeded fifty per cent. since 1829, when they rose to 57.33 per cent., nor have they ever exceeded fifty per cent. on dutiable articles since the same year, when they amounted to 61.69 per cent. During the free trade period they ranged on dutiable articles from 19.56 in 1859 to 27.38 in 1852.

Under the tariffs of the civil war, the average duties on dutiable articles have never exceeded 48.96 per cent., the rate in 1868, and they have never fallen below 32.62 per cent., the rate in 1862. On the total importations the maximum rate was reached in 1869, at 46.55, and after the check of the war, the minimum in 1880, at 29.78.

THE FREE LIST.

A large and increasing share of our imports come in absolutely free of duties. Before 1821 no record was kept of commodities imported except such as were dutiable. In that year the free goods imported amounted in value to $2,017,423, while the dutiable commodities were valued at $52,503,411. The free goods were less than one twenty-fifth of the dutiable articles. In 1831 the free goods were valued at $6,150,680, while the dutiable goods were $89,734,499; so that the ratio had risen to about one fifteenth. In 1841 after a general but not regular increase, the free goods had become worth $61,031,098, while the dutiable articles stood at $61,926,446. In that year almost exactly one half of our commerce paid no duties whatever. By the tariff of 1842 the ratio of free to dutiable articles varied greatly. It was less than one half in 1843, between one fifth and one fourth in 1844, less than one fifth in 1845, and more nearly one fourth in 1846.

The Walker tariff carried the free goods down to less than one eighth of the dutiable articles in 1848. The ratio was even lower for several years, and was below one tenth in 1854. But it became greater, and was more than one fourth in 1858.

The exigencies of the war imposed duties on many necessary articles, and in 1864 the free goods were less than one sixth of the dutiable commodities. In 1867 they fell down to one sixteenth; in 1868 to one twentieth, and they kept at that standard until 1870. The increase since that year has been so great that the ratio became more than one third in 1873, and since that period has steadily approximated one half of the value of the dutiable articles. The exact ratio in 1882 was $210,579,007 to $514,060,567. The tendency to an increase of the free list is one of the marked features in the revenue customs legislation of recent years. The rule of protection is to admit free everything which we cannot produce ourselves, except luxuries.

NATIONAL, STATE, AND LOCAL IMPOSTS.

In 1880 the proceeds of all the imposts and transactions of the national government, outside of the movement of the debt, amounted to $333,526,500. In the same year in the United States for state and local taxation, the sum of $312,750,721 was collected, in addition to special assessments which were not reported. While, therefore, we are studying national income we must not forget that the other moneys collected from the American people are now, since the reductions in the government imposts, even greater than the gross receipts into the national treasury. The sources of the revenue of the states for general, school, and local purposes do not vary greatly. Every state, except Pennsylvania, levies charges upon real property. Illinois, New Jersey, and Wisconsin make these charges light. These four states, as well as others, impose taxes upon corporations, and these latter are becoming an increasing source of revenue in most of the states. In New Jersey in 1883, the railroads paid nearly seven eighths of the state tax.[1] Ohio by its constitution forbids any poll tax, alleging that such charges are grievous and oppressive; and Maryland, Michigan, Kentucky, Rhode Island, and Pennsylvania adopt the same policy, but all the other states include a tax on persons in their methods. Licenses for the sale of liquor have been generally imposed, and in many states

---

[1] The railroads paid $677,557; all other sources gave $140,000.

such fees are charged from hawkers and peddlers. The growth of prohibition has banished liquor licenses from Maine, Iowa, and Ohio; in the latter state the Scott law requires a heavy tax upon all dealers in beverages. Georgia carries its assessment on personal property down to household furniture, watches, and jewelry, and so does Ohio; Connecticut has a like rule. Maryland owns tobacco warehouses from which it collects rents; and many of the states own shares or bonds in railroads, and the title to canals; Missouri has a tax on merchants and manufacturers, Minnesota on seed grain, Texas imposes taxes on certain occupations. Virginia seeks revenue from incomes of a defined class. All of our commonwealths, therefore, derive their income from property on the soil, or from corporations, or from certain occupations, or from a poll tax. As between real and personal property the assessments stood in 1880 in the ratio of seventy-seven per cent. of real to twenty-three per cent. of personal property. The wealth of the country bears no such ratio; but for purposes of taxation the practice has resulted in this division.

Out of the total of imposts, national, state, and local, in 1880, aside from special assessments which are not reported, only thirty per cent. came from customs. Seventy per cent. fell upon land and domestic industry, or capital invested in it, or savings chiefly derived from it. This truth bears plainly and suggestively upon the problem of the right adjustment of national imposts. For commerce should pay its share of the revenue.

CHAPTER V.

THE INCIDENCE OF IMPOSTS.

Why are Charges paid to Governments? — Upon whom do they finally fall? — *Droits*. — Duties. — National Life. — Charges adjusted to Services; to Sacrifices. — Voluntary Offerings. — Direct and Indirect Taxes. — Incidence of the Land Tax. — Taxes on Personal Property. — Imposts on Trades and Occupations. — Stamps. — The Poll Tax. — Articles of First Necessity. — Whisky and Tobacco. — Imposts become a Business Risk. — The Stamp upon Matches. — Cigars. — Effects of Imposts on Consumption. — Sugar. — Tea. — Coffee. — Salt in France and England. — Incidence of Customs Duties like that of Internal Taxes. — Duties become an Element of Cost. — Effect of Supply and Demand. — After the Treaty of Ghent British Manufacturers sold in this Country below Cost. — They sought to control our Markets. — British Surplus of Books and Merchandise. — Silks. — Railroad Supplies. — Bessemer Rails. — Undervaluations prove that Foreign Producers pay heavily to enter our Markets. — Growth of American Silk Manufacture. — Fall in Prices. — The Law of Incidence. — Imposts relative to Earnings and Capital. — The Friction of Imposts. — Cost of Collection. — Imposts should not be a Terror. — Should be adjusted to accord Largest Measure of Freedom in Property, Labor, and Home.

Two radical questions call for answer: first, why are moneys paid to governments? and second, upon whom do the charges really fall? The English speak of internal and external duties. The French name government charges *droits*, rights; with them there are the rights of import, of export, of octroi. Why are these levies rights? Why are these payments duties? You will hear the allegation that the citizen pays so much money for so much defense of his person, and so much for watch and ward over his property. In this view the government is a huge policeman, and nothing more. The state, like the city or town and the county, answers the purpose of a vast engine to put out the fires of violence, to insure against flames real and figurative. Moneys are paid to keep the body from outrage and the property from attack, with some reference to funds of foresight against poverty. This is a part of the truth. Life is to be kept secure and quiet, and avenues are to be held open for getting and amassing wealth. A poll tax is advocated on this ground: that every person owes something to the government, and should pay his share for its maintenance, and then that all property should pay its part of the common cost. But it may cost too much to pick up the farthings of a capitation charge, and the fractions of property may be so far divided that the expense of levying a tax may eat up the whole assessment. With these reservations, however, it is wise and well that the citizen should be a stockholder in the community and the state by contributing to their support. The citizen without property may be regarded as the rock-bottom, from which the structure of a revenue may be built. All above that stratum can be included in any calculation.

But the theory that the state is a monster policeman is only a part of the truth. Society and the state have a life which is of account in and of itself. In order even to the work of police the state must live. The nature of that life makes the difference between Athens and Guinea. Now, when organization is so controlling an element in affairs, institutions signify more and more. They create the field in which persons act and serve. They afford the opportunities for development and progress. They establish the conditions of education, of mechanism, of art, of all which centres in that much-abused word, culture. As the state is a necessity in the rudest condition of man, it is the instrument which contributes largely to his highest attainments. Patriotism may be an instinct, as the love for parents is an instinct, for it is part of the very breath of existence. It is certainly true that in the broadest and ripest stage of civilization which the world has witnessed, patriotism became the chief and noblest virtue. The most dutiful son is not he who relies most on his father or mother, but he who does the most for them. So the true citizen is not he who seeks to get the most from the state, but he who tries to lift up the commonwealth to the worthiest standard.

This theory of the commonwealth does not call for frequent interference in personal affairs, for meddling in private concerns. It is the simple recognition of the course of history. The life of nations is distinct from the existence of their leaders, of their multitudes, — something different from their creeds, from their conflicts, from their extensions, and their aggrandizement. Science has not yet defined the elements of human life, but it is all about us. National life has been the manifestation which has rendered all the centuries luminous. The soul which breathed through Egypt is as visible as that of any one of the Pharaohs; the greatness which was Athens had a spirit as subtle as that of the authors and the artists who were born of it. The England of Henry the Eighth and of his daughter, of Anne and of the Georges, was as real an existence as any bluff Englishman of either age. On this continent is growing up a power which is other than its units, is broader than its parts, is vital in a sense as exact and absolute as the life of any American from ocean to ocean.

This national life is a thing to be fostered and developed. Money does not make it, but it helps sustain it. Wealth is not its condition, but it affords helps to broaden and elevate it. Every citizen owes to his land love and devotion, and the share of support which he is able to give. How one town becomes thrifty and enterprising in its people, and how education advances and manhood takes on fresh value, and society flowers and bears fruit, while near to it a neighbor sinks lower and lower in all which renders this world beautiful and productive, all of us may see. How one state or province runs the race of vigor and swiftness and grace, while the other lags behind and plays the sluggard, the chronicles constantly tell us. How one nation marches in the forefront of civilization, and another gropes and grovels in middle-age darkness, is the spectacle of the globe.

He fails to appreciate true manhood who regards the individual simply as a farmer or a mechanic, a lawyer or a preacher, a student or a toiler; for over and above his tasks he is a man first of all. Just so the state has its tasks, but it has a life broader than they can be; and in order to perform them, that life must be noble and worthy and many-sided. Even into the humdrum matters of revenue this thought has penetrated. We must give unto Cæsar the things which are Cæsar's, because government is our roof-tree, and because the character of it goes far to determine our own character. Because there is a national life, the levies upon a people become *droits*, rights, and the payments which the citizen makes are indeed duties.

SERVICES AND SACRIFICES.

Two claims have been asserted relative to the imposts of government: first, that they should be adjusted in the ratio of the services of the state to the individual; and second, that equal sacrifices should be required of every person for the state. Both propositions involve elements difficult to solve, and calculations wholly at variance with the simplicity which must be maintained in any effective revenue system. The state must be sustained, and the support must be adjusted so as to cause the least possible burdens to the citizen, the least obstruction to his operations, the least check to the movements of society. If a plan can be devised by which government can secure its revenue with certainty upon conditions which come very near to voluntary offerings by all the people in such degree as they may be able to contribute, we approach very closely to the ideal state — to absolute freedom.

DIRECT AND INDIRECT TAXES.

Taxes have been defined as direct, on the assumption that such are finally paid by those upon whom the assessment is imposed, and as indirect, because the latter are collected back by him who advances the sum. But the classes of imposts which come under the one definition and the other have varied under the explanations of different writers. Locke, for example, insists that all burdens fall ultimately on the land-owner.[1] The classification has some conveniences, although it has little accuracy. In whatever form revenue is collected, the payer will seek to throw a part, if not all, of the burden upon some one else. In practice taxes upon real and personal property and upon income and occupations are accounted direct taxes; those imposed as license for dealers in liquors and other commodities and charges on articles of consumption, are accounted indirect taxes. We shall find, however, that the taxes called direct are those which often are multiplied the greatest number of times, and are farthest removed from him upon whom the payment is finally cast.

[1] Works, vol. iv. p. 55.

INCIDENCE OF THE LAND TAX.

The land tax, as we have seen, has been found to be that which in all times and in all countries, has been most generally relied upon for a large part of the public income. This may be collected upon a valuation fixed once for all, and not subjected to variation from any change in the conditions of trade and production, as has been the rule in Britain and in France; or the assessment may be annually revised, as is the practice in the American states. The levy may be upon the assumed selling value of the property, or upon its products, gross or net, as was the method in Egypt and in Europe at an early day. Stability of returns and the absence of visitation are the recommendations of the permanent valuation. Greater fairness follows from frequent revisal and correction. When the charge is levied upon the products, it falls to some extent upon the skill and industry of the cultivator rather than upon the soil. By whatever system assessed, the land tax has always been the occasion of complaint. In France and Britain criticisms upon the valuations and upon the rates collected are frequent in journals and before the Assembly and Parliament. These come from those who allege on the one hand that the soil does not pay its fair share of the revenue; and on the other from persons who feel that by a change in conditions the ratio of taxation has become undue in their case.

The incidence of a tax on land varies according to the use of the assessed property and according to the demands to which it responds. The pleasure park of a capitalist, and the mansion of the rich owner, as well as unproductive land in general, will bear itself whatever impost may be placed upon either. The owner is the consumer in the case of the park or the mansion, and he cannot call upon any one to help him pay. For unproductive land the owner is looking for profits in the future, and he adds taxes and interest to the capital. Because this class of property remains valued under a scheme which fails to recognize present prices, complaint is loud in Britain that grave injustice is done.

All business property feels the same influences as attach to other forms of investment. The plants of factories and furnaces, of warehouses and merchants' stores, pay a tax levied upon them, and it passes at once into the account of expenses of the manufacturer and the dealer. They advance the sum, but they include it in the outlay upon which they are entitled to profit. The case is the same with the farmer who raises products for profit and not for pleasure; the tax becomes an element in the cost. The tax of the producer follows the product through the hands of the merchant, who adds his own tax, to the retailer, who also adds his land tax.

The tax on homesteads and tenement houses is still more frequently multiplied. The operator in the factory or the shop pays the tax if he owns his house, or he finds it included in his rent if he is a tenant. He tries to get this tax back in his wages if he can. It thus is joined with the tax on the plant which the manufacturer has paid. It attends the commodity into the hands of the commission merchant, who must get his profit on it, into the wholesale store, where another profit is added to the element of the tax, to the retail dealer, who must augment it, to the peddler, who again wants his profit upon it.

But it occurs that one commodity is a raw material for many another article. The original commodity carries the land tax with it through all the exchanges of trade, and all of these increments must attend it through the modifications of form and use which mechanism may give it; but into these modifications new charges on land appear from the plant, from wages, and from the profits of managers, and the land tax again to which these managers are subject.

The land tax must be more multiplied than any other form of impost for the reason that land lies at the bottom of all production. Any impost upon it enters into food and shelter for every producer. No commodity can change form without drawing into itself fresh land taxes. No exchange can take place without involving land imposts for the food of the trader, for the store in which he deals, for every movement of the commodity. Every middle-man multiplies the land tax. Every increment grows not only by its own magnitude and that of its predecessors, but also by the greed for gain of every person who handles the article. The snowball gathers size by every revolution. Except in the single case of the home, and most of all the home of the rich, the land tax is more remote from the actual consumer of the matter taxed than any other impost levied in any country. The anomaly is that such a charge has been named a direct tax.

The land tax becomes a vital part of the cost of every article produced, and the tendency is to multiply it in the degrees sketched. But the landlord may find that tenements are in excess of the demand, and although a tax may be even increased, he may fail to cast any part of it upon the tenant; he may be compelled to accept the full burden himself. The mechanic may discover that although his taxes or his rents are advanced, the demand for his services does not grow in the same measure, and may rather be less; in that case he cannot get any return for the tax, but must take it out of means perhaps appropriated to other purposes, and his children may be deprived of school-books or of comforts of dress. The factory may learn that the market is glutted with its goods, and the charge set over to meet the land tax must be dropped with perhaps other items, and the commodities sold at such a price as can be got; so the charge of the government must come out of the stockholders, or out of past savings. The experience of the middle-men may be the same.

They may be unable to cast the tax upon buyers, and may have been forced to pay it to the producers; and it must be settled out of their gains or set to the account of loss. The retail dealer will have the like story to tell. It is the conflict of traffic. The impost enters into the cost, and the problem who shall pay it is the problem of trade, whether it shall show a profit or a loss. That is largely settled by supply and demand.

The assumption that the land tax is a direct tax has pervaded many systems of revenue. The truth is that no impost can be more pervasive, can enter into commodities in so many forms, and therefore be aggravated so much and cost the consumer as well as the producer so heavy a payment. It is a blanket mortgage which covers every industry, every saving, every exchange, every employment, every use, every consumption. Involving large costs to levy and to collect, it has been maintained because it is simple, attaches to visible and tangible property, and is sure and steady. The idea that the soil belongs to the state, has often been proclaimed to justify the charges levied, and a modern theorist advocates the imposition of all taxes on the land for this reason.[1]

TAXES ON PERSONAL PROPERTY.

Assessments upon personal property may be followed in much the same manner. On fixed capital, which is not offered for loan, any impost must be

---

[1] Henry George, *Progress and Poverty*.

paid by the holder, for he has no means to bring others under the burden. But if capital is offered for loan any impost will in some way be charged to the borrower. The imposts on national banks have always been included in the expenses, and dividends have been sought beyond these charges. Imposts upon household furniture, on personal ornaments, on articles not contributing to production, may be regarded as finally paid by those upon whom they are levied. But even such a tax becomes part of the cost of living of the contributor, and he will try to get it back in some form. An income tax upon those who have retired from business, or are unable to take part in affairs, is finally paid by the person assessed; but all charges on incomes derived from production and traffic pass into the costs of business, and a constant effort is put forth to recover them. In the case of those who are the immediate subjects of the levy, it has been alleged that the income tax checks savings, and becomes therefore fatal to its purpose. But all imposts which cannot be recovered have something of the same effect.

IMPOSTS ON TRADES AND OCCUPATIONS.

All imposts upon trades and occupations, all license, and most stamp taxes, belong to the class which pass into the cost of business, and thus are duplicated to the people while the government gets its first levy only.

THE POLL TAX.

The poll tax, separate from considerations of income or vocation, is probably that impost which really falls finally upon him to whom it is assessed. It is sometimes paid, as in the case of the road tax in this state, in labor. Its rate is seldom large by itself, for it is adjusted to the poor as well as the rich. The friction from it occurs from this universality and the cost of levying and collection. The term, "direct tax," may more properly be given to this impost than to any other.

ARTICLES OF FIRST NECESSITY.

The internal imposts on articles of first necessity are always recognized as indirect, as advanced by the dealer and collected back from the consumer. In normal conditions this is true. Yet it is far from uniformly the case. The seller seeks to get a return from his whole investment, whether in imposts or other items of cost. But he cannot always do so. He must accept the conditions of the markets. During the prevalence of the highest internal taxes in this country on many commodities, reports occurred that sales were effected at less than the amount of the government imposts. This was found to be the case with whisky and tobacco. Inquiry would sometimes develop fraud, sometimes towards the government by failure to pay the tax, and sometimes towards the purchaser, in that the articles were not what they were alleged to be. But cases were discovered where the tax had actually been fully paid and the articles were of the standard quality, and where the necessities of the seller compelled him to accept in ready money much less than the cost including the tax. The experience is of not infrequent occurrence; a producer or a dealer is forced by stress of his obligations to sacrifice a part of his commodities to maintain his credit and carry on his business. This incident of production and of traffic becomes a factor in transactions, great and small. Recent auctions of manufactured articles in this country express the excess of supply over the immediate demand, and the attempt to create an equilibrium. Similar auctions are common in imported goods of many descriptions. The seller takes the risk of accepting a price below cost, but he finds also in some cases that the buyers are more numerous, and their demands greater than will meet the cost; then profits accrue. This process illustrates how the payer of an impost must put it with other items of cost at the hazards of business. He may get it back in whole or in part, or it may fall upon him finally. He may sometimes find the impost come back manifold.

The counter proposition finds many illustrations. When the cost of production is reduced, it may take quite a while for the price to fall in the like ratio. The producer and the wholesale dealer struggle to retain the whole advantage of cheaper methods. Imposts follow the same law. He who is relieved from them makes no haste to surrender the gain to any one else. He tries to keep it as long as he can. Gradually competition compels him to yield more or less, until in time by cheaper production the supply is increased in larger ratio than the removal of the impost, or the cheapening of the cost; then the consumer derives more benefit than either item will by itself express. Or as the more common instance is, the equilibrium of supply and demand is soon established on a new basis, and the producer and the consumer share in the advantage of the tax abolished. The removal of the stamp upon matches at first was followed by no change in price; soon the price fell more than the rate of the tax. Manufactories were increased, and small producers entered the field from which the operation of the impost had excluded them. The market fell below the difference created by the removal of the tax. The price will be determined by the sharpness of competition. The experience has been similar in tobacco and cigars. Workmen first required a share, if not all, of the tax removed, while the manufacturers were also inclined to keep the difference. But dealer after dealer has conceded more or less of the sum formerly paid in impost, and the wholesale dealer and the retailer, if not the consumer, get the benefit.

EFFECTS OF IMPOSTS ON CONSUMPTION.

When the impost enters into the price of the article, the consumption is as a rule diminished, and to that extent the demand lessened, and thus the effect is counteracted in some degree. On the other hand, the removal of the tax cheapens the commodity, the consumption as regularly increases, and if the supply cannot be made greater the demand affects the price. The effect of a small impost on the use of articles of prime necessity can be studied in the statistics. In Great Britain, from the beginning of the century to 1859, the imposts on sugar ranged from 29s. in 1815–1819, to 14s. in 1855–1859, on the hundred weight. Prices followed nearly, but not quite, the movement of the impost. The average consumption of each individual rose from 16 pounds 3 ounces in 1815–1819, to 34 pounds when the tax was abolished, and has since risen to 40 pounds to the individual. The figures with reference to tea are still more curious. In Great Britain, since 1805, the duties on tea were about three shillings a pound, and became nearly four shillings in 1815–1819. They have fallen to one shilling in 1865–1869, and are now sixpence a pound. The consumption of tea was a pound and four ounces in 1815–1819, the period of highest duty, and has grown, especially since 1850, until it has become three pounds, and is moving on towards four pounds for each individual.

In this country tea is not so much in favor as a beverage, and our people show no considerable increase in consumption, whether an impost is or is not levied. The rate of consumption was in 1882 1.46 pound to each person, and in 1866 it was as low as

.49 of one pound.[1] Coffee is much more the American beverage. The price has not varied in accordance with the imposts. On the contrary, when the duty was four and five cents a pound in 1862, the price was 11.3 cents; and after the duty was removed the price advanced to 19.3 cents in 1874. The consumption has fluctuated greatly, being as low as 2.24 pounds *per capita* in 1863, with the price at 12.5 cents, and as high as 8.07 pounds *per capita* in 1859, with the price at 9.4 cents a pound. In 1859 no impost was levied; in 1863 the duty was five cents a pound. But again no impost has been levied since 1870, and the consumption has advanced, with some checks, to 8.25 pounds to each person in 1882, when the price fell to 9.8 cents a pound.[2]

The explanations of the advance in the prices of coffee here after the abolition of the imposts have relation to the production in Brazil, which is our chief source of supply, to the export duty in that country, and the causes affecting the markets of the world. The belief that the demand would be considerably increased here by the removal of the duty led our own merchants to seize the profit and join in the advance.

In France it has been learned that the reduction of one half in the price of salt by the reduction of taxation has multiplied the quantity consumed *per capita* by two and a half times. The quantity con-

---

[1] Bureau of Statistics, table 25, No. 3, 1882–3.
[2] Bureau of Statistics, table 28, No. 3, 1882–3.

sumed is yet only two thirds of that used in England, where no tax is levied upon it.[1] The salt tax is one of the burdens of France. It confessedly restricts the consumption of this article of prime necessity, and both in agriculture and in the household affects the health of the people.

In internal imposts we have seen that the charge is disseminated as far as possible by him who first pays it. He will try to buy for less price raw materials entering into his products, in order to meet the impost, and he will seek to collect it as many times as he can from buyers and customers. The mechanic who pays a land tax seeks to get it in wages, the landlord will collect it from his tenant, the trader will estimate his license or tax in the expenses which he must recover, the lawyer asks the price of stamps from his client, and the burden rests upon him who cannot roll it off upon some one else.

INCIDENCE OF CUSTOMS DUTIES.

The incidence of charges upon importations does not differ in character from the incidence of other government imposts. Leaving out of account for the moment whatever influence may be exerted upon the production of a country, the duties are paid by the foreign manufacturer or exporter, or by the domestic importer or the consumer, in whole or in part, according to the demand for the commodities upon which the rates are levied. The effort may be to throw the

[1] De Parieu's *Traité des Imposts.*

charge upon the consumer, but the conflicts of trade prevent this result in most cases. If the demand were always equal to the supply, or in excess of it, the consumer must pay the impost. But the supply frequently keeps far ahead of the demand, and the producer must adjust his prices accordingly. He must take what he can get for the wares upon the market. He may refuse to offer any more unless he can get his own prices; but unless he can afford to hold his commodities indefinitely, he must accept the conditions of trade, even if he has to suffer a loss.

During the period just after the peace of Ghent, British producers threw their goods into this country with the deliberate purpose of breaking down competition and holding our markets for themselves; they notoriously fixed prices far below the cost of production, for the object of crushing out the rising manufactures. They accepted cheerfully the payment of the imposts, and created a cheap market for the time, in the hope of establishing a dear market for the future. The process is kept up systematically, for objects which can be understood. It often happens that the best British editions of fresh works can be bought in this country, with the imposts added, at a less price than they are offered by the publishers in London or Edinburgh. The reason is that the demand at home has been carefully measured, and rather than permit a glut to occur there, the surplus of an edition is shipped hither, and sold at a low price to close out the transaction. In this way the

British market is kept firm, while something is received from the copies exported. The process prevails in other trades. When the demand at home falls off, British and European manufacturers send their excess of production to us; and the auction rooms of New York and Boston, or the counters of interior stores, are made attractive at prices less than are asked for the identical goods in London, Birmingham, Paris, Berlin, Vienna, or Florence.

But the case will arise when the supply abroad is not above the demand there and here. The manufacturer, carefully gauging the requirements of the markets, discovers that he can collect not only his immediate cost of production, but also all additional charges, and a round profit. He seeks all the profit which he can get. The buyer wants the commodities. The wholesale purchaser has to pay the advance. If he makes his purchases wisely, he finds that he can collect the augmented charges from the retail dealer, and he does so. The retail dealer in turn recovers them from the consumer. But it may happen that the wholesale dealer misses in his calculations, and he is compelled to close out his venture by accepting the impost and more himself; or the retailer may discover that his supply is in excess of the demands of his market. He again may have to stand the duty, and more too. Frequently this experience varies on the same lot of goods. On a part, the dealer, wholesale or retail, may be able to make the customer stand the portion of the price answering to the impost on a share of an importation, and on the remainder left upon his hands when the season closes, he may be compelled to bear the burden. The average may be sometimes in his favor, and sometimes in favor of the consumer.

The illustrations are commonplace. Fancy silks from Lyons are crowded into our markets, and fashion renders them salable for a time. The purchaser is glad to pay the imposts. The fashion passes away; the foreign producer is caught with a stock on hand which he cannot carry; he thrusts them on the market regardless of cost. The commodities which yesterday sold at seven dollars a yard at retail are offered at one dollar. These variations are more common in dry goods, and such commodities as are affected by fashions. They extend, however, to many of the branches of traffic. When the rush for building railroads is at its height, wares required for construction and equipment are sought for, and the seller can make the price. Soon the rush ceases; the supply created for the greater demand is found to be much in excess, and the buyer who can pay cash promptly is master of the market. He in turn fixes the prices, and he is careful to see that the imposts are thrown back upon the producer or his immediate representative. The history of Bessemer steel rails is classic. The price was $150 a ton, and Americans bought them at that price. The duty was fixed at $28 a ton, and the consumer undoubtedly paid it. But soon like rails were produced here at home. The foreign maker was compelled to lower his charge. The fall was gradual, and the buyer kept paying the duty. Soon transactions were made directly and in terms with the duties paid by the foreign producer. Such transactions are on record; but the whole market was affected, and the price tumbled until these rails are sold at $33 or $34 [1] a ton, and the producer keeps on accepting the situation, and allowing the American imposts to be thrown back upon him. In England such rails sell to-day at $25 a ton, in the United States at $34. The duty is $17. It is obvious that, with transportation added, the British producer must bear the greater part, if not the whole of the imposts.[2]

The incidence of customs duties does not vary, therefore, from that of other imposts. The effort is constant to throw the charge upon the consumer, but various influences combat that result. The sum of these influences constitutes the relations of supply and demand. To assert that the consumer always pays the impost is to allege that every investment brings back full returns on all its parts at all times. Experience proves that the truth is far otherwise. The foreign exporter estimates the impost as one of the elements in the cost of his articles in the market which he seeks. He starts with a calculation which will give him large profits. Even in average years he is compelled to accept less than his reckoning.

[1] *New York Bulletin,* January 23, 1884.
[2] Bureau of Statistics, table 37, No. 1, 1882–3.

In many instances, although the aggregate of his business may be remunerative, he accepts a loss to guard his interests in other directions, or even to open an inquiry for his commodities. But when the supply is increasing, when it has passed the point of equilibrium with the demand, he changes the bases of his estimates; he reduces his items of cost; he finds that some one else can produce competing commodities at a rate to win the market; he yields first one and then another share of his margins, and for a long period he may be compelled to sell without getting back his original outlay. He may be driven to this policy because it may be cheaper for him to use his machinery, even at a loss, and to keep his force of skilled workmen, rather than suffer the one to be eaten by rust and the other to be scattered.

Officers of the treasury have of late exposed striking instances of undervaluation of commodities imported into this country. In many cases silks are invoiced at prices far below the cost of manufacture in Lyons. The same is the case with some woolens, and with various miscellaneous merchandise. By maintaining their own agents in our ports, foreign producers are able to make their own valuations, and to gain advantages for competition here far below the rates in their own home markets. These official statements are the demonstration that in some way the prices of such foreign commodities in our markets are below the prices at the door of the manufactories. The explanation is that the foreign producer

THE INCIDENCE OF IMPOSTS. 155

accepts the whole burden of American duties. In his anxiety to secure at least a part of our trade, he values his commodities far under the wholesale prices at home. He does more; he carries that valuation below the possible cost of production. His object is to escape a share of the duties which are adjusted according to the value by invoice. Whether he violates any law of this country by his devices or not, he presents a very striking demonstration of the fact that the consumer does not always pay the duty, and that the foreign producer often goes great lengths in order to guard his customer in this country from that charge.

Silks have been instanced as one of the classes of merchandise with reference to which this process of undervaluation is alleged. In 1860 there were only 136 silk manufactories in the United States, and they employed 5,435 persons, and produced $6,607,771 worth of fabrics. In 1880 these factories numbered 382, employing 33,337 persons, and producing $34,519,723 of finished goods.[1] In 1860 we imported all but thirteen per cent. of the silks consumed by our people; in 1880 our factories furnished thirty-eight per cent. of all the silks of every kind which decorated our homes and the persons of our inhabitants.[2]

[1] Report of W. C. Wyckoff in census of 1880.

[2] Suppose that a five per cent. duty is imposed on foreign silks, and that, in consequence, after a certain interval, half the silks consumed are the product of native industry, and that the price of the whole has risen two and a half per cent.; it is obvious that, under these circumstances, the other half, which comes from abroad, yields

In ribbons and some other styles our factories met almost the entire demand. This domestic competition has been the cause of the undervaluations of which we have spoken. In the markets of our various cities the result has been felt in the constant reduction of prices. That reduction has been, on the average, not less than twenty-five per cent., and frequently is as much as thirty per cent.[1] Thus, by the effect upon the foreign manufacturer and by developing home production, duties are thrown far away from the consumer upon him who bids highest for the market.

The rule about duties is precisely the same as in other government charges, in other matters of outlay in business and traffic. The effort is to include the imposts in the receipts for commodities, but shrewd sellers reckon on the average sales more than on any single transaction. The loss on one commodity or on one sale may be the inducement to the customer for many large operations. In any specific sale it may not be easy to say whether the result is loss or gain. The assumption is false that in every sale the items of cost, whatever they may be, are met by the buyer.

Whatever will raise the supply above the demand must result in advantage to the consumer. If that

---

the state five per cent., while the tax levied from the consumers on the whole is only two and a half per cent.; so that the nation in the aggregate is at this time losing nothing by protection except the cost of collecting the tax, while a loss equivalent to the whole tax falls upon the foreign producers. — Sidgwick's *Political Economy*, p. 492.

[1] Letter from W. C. Wyckoff to Hon. J. A. Kasson.

excess is rendered permanent, a fall in price must follow; but if the ratio is changed without creating such an excess, the consumer will still find that the producer or the dealer must reduce his charges.

THE LAW OF INCIDENCE.

The law of incidence may be clearly stated. The tendency is first to charge every impost to the final consumer of the commodity affected; thus, in articles which enter into new modifications, the tendency is to throw the charge forward upon the last purchaser. But against this tendency acts any increase of supply relative to demand. Because land cannot be, as a rule, augmented in quantity, the imposts upon land used for raising crops for sale, or for the homes of those engaged in labor, are cast upon production and producers, and thus upon consumption. Upon capital engaged in manufactures or farming or in exchange, the tendency is the same, because the sum of capital increases slowly. In the case of commodities, the incidence will depend upon the ease and rapidity with which the supply can be increased relative to the demand. Duties on tea and coffee have been repealed in this country without immediate reduction of price, but in time a part of the benefit has reached the consumer. An addition to the duties has not always been placed upon the price. When the impost can be charged upon the consumer, the effort always is to treat it as an element in the cost, on which a profit is to be collected in every change of owners. This operation magnifies the profits in the branch of trade so affected, and when those are carried above the average, competition enters to adjust the equilibrium. With the publicity which attaches to production and trade in these days, any considerable increase in profits in one branch immediately increases the competition in it, and leads soon to such an augmentation of supply that the consumer gets the benefit.

WHAT CLASSES PAY IMPOSTS?

Inquiry is often raised concerning the classes upon whom certain imposts fall, dividing these classes according to their earnings or their capital. The land tax is by theory assessed in the same percentage upon all property, — on the hovel of the poor and the mansion of the rich, on the few acres of the small farmer and the splendid park of the capitalist, on the little shop of the cobbler and the vast factory of the millionaire. The percentage is the same, and the result is supposed to be equality. But the rate which may seem small to the capitalist becomes a grievous burden to the man struggling to hold the title to his little place. In addition the large capitalist understands better how to make a tenant or a customer pay his taxes than does the owner of a small homestead whose thrift is his only capital. Yet further, the process of casting off these imposts upon others brings the larger share of them upon the productions and the traffic which concerns the most people. It becomes true, therefore, that except in the instances of vast parks and costly mansions and unproductive property, the land tax reaches whatever is raised or made, or bought or sold, and thus enters into whatever is eaten or worn or taken into the home. The land is one of the first necessaries of life, and a tax upon it covers all other necessaries. Internal taxes upon articles of prime necessity are recognized by all as falling most heavily upon those who depend for their livelihood on their daily earnings.

One other consideration concerning the land tax deserves to be mentioned. It must be paid in a lump for the year. That rule renders it especially heavy for those who struggle to get their money. The result is that cases are many in which the owner, being unable to raise the means to meet the tax at the time fixed, loses his little home or shop or farm. Even in this country the sales of lands for taxes are very numerous, and occasion misery and ruin. Ignorance of the requirements of law has brought more than one piece of property to the hammer. The policy of the government must be to insist upon prompt payment. It can take no account of temporary troubles, of sickness or absence, or failures to sell crops or wares. The tax-gatherer must have his levy, or he must take the property or report it for sale.

Doubtless these inconveniences have been the occasion of the devices which have been tried for dividing imposts, for calling for payments for licenses to trade, for particular occupations, for some substitute for large demands at a single time. The hearth and window taxes were devices for this purpose as well as for increasing the payments of the rich, but the inquisitorial methods involved in reaching the information essential forbade that such imposts should ever become popular.

Since we have found that relations of supply and demand of commodities determine in large measure where shall be the incidence of all imposts, and that the holder of an excess must pay, while the needs of the purchaser may make him pay, the assertions that all taxes fall upon the land, or that labor must in the last analysis undergo all government charges, or that consumption is alone finally assessed, cannot be sustained. Imposts become a part of the cost of every article, either through the land tax or through special assessments or through licenses or through customs duties, or through more than one of these charges. Like every other element of cost they may become part in either profit or loss. They may be borne by the producer, the middle-man, or the purchaser. In any event they are paid out of no particular fund. They may come out of savings in the form of money or in the form of land, or may fall upon the wages or salaries or receipts of current labor, or, finally, they may take the form of debt and be paid at last by the sale of gathered property, real or personal, or stand unpaid as a debt. For further analysis, this debt may as a loss stand against savings, current earnings, or by a bankrupt be thrown over to be again charged off against the one or the other. Protective duties tend to stimulate production, and unless the demand is increased in like measure, they must fall to just the extent of this stimulation on the foreign producer or his agent.

THE FRICTION OF IMPOSTS.

The incidence of imposts is to be measured in other effects than in mere money. In every charge made by the government the latter is brought into contact with the citizen, and some friction must result. This friction is one of the elements of cost of public charges. In levying taxes upon land, the state touches every owner at least once in every year. But this property is visible, and the visitation may be external, and is not domiciliary. But when the levy reaches furniture and personal articles, inquiry must be close and intimate. In movable property, generally, difficulty arises in determining values and titles. Still more searching must be the question if imposts are to be made upon incomes, which the individual himself must study carefully and long to determine accurately. A single commodity, like salt or tobacco, may be followed with less of inquisitorial methods. But every impost on internal production, on individual trade or traffic, or savings or earnings, must depend for efficiency upon scrutiny which must enter home or shop, and private bureaus and secret papers. The methods tend inevitably to be arbitrary, or they incline to favor the persons who will seek to defraud by concealments and understatements. Thus personal declarations are invited and relied upon in several states relative to personal property, and only when suspicion is created investigation occurs and penalties are imposed. American experience relative to the income tax proved that its methods were hostile to our traditions, and to our spirit of personal liberty.

COST OF COLLECTION.

Imposts of this class which require minute inquiry, and personal visitation, and constant police, are in practice the most costly to levy and to collect. The poll tax has been advocated because it interests every person in the government; but it has always been found to be expensive in its administration. Montesquieu pronounces the tax on persons more natural to servitude; that on merchandise more natural to liberty.[1] The expenses attending any system of revenue will be affected by the extent of the territory and the density of the population. Thus in Nevada the state taxes are collected upon an allowance to the collector of fourteen per cent. This policy comes very near to the old plan of farming out the revenue.

The customs system requires officers only on the frontiers of a country, and involves a smaller force than imposts gathered from the citizens in their

---

[1] A poll tax is natural to servitude; a tax on commodities is more natural to freedom, because it has a less direct connection with the person. — Montesquieu, *Spirit of Laws*, book xiii. chap. 12.

homes. It has been found in practice the system involving the least expense in administration. It is claimed for it that for these reasons the friction is far less than under any other policy of revenue. In Britain the cost of levying and collecting the customs is five per cent., in the United States 3.7 per cent.

IMPOSTS SHOULD BE FELT AS LITTLE AS POSSIBLE.

The tax-gatherer is the traditional enemy who is classed with death. The citizen is able to avoid neither the one nor the other. Yet one school of economists has urged that he should be seen in every community in order that the tax-payer may feel and know the sums which he contributes. The plea is akin to the terrible examples of crime and degradation that are paraded before those whom we would control in the right way. But this governing by terror is better suited to former ages than to our days. That Southern statesman who testified that our national government had been felt before the war only in blessing, bestowed the highest eulogy possible. No more reason exists why the money exactions of a government should be felt by the citizen, than why its administration of justice should touch every one palpably, and so as to arouse his attention. Personal liberty is most complete when no outward pressure is appreciated in any way. Courts are held, but in order to be assured of their value, it cannot be wise to inflict some yearly burden upon the body of the people. Legislatures are well, but the annual hazards of change and disturbance are not accounted advantages. A police force is a necessity in the community, but no one believes that it is essential that it shall summon innocent and guilty alike, and parade arrests indiscriminately, in order that citizens may feel and know that such a force is maintained.

A system of revenue is like any other branch of government. It should do its work noiselessly, without annoyance to the citizen, without interruption of industry or traffic, without unnecessary burdens of any kind. It should be like the sun, appreciated for its light and fructifying power. Homes should be exempt from its visitations; it should touch no person aggressively; it should act openly and not by secret inquisition or by arbitrary methods. If freedom is a blessing, imposts should be adjusted to accord the largest measure of freedom to every citizen, in his property, in his labor, and, above all, in his home.

CHAPTER VI.

FREEDOM OF PRODUCTION.

Imposts obstruct Commerce. — They obstruct Production. — The Statesman must aim First at Freedom for Production, not for Trade. — Quesnay: Agriculture the Only Source of Wealth. — The Mercantile Theory. — Locke. — Adam Smith. — Agriculture, Manufactures, Commerce. — Production different from Transportation and Exchange. — How to build a State. — Distribution and Consumption. — Freedom renders Labor Fruitful. — Burke: "The Revenue is the State." — Labor before Exchange. — Domestic Industry Stable. — Commerce Fitful. — Homes. — Henry C. Carey: Diversity of Industry. — Increase of Production. — New Industries offer Fresh Prizes. — Alleged Overproduction. — Sidgwick: "Society is always in a Condition of Underproduction." — Agriculture and Manufactures. — Statistics of J. R. Dodge of the Agricultural Department. — The Tariff and Production. — Pig Iron. — Manufactures in 1850 and Subsequent Decades. — Mining Industries. — Wealth *per capita*. — Gladstone: the American Republic "the Wealthiest of all the Nations." — Testimony of Bismarck. — Carlyle. — The Tax-gatherers should touch Production at the fewest Points. — Duties on Imposts limited to the Frontier. — Leave all the Rest of the Country untouched. — No Inquisition.

THE charge has been put forth that imposts on importations are obstacles in the way of free commerce. The allegation is true. Collections from any branch of enterprise constitute just in so far a restraint. Customs duties are a check on free trade. The converse is more emphatically true. Imposts on production are a restraint on production. Commerce and production are so closely allied that what affects the one will more or less reach to the other. Yet they have diverse interests, and each has its own sphere and its own risks and burdens. Any system of revenue must affect production. As we have seen, a land tax enters into every article which comes from the soil or rests upon it. It penetrates food and raiment and home and school. It is multiplied from the cotton boll to the finest fabric, from the coal and the ore to the machine which does everything but think. Something of this multiplication attaches to every form of impost. But it is least, just in the degree that the impost is removed farthest from the work of the husbandman, the artisan, the operative, the producer of any class. Even if the consumer alone is regarded, his burdens are diminished just to the extent that the impost is placed nearest to him. · Political economy must start with studying production, not consumption. The statesman must aim at freedom, not first or chiefly for trade, but for production. Now what is essential in a revenue system to secure this freedom?

Often the various processes of commerce are reckoned as a part of production.[1] But, for simplicity of language, although transportation may render useful commodities which are at the starting-point without exchangeable value, it is better to regard production as that which transforms material or originates utility, while exchange, commerce in all of its variations,

[1] Henry C. Carey, vol. i. chap. i.

only changes the place or ownership of commodities. Thus there is a clear line between agriculture and mechanism in all of its types, on the one hand, and trade on the other; between production and commerce.

SOURCES OF WEALTH.

Quesnay and the school of French thinkers, styled the Economists, taught that all wealth proceeds from the soil, and that agriculture is the only production. The next step was that of the commercial school, which has exaggerated commerce, and claimed for it the commanding rank in the world's pursuits. Yet it is notable that the mercantile theorists insisted upon government restriction and direction of foreign trade. Locke was the real prophet of the modern era, for he insisted that labor lies at the root of all wealth. The chief indebtedness of mankind to Adam Smith is that he expanded and made popular this doctrine, and thus brought labor up to its true relation. He illustrated how labor takes the forms of nature and adds value to them, and thus becomes the chief element in creating wealth, in its modern phase and extent. If he did not carry his analysis through the complex development the fault was that of his time. With the vast strides of invention and mechanism classification asserts itself. Manufactures have outrun every other branch of industry and enterprise. Agriculture, necessary as it is, and lying at the base of all life, has fallen into a second place, measured by money, and commerce is their servant. These three, — agriculture, manufactures, commerce, — but the greatest of these is manufactures. So great is the development of commerce, that it deserves to stand apart, and the allied interests also demand separate classification. They are genuine production. Traffic is different from making things. Scientific accuracy justifies the distinction, nor is there any difficulty about it in common practice.

The producer stands apart from the middle-man. Transportation is not included in production. Commerce domestic and foreign, the whole field of exchange, lies outside of mechanism and agriculture, the making of things. To make differs from carrying and selling. Values may be changed by transportation. Internal trade increases riches, but it is not production. Foreign commerce is often a fountain of wealth, but it is not the steady stream which flows from every hill and valley, from every mine and well, from every sinew and muscle. Agriculture, manufactures, mining, industry applied to earth or matter, to change forms and fit them to use, are production. This is the magician of this age, the creator of wealth, the prophet of a higher development for mankind.

You are to build a state out of the materials of human society.[1] You possess the soil of a great continent. Whom would you summon? You invite first the cultivators of the earth. You provide for feeding the population which you will gather. You

---

[1] See Plato's *Republic*, book ii.: "Let us build a city in thought."

clothe the workers and their families, and shelter them. Then you arrange for tools and implements, then for improved homes, for schools and churches. Art will follow, and all the adornments of life. You fashion your political institutions; you seek to develop wealth and culture; you are busy with production in its many forms; you do not trouble yourselves about consumption; that will take care of itself; your aim is to furnish everything essential for human comfort. Some of these things will have to be secured from abroad, but you must first make something to exchange for whatever is brought in. You can get nothing without paying for it, either in commodities or in money in hand or promised in the future. Your traffic is based on barter. Your production may be fresh and ready for exchange. Gradually you will gather a surplus, and put it into money. You may want to buy in advance of your production, and then you will create a debt which you will pay out of the results of future labor.

But you begin, not with trade but with production. Your care is for production and not for consumption. The class of population that you seek is that which will make something, will add to the results of labor, either from the soil or from some handicraft. Accumulated production is capital, and you may have use for that. You must ally it with active production, to keep up growth and progress. All the while consumption will be going on. But that is an incident, and not the condition of prosperity.

You may estimate that production greatly exceeds consumption, and your wealth will grow just in that ratio. You may find consumption exceed production, and just in that ratio you will become poor. In production in certain types consumption is an element, but you are not seeking the destruction of raw materials but the creation of the higher style of commodity. Consumption is thus a necessity. You consume food not as an end but to produce strength. You enjoy music for the pleasure which is immediate and the impressions which pass into the being.

Sismondi alleges that production is a good only as it is followed by corresponding consumption.[1] Then economy is not a virtue, and the accumulation of wealth is not a good. But the common sense of mankind approves of the reasonable saving of earnings, the laying up of property, the careful keeping of production above consumption. A French writer insists that "the happiness of states depends less on the quantity of products than on the manner of distribution."[2] But you must plant and reap your crop before you can garner it; and you must gather it in before you can distribute it. The increase of production does not interfere with wise distribution. On the contrary, the very increase has developed the study of the best laws of distribution. But this process looks again to saving by all, and to the augmentation of wealth among all classes. True science as

---

[1] In *Commercial Wealth*.
[2] M. Droz, quoted by Blanqui, p. 479.

well as benevolence will seek to provide comforts for every human being.

But in no case is consumption the aim. It is the strength, the comfort, the pleasure, which you seek. For these you strive to increase the volume and variety of your commodities. The excess of such commodities above the demands of the hour constitutes the wealth of an individual or a nation. This excess of production over consumption is the triumph of civilization, the measure of progress, the indication of national power and greatness.

Now political economy can do no better service than to contribute to production, and to its excess over consumption. We have agreed that the government should touch the citizen at as few points as possible. But just in the degree that it must touch him it should be its task to incite to the augmentation of the objects of human desire. To that end it should take from him as small a share of his industry as will serve its purpose. For the results of industry when not consumed and exhausted contribute to new results often in an arithmetical ratio and sometimes even in a geometrical ratio. The best service which capital or the products of labor can perform is to fructuate in the pockets of the people.

Production comes as near absolute creation as is possible for man to attain. The miner takes the ore out of the earth, and it adds to the wealth of the world. It is iron, and it becomes under the mastery of mechanism the machine which drives the locomotive or the factory. It is gold, and it measures the possessions of mankind. The farmer out of the soil brings food for his own and other lands. The fibers of vegetation or of animals are fashioned into raiment. Comfort and convenience find servants in the metals which were shapeless, in the forests which sheltered wild beasts. Nature has no element which is not subdued. The barbarian becomes the civilized man. Out of work blossoms all art and all culture.

FREEDOM OF LABOR.

Free labor is that which is most productive. The condition of the South to-day proves how much more freedom can contribute to the general as well as individual wealth, than any system of enforced toil. It is not at the fountain where water gurgles up in flowing streams that the thirsty man will pledge his fortune for a drop. Sahara makes every particle of liquid precious as gems. About the mines you pick up nuggets of gold and silver as curiosities. You do not carry coals to Newcastle, because there production is most free from restraint. In the orchard, fruit is cheap. In the harvest field, Ruth may gather food from the loose remnants of the husbandman's garnering. Yet a little thing may determine whether a mine shall be worked, whether a farm shall be cultivated, whether industry shall strive for its rewards, or shall fold its hands and sullenly refuse to contribute its skill to the general wealth. Holland taxed its land until its people surrendered to despair.

Spain by its grievous charges crushed out the spirit of its producers. The Flemings groaning beneath the oppressions at home carried manufactures and consequent wealth and progress to England. Britain invited and encouraged the immigrants, and knew the secret that the making of things is the beginning of trade and of riches.

Whatever limits the liberty of the citizen restricts his labor and the results of it. In Turkey, property is subject to infinite risks of government impositions, and the subject cares little for regular toil, and lives on scanty sums. He hoards what he can get in gems or coin, or other forms which he can readily conceal or remove. He does not set it to work in shop or factory. The nature of the government has been generally the measure of the development of industry and of its gains. In his discussions of the French Revolution, Edmund Burke declared that "The revenue of the state is the state." Beyond all question, the spirit which enters into the revenue system of a government is a fair type of that which directs all legislation and administration. The struggles for money are the chronicles of man. The state which watches over the citizen will guard well his labor and its rewards. If in every stress a government seeks to defend and encourage its toilers, it will exhibit the best qualities possible, for Burke says again: "The revenue, which is the spring of all power, becomes in its administration the sphere of every active virtue."

LABOR BEFORE EXCHANGE.

Labor, and not exchange, is the beginning of all prosperity. In all lands, the numbers engaged in toil are greater than those devoted to trade. In this country, with our marvelous domestic traffic, supplying the needs of fifty-five million people, who spend more money than any other like number in the world, the share of the population engaged in all branches of foreign and home commerce is considerably less than one eighth. The exact figures are 1,810,256 persons engaged in trade and transportation against 17,392,099 in all classes of occupations. At the same time 7,670,493 persons are engaged in agriculture, and 3,837,112 persons in manufactures, mechanical and mining industries. Or again, in simple production are employed 11,507,605 against 1,810,256 in trade and transportation. Our total foreign commerce at its highest is, of imports $724,639,574, and of exports $833,925,947, or in round numbers, $1,570,000,000, less than a third of the value of our manufactures, while our exports are between one sixth and one seventh of our manufactures. Even in Britain, the most commercial country in the world, the imports are only equal to three eighths of the manufactures in annual value.

As a mere proposition of numbers and of values, the government ought to consider most the producers rather than the traders, in its laws of all kinds. We have also seen that labor in its various forms, all the diversities of production, enter first into the conditions of personal and national prosperity. Other considerations belong in this argument. Every moral excellence is based on industry and thrift. Not every person can engage in trade, but every one can do some work, can lend a helping hand to make something. He can till the soil, or gather in crops, or care for cattle or poultry. He can assist in factory or shop; he can turn out a pin, or set a type, or drive a nail, or carry a hod. Those homes are happiest where some at least are regularly occupied in some remunerative employment; for out of these homes arise the persons who become our students, our thinkers, our artists, our producers, our masters in invention, in development. That employer was not fully right who set an apprentice to carry bricks from one spot to another, and then to return them again, simply that he might be occupied; but productive employment is a good thing in itself, over and above its rewards.

Where the creek turns water-wheels and keeps busy spindle and loom, where steam fashions fabrics, where iron and steel take on forms of usefulness and power, where human needs are provided for in their greatest diversity, it will be found that brains in the largest ratio are active and fruitful, most persons become able to help others as well as themselves, and the most genuine and steady progress is made in the direction of the best civilization and the most worthy manhood. The largest production, it is to be observed, is in this country in the largest cities, — not simply the greatest quantity and value of manufactures, but the greatest ratio to the persons employed, for the chief seat of our manufactures is first in New York city, and next in Philadelphia. But wherever mechanism is most skillful, and manufactures most varied and most extensive, there in this land, and in all lands, you will find the richest blossoms of all which progress has brought to humanity. Our theme does not carry us to the dens which disgrace every commercial port, to the degradation which gathers on dock and about harbor, to the shamelessness which dares the day, and has dared the night, wherever sailors seek a port, since Ulysses roamed the sea in dissipation and adventure.

But virtue seeks home and its quiet and training and pleasures. Production thrives at home. Commerce is changeful and wandering. It craves excitement and novelty. Prosperity resting on it alone has always been unstable. The scepter has passed in turn along the Mediterranean to Spain and Holland, and now to Britain. Venice wedded the Adriatic, but has left no daughter to adorn her palaces. Spain derives consequence to-day from insults to Alfonso in Paris. Britain relies upon her arms and her diplomacy to hold control of the commerce of nations against a competition which threatens her at every point. Fitful as the ocean, which is its element, commerce is a coquette who cannot be trusted to enrich and beautify home for all time. Measure the duration of nations; you will find that the peoples who knew the secret of long life have been those that relied upon their own productions, and made commerce an incident and not a chief dependence. That is the counsel which Egypt utters from her pyramids, which China has written in her strange characters, and holds at this hour before the eyes of mankind.

Let Americans study to build up homes, to root the national prosperity in our own soil, to make every citizen a producer, and to broaden the base of our wealth so that no shock from without can shatter it, or even shake its steady strength. Wars may yet come, and the plea which after the Revolution, and after the War of 1812, led our people to seek to clothe themselves, as well as feed all on our soil, and to prepare to equip armies and to maintain navies, has still its force. But wider than any preparation for conflict is the task of maintaining a free and prosperous people, for extending comforts to every household, and for guaranteeing a livelihood to every son and daughter of the Union. Production is the beginning of wealth; from it must come the means to buy abroad, as well as to lay up savings for future exigencies. The farmer who has the largest crops is he who can spend the most money. It is the mechanic who earns most by his labor who can purchase the most of the results of other people's toil. It is the operative who works regularly who has the largest surplus to invest in comforts and luxuries. The merchant knows that when agriculture is fortunate his trade becomes most profitable; when manufactures are successful, commerce widens, and reaps richest gains. Traffic varies with the crops, and with production generally. The statesman who seeks to create commerce, apart from the diversity of home industry, undertakes the task of sailing a ship with its masts downward, of navigating a steamship with its hull reversed. If it were true that more revenue could be collected by a system which should foster commerce at the expense of production, surely common sense could not approve of it. Rather would the exclamation burst forth in the sharp tones of Pitt on the stamp tax: "Shall a miserable financier come with a boast that he can fetch a peppercorn into the exchequer, to the loss of millions to the nation?"

DIVERSITY OF INDUSTRY.

Henry C. Carey calls attention to the fact, which is the secret of much of the mechanical development of our times, that "labor is improved in quality by division, and this quality tends to diminish the quantity required for producing any commodity." The more skillful the mechanic, the briefer the time within which he can accomplish a given result. This reduction of time is a cheapening of the commodity produced. This is the process that has given to the American people, and to other countries in a less degree, such additions to their comforts, which have made home so attractive, and have lengthened the average of human life by removing many of its hardships. To this increase of production the philanthropist must look for such an amelioration in human conditions as will fight the battle against poverty to the point, if not of its banishment, at least of a mitigation of its pains. When every nation shall work out its share of this task, some benefit must accrue to every other. With the frequent intercommunication between all parts of the world, the tendency is for any abundance in one land to overflow into every other. The wealth of the Indies, when first introduced, pervaded by degrees every channel of commerce. The better wealth of food and raiment and household comforts cannot be limited in any narrow grooves. The higher the current can be carried in any country, the greater the flow into every other land.

The best contribution which any people can make to the general good is not to trade, but to produce, — not to make haste to exchange commodities which exist, but to add to the common store, which will be sure to be exchanged as the supply reaches the proportions of plenty. Malthus testifies that "a decided elevation in the standard of the comforts and conveniences of the English working classes" was caused by the unusual succession of fine harvests in the fifty years from 1715 to 1765.[1] Provide the commodities, and they will surely be distributed, even to the poorest.[2]

[1] *Political Economy*, p. 225.
[2] So far as we limit our investigation to cases where we may as-

With every new industry fresh prizes are offered for skill and efficiency. The army of persons seeking work is met with novel invitations and promises of additional compensation. The pressure on the old vocations is diminished, the rewards in them must tend to increase, the whole surface of society feels the coming of a new spirit which stirs it with activity. Every addition to production offers more to be distributed, and carries the share which labor can receive upwards. This share is not given simply to those engaged in the new industry; it tends to a general distribution, and all occupations are benefited. Every added industry, like every new regiment organized during the war, summons fresh recruits, and augments the force of production and its aggregate volume.

ALLEGED OVERPRODUCTION.

The champion of commerce discovers a Gorgon in the form of overproduction. He tells us we must beware of developing home industry because the markets will not take our commodities. In no country where population is so great and soil so various and occupations so diverse as with us is it possible to produce too much in the aggregate. Always somebody can be discovered who is in want. He has not earned enough to pay for that which he would like

---

sume that the primary needs of the human beings considered are an approximately constant quantity, we may clearly lay down that the possible maximum of saving increases as the gross produce of labor, but in a greater ratio. — Sidgwick's *Political Economy*, p. 160.

to have. The equation of commodities to each other may be temporarily amiss. But so long as everybody has not everything which he wants, the pretense of overproduction is an economical crime. We may build too many railroads; we may weave too many calicoes; we may turn out too many blankets and carpets; but the reason is that the production of some of our people has not been adequate to enable them to take their share of travel or freight or calicoes or blankets or carpets. Instead of curtailing production, what we need is greater variety of manufacture, a more diversified industry. The trouble is that the supply is not in sufficient variety. As the most recent and one of the most instructive of British political economists, Sidgwick, in his volume recently published, wisely insists: "Society is always in a condition of underproduction."[1]

Famine finds welcome in lands of a single crop, not in the countries in which agriculture is varied. The stress for food which sent the Jews to Egypt was where the dependence was chiefly upon grain. India and the districts of China, which rely in great part upon rice, are the scenes in which starvation revels most frequently, and with most sweeping slaughter.[2]

[1] Page 380.

[2] In a single year in the administration of Lord Cornwallis, ten millions perished (in India) of starvation. In the famine campaigns of 1873, 1876, and 1877, a population of eighty millions were successfully defended at a cost of eighteen millions sterling. The average daily number who received gratuitous relief was 900,000; while the average numbers employed on relief works were 1,680,000. — "The Indian Crisis," *Quarterly Review*, July, 1883.

Ireland has paid the penalty of looking to potatoes as the one crop for food. The warnings have been terrible and often repeated, that peoples cannot trust to one article of farm products. Eastern lands have suffered most severely because there the lack of wisdom has been perpetuated. But in other countries also the dependence upon one article of food, whether upon fisheries, upon wheat, upon pork, brings sooner or later the penalty of poverty, if not of actual famine. Industrial disasters in like manner fall upon districts which are devoted to an exclusive industry. Long ago a French writer called England *la terre classique des crises industrielles*.[1] Manchester was almost ruined when cotton could not be gotten at the opening of our civil strife. Lyons has been reduced to grave stress by the failure of the silk-worm. When a crisis comes in the iron trade Pittsburg smokes fade away, and its furnaces become silent. The folly of putting all one's eggs in one basket has passed into an axiom.

The world has never yet produced as much of all commodities as could be consumed. In this branch or that, an excess has doubtless been created, but the trouble has been that labor has not been sufficiently diversified, and that a mistake has been fallen into with reference to the ratio of commodities to each other. In the world at large, and in any particular land, this has been the difficulty. Civilization has taught no more important lesson than that the con-

[1] Fonteyraud, quoted by De Parieu.

dition of all, and especially of the poorer classes, has been improved just as new industries have been introduced, and therefore just as the aggregate of production has been increased. In a purely agricultural period the enjoyments which mechanism brings later are unknown, and so in a purely agricultural land or district before the modern facilities for communication, such luxuries were comparatively few. As manufactures are developed, more persons are employed, or at least the sum of their earnings is multiplied; the articles manufactured pass into consumption, and wealth is augmented. As this process goes on, countries become rich. It is the only method by which men have learned to add to their enjoyments and their possessions. The number of persons suffering from poverty and the degree of abject degradation have been diminished in the precise ratio in which industry has been diversified among men. In any particular land the elevation of the lower elements of the population has gone forward from the same causes. The fertility of the soil may enable a newly settled country for a while to prosper on agriculture alone, but the time comes very soon when all who can profitably engage in tilling the soil are thus occupied, and a path must be found for them to go on to self-support and to wealth in other fields. Too many may crowd into a single vocation, or its product may lose its profitable ratio to the general demand. Then new occupations must be substituted, and the sphere of production must be enlarged. That is the necessity in this country now. When in the old countries the markets are over supplied, the manufacturers themselves, or their agents, ship the surplus to some other point, and sell it at any price which it will bring. This relieves the glut, keeps the mills or furnaces busy, and guards the demand from falling to a ruinous standard. American producers have not yet indulged in this policy regularly and with deliberation. They keep their products on hand and refuse to sell except at a fixed price, or crowd the home market. They have not reached out far enough to prevent their efforts to relieve the glut from affecting the current demand. The recent auction sales are subject to this criticism. They have taken the goods off the hands of the manufacturers and their agents, but they have gone in chief part into the very quarters from which the demand for the future is looked for. British manufacturers push their surplus as far away from their regular markets as possible. Then they try to get as high a price as may be, but they seek first to keep their regular markets unaffected by the forced sales. Our American manufacturers must learn to practice the same arts. Their exports would be largely increased, if they would ship their surplus systematically, and sell abroad at such rates as would capture and hold purchasers. The process has begun; it can be carried much farther with good results. Such a system is better than to shut down mills and furnaces, for prices can be always attained which will involve less loss than such stoppage. An export trade can be established of increasing magnitude, and thus help to the development of home industries in other branches.

For in every land the cure for apparent overproduction is not to stop work and moan over excess of commodities. On the contrary, the secret of prosperity is to create new manufactures, and to afford occupation to more people, and thus provide them with means to buy enjoyments with which they are not yet familiar. There is no overproduction in this country; in fact, there is need of extending the operations of industry, and creating the means by which a larger number shall be able to make life brighter and more easy. The sewing-machine has added to the comforts of millions; the cheapening of dry goods has clothed men and women with a neatness and variety which in other days were the distinction of only the very rich. Our homes are all decorated with conveniences and treasures which invention and diversified labor have bestowed upon us. These comforts and others like them are to be extended to those who are now without them, by continuing the same process, by extending industry into new walks and providing occupation for many now idle, and directing wasted energies into beneficent directions. Adjust the ratio of production correctly, and experience will do that, and any apparent excess will find consumers, for poverty will be driven farther and farther into retirement.

Now, this extended production has another advantage. It sets to work persons who otherwise would be idle. It turns to use, in connection with labor, capital which has been content to rest in bank or to be risked in speculation. With every new industry a field is found by individuals who have played the idler, or have waited for their opportunity. Men have special tastes and aptitudes. A witty scholar has defined idleness to be ill-directed industry. Beyond question the idle singer of a summer day may have in him the qualities which will conquer success in some occupation which enlists his tastes and his genius. Every invention enlists fresh recruits in production. Every new vocation rallies some men who have stood idle in the market place.

AGRICULTURE AND MANUFACTURES.

Adam Smith pointed out to the American colonies the duty of devoting themselves to agriculture.[1] Say believed the true policy of this country was to cultivate the soil, to become another Poland. A French essay advocating a commercial treaty with the United States insists that this is still our true policy. Before the Tariff Commission last year a distinguished professor of political economy declared that: "If it were true that all of our population would, under free trade, take to agriculture, it is mathematically certain that agriculture would support them all better directly than under the present arrangement."[2] This

---

[1] *Wealth of Nations*, p. 293.
[2] *Report of Tariff Commission*, vol. ii. p. 2319, Professor William G. Sumner.

is the theory at the bottom of the commercial system of revenue. Our agriculture is varied, and it is fruitful; it has advanced with giant strides. It has attained a magnitude which at the outset would have been believed impossible. Yet its products are only a little more than one half in value, if they are so much, of the annual products of our manufactures. In 1880 the products of our manufactures reached the monstrous sum of $5,369,579,191. Our agriculture amounted at most to $3,600,000,000. The former figures are taken from the tenth census; for the latter, I am indebted to the statistician of the Agricultural Department, Mr. J. R. Dodge.[1]

[1] The following is the statement for which Mr. Dodge is entitled to acknowledgment and thanks: —

UNITED STATES DEPARTMENT OF AGRICULTURE,
DIVISION OF STATISTICS,
WASHINGTON, D. C., *June* 28, 1883.

SIR, — Yours relative to annual value of productions of agriculture is received. You are aware that the census compendium gives an aggregate of "estimated value of all farm productions (sold, consumed, or on hand), for 1879," namely, $2,213,402,564.

These figures are taken, probably by ninety-nine persons in a hundred, as the entire value of all agricultural production in the United States. This is very far from the fact, for these reasons: —

1. The productions of the immense areas of public lands, beef, wool, etc., are not included, or those of private lands not in farms, in the older states.

2. Milk, meat, poultry, and eggs produced within the limits of towns and villages, and all products of small tracts in the country less than three acres (unless having a value of $500), have no place in the census aggregate.

3. The census tabulations, which include only products of land in farms, are further limited to products named in the schedules. There

These figures teach marvelous lessons. Our agriculture has been fostered by our manufactures. Our farms are as numerous and as well cultivated as they could be if all of our people were devoted to the soil.

are many productions not designated in the census tabulations. It is only intended to sum up the values of the products therein named. Is the corn fodder grown on 62,000,000 acres of land of no value? Is the straw of 56,000,000 acres of small grains valueless? The number of farm animals is given, but the value of domestic animals and poultry slaughtered during the year is not mentioned. The value of orchard fruits evidently includes that which is sold, probably, in most returns, limited to apples and peaches named in the schedules, and not including the immense quantities consumed or given away. Then there are numerous small crops, not included in the tabulation, like peanuts in Virginia and Tennessee, peppermint in New York and Michigan, which are not represented in the aggregate. Hop roots have been of some value this year, but they never get into a census. The nuts and wild fruits and medicinal plants of farms and public lands would be included in a broad definition of the products of agriculture.

Now this is too large a subject for consideration in a paragraph or two, and I have no time for proper elaboration; yet I may name an approximate estimate of all the productions of the land area of the United States, without placing an exact value upon each, at the round sum of $3,600,000,000. This is for the census year, and the relations of quantity to value are such that the difference in recent years would probably be small.

If meats are not included, for fear of duplication of values, there is immense depreciation of the aggregate, for the pasturage, which makes three fourths of it, is not reckoned. Corn is only used for "finishing" the best class of beef, and for a few weeks' final feeding of swine, and half of it is fed to work animals and used as food of man. The duplications of value from this cause are small compared with the omissions in the constituent values of the census aggregate.

Yours respectfully, J. R. DODGE,
Statistician.

HON. ELLIS H. ROBERTS.

Invention in mechanism has simplified the tasks of husbandry, has reduced its drudgery, and diminished the number of persons required in its operations; but aside from such considerations, only about so much agriculture can be developed in any country with a given population. Farmers are not the best customers of each other. When a certain average has been reached, the tendency in all lands is to stop breaking new ground, to be content with the crops planted, to rest upon the homesteads as they are. As the population increases, a fresh impetus is received; but without any growth of population, agriculture loses nothing of the sum of its production by the establishment of manufactures.

The statistician of the Agricultural Department, J. R. Dodge, has enforced this principle by dividing our states according to the number of their inhabitants engaged in agricultural pursuits. The first group has farmers to the extent of less than thirty per cent., and the land there is worth $38.65 an acre. In the second group from thirty to fifty per cent. are farmers, and the value of the land is $30.55 an acre. In the third group the farmers number from fifty to seventy per cent., and the land is worth $13.53 an acre. In the fourth group the states are chiefly agricultural, and seventy per cent. of the people are employed on the soil, while the land is worth an average of only $5.18 an acre. In the first group, moreover, the value of the products of the soil is $457 *per capita* to the cultivator; in the second group, $394; in the third group, $261; and in the fourth group the annual products fall to $160 *per capita.*

Some of you know the history of many a farm. While the whole family work it, the product reaches a moderate sum. All the mouths are filled, but there is nothing over. All the boys work; some with hoe, and some with scythe, and some with flail; the girls spin and mind the dairy. A factory or a mill is started in the vicinity, and one or two of the boys go off and get employment. The old farm produces just as much without them. The fields are mowed by machinery, threshing is done by horse power, the value of the farm is increased, and the wages of the boys who have left it are added to the riches of the family.

We stand in the centre of the foremost commonwealth of the Union. It is not only first in its commerce, but first in its manufactures, and first also, or nearly so, in the value of its agriculture. The conditions which surround us confirm the principles. Manufactures are not built up at the expense of agriculture. On the contrary, they are often a new creation and an absolute addition to production. The old fable tells how dragon's teeth were cast upon the earth, and they sprung up into men. Manufactures are the dragon's teeth which everywhere spring up into extensions of population and of wealth.

You may see to-day, in the far East, the agriculture of the time of Homer. The plow is little more than a pointed stick driven into the earth at a sharp angle. Threshing is yet done by the feet of oxen on the hard ground. On the farms of Dakota and California steam-plows turn the soil, and wheat, in fields of thousands of acres, is cut and gathered and loaded into wagons by machinery. If we relied upon the Eastern methods, where would we get our food? But for the implements which invention and mechanism afford, how could our fifty-five million people live? But it is not in this way only that manufacture helps agriculture. It encourages it and varies and thus enriches it.

Without a mill or a furnace or a factory in this county or in this state, our farms would not produce as much in quantity as they do now, for the inducement to labor would be less, and the value of products would fall off to a very large degree. Burn every mill, shut up every furnace, and your farms would produce no more, and as you would have no market, you would find it hard to sell your product at any price.

As population grows, the earth brings forth by culture new crops, vegetables, fruit, and the like, perishable and not capable of transportation, but among the most profitable for the farmer. Thus farming gives larger profits just in the degree that manufactures are established near by.

Whether we take the number of our farms or their value, we shall find that the agriculture of the United States has increased about threefold since

1850. In that year the number of farms was, in the United States, 1,440,073, and their value $3,271,575,426. By 1880 the number had advanced to 4,008,907, and the value to $10,197,096,776. In the same period our manufactures had advanced in annual product by five and three tenths times — from $1,019,106,616 to $5,369,579,191.

What is the dream that even our agriculture, grand as it is, could be a substitute for the manufactures which enrich our fifty-five million people? How could the less stand for the greater? The allegation is that the profits of manufactures greatly exceed those of like capital and labor in agriculture. Something of this is true. How, then, could the less remunerative support the better and more rapidly growing interest?

THE TARIFF AND PRODUCTION.

The tariff has been one of the influences which have affected our production. In the period of low duties, of practical free trade, our industries languished; they have been wonderfully developed in periods when the duties have been protective.[1] Pig iron is one of the typical products; it enters into so many articles, and

[1] "In spite of this sombre picture, the prohibitory system carried in itself the germs of a renovation which has greatly diminished its disastrous effects. The incontestable impetus which it gave to production in England, France, and Holland, especially at the beginning, contributed much to raise the rate of profit in all the protected branches of industry, and made immense amounts of capital flow in, which also soon became insufficient." — Blanqui's *History of Political Economy*, p. 320.

it comes so readily from the soil with the application of labor in its simplest form in one process. In 1810 we produced 53,908 gross tons of pig iron and cast iron. By the compromise of 1832 the fires were put out of fifty-seven of the fifty-eight blast-furnaces which were then in existence. In 1840 the product of pig and cast iron was 315,000 gross tons. Under the free trade policy the production of pig iron showed no rapid extension, and all the industries dependent upon it felt the check. Thus, from 1854, the culmination of the effects of the Walker tariff, when the annual product was 736,218 tons, this industry remained practically stationary, and in 1861, at the time of the change to a strong protective system, the product was 731,544 tons, — less, actually, than in 1854. Within the next seven years the product ran up so as to become 1,603,000 tons in 1868. The increase has been signally steady ever since, until, in 1882, no less than 5,178,122 tons were produced. In 1883 the product was 5,146,972 tons.

During the past ten years the British furnaces have added 1,751,266 tons to their product, an increase of less than thirty per cent. Within the same time our furnaces have added 2,324,564 tons to the annual product, or an increase of nearly fifty per cent. So that under our present revenue system our growth in the development of iron in its simplest form is both absolutely and in percentage far greater than that of Britain. In manufactured, or finished iron, the gain in the United States has been so remarkable, that in 1882 the production in this country was very nearly equal in total volume to the production of Britain. The case is identical in Bessemer steel rails, and in steel products generally.

These specific illustrations might be multiplied indefinitely to show that in the interval of the Walker tariff and its successor of 1857, the development of our industries was checked, and that it has been revived and greatly extended under the protective policy restored in 1861. But a broader comparison is at hand, upon the total productions of the nation at different periods. The census presents the total results of our manufactures in 1850 at $1,019,106,616, and these are the first full and complete figures gathered upon official authority. It is easy to see that the rate of growth during the preceding decades must have been very large to reach such magnitude from the poverty of our beginning. From 1850 to 1860, the growth in annual production was up to $1,885,-861,676, or just about eighty-five per cent. for ten years. Then came the terrible civil strife, exhausting the life-blood of our young men, and destroying values in many of our states; yet by 1870, the manufactures of the nation were in gold value, $3,385,-860,334, or an increase of $1,699,998,658, and this is seventy-nine per cent. or nearly equal to the preceding decade of entire peace.

In the decade from 1870 to 1880 the increase in production was up to $5,369,579,191, an addition of $1,973,709,857. This increment alone is nearly fifty per cent. of the annual production of the manufactures of Great Britain, is within one third of the total manufactures of France, and within one seventh of the annual product of all the German manufactures. In mining industries, we have by far outstripped all rivalry. For statisticians agree that of the world's mining wealth we produce thirty-six per cent., and Great Britain thirty-three per cent., while all other nations produce only thirty-one per cent.

Statistics furnish even a broader demonstration of the expansion and fruitfulness of all our industries. For investigations based on the census show that while the wealth of the nation was only $308 a head in 1850, it was $514 in 1860, showing an increase of sixty-seven per cent. It arose to $624 in 1870, with an increase of twenty-one per cent., and in 1880, by an increase of thirty-nine per cent., attained the magnitude of $870 a head. The total wealth of the United States reached in 1880 $43,642,000,000,[1] just in excess of the aggregate for Great Britain, which stood at $43,366,000,000. France was at the same time worth $35,898,000,000, and Germany $29,403,000,000.[2] "Chambers' Journal" for January, 1884,[3] declares that statisticians after calculations "pronounced the United States to be not only potentially but actually richer than the United Kingdom," although the American wealth *per capita* is placed at £5 less than the British average.

[1] Bradstreet, January 12, 1884.
[2] Mulhall's *Balance Sheet of the World*.
[3] The same figures are given by the London *Times*.

Mr. Gladstone, in his notable article in the "North American Review," October, 1878, on "Kin beyond Sea," declared that the census for 1880 would exhibit the American Republic "as certainly the wealthiest of all the nations." He cites the annual production of the United Kingdom at £1,000,000,000, or five times that number of dollars; our manufactures alone in 1880 exceeded this sum in total production, while our agriculture with $3,600,000,000 is to be added. Mr. Gladstone was justified in saying: "While we have been advancing with this portentous rapidity, America [*i. e.* the United States] is passing us by in a canter. Yet even now the work of searching the soil and the bowels of the territory, and opening out her enterprise throughout its vast expanse, is in its infancy. The England and America of the present are probably the two strongest nations of the world. But there can hardly be a doubt, as between the America and the England of the future, that the daughter at some no very distant time will, whether fairer or less fair, be unquestionably yet stronger than the mother.

"'O matre forti filia fortior.'"[1]

The great British premier is not alone in his recognition of our marvelous material development. The German chancellor, who has accomplished so much for his own country, and who proves his convictions by adopting our example, has officially put on record his testimony. In the Reichstag, May

[1] *North American Review*, October 1878, p. 181.

14, 1882, Prince Bismarck used this expressive language : —

"The success of the United States in material development is the most illustrious of modern times. The American nation has not only successfully borne and suppressed the most gigantic and expensive war of all history, but immediately afterwards disbanded its army, found employment for all its soldiers and marines, paid off most of its debt, given labor and homes to all the unemployed of Europe as fast as they could arrive within its territory, and still by a system of taxation so indirect as not to be perceived, much less felt. The United States found every year a great and growing surplus in its treasury, which it could expend upon national defenses or national improvements. While the American Republic was enjoying this peculiar prosperity, the countries of Europe, which America most relieved by absorbing their unemployed population, were apparently continually getting worse off." "Because it was his deliberate judgment, that the prosperity of America was mainly due to its system of protective laws, he urged that Germany has now reached that point where it is necessary to imitate the tariff system of the United States."

WHY CHANGE OUR SYSTEM?

With such results why should Americans seek to disturb a revenue system under which they have won unparalleled prosperity ? Why should such home production be endangered for the uncertainties of the troublous seas, for commerce which no nation has ever yet secured except by maritime warfare, or held except at the expense of costly navies ?

This is material progress; but how much of assurance is there in the ringing declaration of Carlyle? "Show me a people energetically busy, heaving, struggling, all shoulders at the wheel, their hearts pulsing, every muscle swelling with man's energy and will; I will show you a people of whom great good is already predicable, to whom all manner of good is yet certain, if their energy endure. By very working, they will learn; they have, Antæus-like, their feet on mother fact; how can they but learn?"[1]

The tax-gatherer is the agent of restraint at every point which he touches. He should approach production at the fewest possible points. He cannot make a demand which does not just in so far affect personal liberty. If to enforce his demand he must enter the home or the shop, must scrutinize the habits and earnings and savings of the individual, the inquisition grows to be a grievance. The government which meddles least with the citizen accords to him the broadest freedom. The fewest inquiries it addresses to him who is guiltless of crime and the least it touches his property, the most faithful it is to its obligations. Despotism thrusts itself into all personal concerns, and exacts contributions at many points. The distinction between a free government and despotic systems is just here. The ear of Nero, which listened to every gasp and sigh of the prisoner, is the type of tyranny everywhere. It watches and

[1] *Past and Present.*

it suspects and it surrounds the citizen. Fouché and his police sought out the thoughts of the French people. The Oriental supervision of the subject extended to homes and industries, to person and to property.

But inquiry into the political conduct of men is less sweeping, and may even be less annoying and offensive, than restriction of their labor and of their food and clothing and private acts. The American people, under the internal revenue system, have found inspectors and assessors ask for a report of their productions, to assess the tax on manufactures; for a statement of their sales, to levy an impost upon them; for an exhibit of all their gains, to determine the tax on incomes; for a presentation of the property of the dead, so that the government might take its share from the bequests to widows and orphans and other dependents. The tax on land requires a constant assessment of its advance or fall in value, and in some states the citizen is called upon to make a schedule of all his possessions for the guidance of the tax-gatherer.

Every such approach within the privacy of the citizen is an infringement of his liberty. It may be necessary for the purposes of the state, but it constitutes just in so far a limitation of the independence of the citizen. It is the sound of fetters and of shackles.

In all lands just as the tax-gatherer has been brought most closely to the subject, and his visits made most frequent, the complaints have been loudest. The share of earnings or savings taken has been one of the grounds on which the methods of different periods have been measured. But the nearness of the infliction, the decree of inquisition insisted upon, the closeness to the home and the person incident to any plan, have been the standards by which systems have been characterized.

The special distinction of a duty on imports is that the collection is made once for all. The inquiry relates simply to the introduction of commodities within the borders of the nation. It limits itself to the national frontier. It does not propose to enter the home or the shop of any citizen. It announces that it will collect revenue from that which is brought into the country. It invites the importer to make his declaration of quantities and values. It permits him to deposit the merchandise in a government warehouse until such time as he may wish to put it upon the market. Only at that time is payment required. Such payment is an advance by him for the retail dealer, who in turn advances his share for his customers; or, as we have shown, it may be a payment really for the foreign producer. At all events, the individual tax-payer has the choice of meeting the charge or not. He may, if he chooses, refuse to buy imported goods. At one period some Americans, in their hatred of slavery, entered into a compact not to consume any article produced by slave labor, and therefore rejected importations from

Cuba and Brazil and other slave countries. The citizen may therefore choose for himself whether he will undergo the charge made by the laws. He may even avoid relations to the customs if the business of importer is irksome to him. He can so direct his selection of articles of food and clothing and household wares as to reject such as are subject to duty. The individual may thus in the last analysis determine for himself the share of the burdens of the revenue which he will assume.

The contrary is the case with every other system of revenue. A person cannot well avoid the tax on land in some form. He may decline to own a farm or a homestead, but he must yet pay his tax as a tenant, or if he seeks as a boarder and lodger to limit his contribution, he cannot escape it; for he must enable his landlord to meet the demands of the tax-gatherer. The theory of every direct tax is that it is operative at once, and is imperative.

The nation that establishes custom-houses on its frontiers and there collects its revenue, may be criticised for erecting a wall about its territory. But if it levies no tax on any process of production, if it requires nothing from its citizens except at that point, it presents as complete a spectacle of freedom as is possible on earth. It affects in no way the choice of vocation by its people. It leaves every man absolutely free to employ his industry as he chooses. It makes no inquisition into any act of its citizens, and they may execute their papers exempt from any charge by the treasury, and may divide their property by will without contributing any part of it to the government.

Charge, if you will, that the government maintains a cordon of officers on its borders to watch what comes in. It does not for its revenue send detectives into homes; it does not ask what its citizens eat or wear, or what they make or raise, or how they deal with each other, or what they do with their property at death.

CHAPTER VII.

COMMERCE BROADER THAN BARTER.

Shall a Revenue System protect Production or Commerce in Largest Measure ? — The Balance of Trade no Mystery. — The Individual who buys more than he sells tends to Bankruptcy. — Commerce confers Value. — A Nation's Trade only the Sum of that of its Individuals. — Capital, Earnings, Debt. — The American War Loans. — Say. — Mill. — Blanqui. — Coin and Bullion. — The School of Free Trade. — The Attitude of the Nations. — Buckle. — Broad Humanity. — Profits of Commerce. — Balance against Britain. — Margin of Gains. — The Carrying Trade. — British Capital Abroad. — The World's Banker. — France. — American Commerce. — Immigration. — British Exports and Imports. — Exports and Imports of the United States. — Comparative Growth since 1865. — Admission of Sir Thomas Brassey. — "MacMillan's Magazine." — Mr. Gladstone's Prediction of the Commercial Supremacy of the United States. — No Reason to change our Policy. — British System does not even promote Commerce.

WE have reached the conclusion that freedom of production is the first necessity for any people. Next to it, but secondary in every respect, is the absence of restrictions on trade, foreign as well as domestic. Government cannot help in its legislation and its administration touching the concerns of the people. Theorists may plead that the state shall do nothing to restrict commerce; the corollary of their plea is that every burden shall be cast upon production. The opposite claim is that every revenue charge shall be adjusted to favor production; it inevitably follows that some imposts shall fall upon commerce. The two schools of revenue legislation are divided by this line, in truth: shall the revenue system favor production in largest measure, or shall it exalt commerce to the first place in its favor?

The controversy is between these two policies. The combatants are free production on the one hand and free trade on the other. The adjustment of imposts is to extend protection and encouragement to the one or the other of these two great interests in preference to the other. Our argument has been that production is more deserving of favor than foreign commerce, because it lies at the basis of all prosperity, personal and national; because it employs more persons; because it carries comfort into more homes; because it develops in largest degree the best elements of society and of manhood. Commerce will not be overlooked in any nation in this age. The seas are white with its sails and with the fleece of its smoke. The merchants roam over all lands and dictate the policy of great nations. They beat down the resistance of China and force opium upon the unwilling people. They penetrate the heart of Africa to establish factories for the distribution of their commodities. Cabinets study how to make easy the paths of traffic. European powers rival each other in grasping by diplomacy and force for control over the countries of the East, in order that profit may be gained by commerce.

THE BALANCE OF TRADE.

One problem of trade underlies the questions of revenue which are connected with foreign commerce. Mystery has been thrown about the balance of trade, until the claim that it rests on a basis different from the relations of debit and credit in private transactions is put forth with an audacity which has overwhelmed not a few thinkers and legislators. All trade is barter, we are told, and commerce must bring profit to both sides, and every import must have its offset in exports. You cannot sell unless you buy, insists our opponent; and the pretense that an adverse balance of trade is a detriment, he alleges, is a fallacy. If buying beyond your means is a blunder and may be a crime; if running in debt without hope of payment is inexcusable in morals and in practice draws after it its own punishment, then an adverse balance of trade is a threat of disaster, and may signify, if long continued, industrial as well as commercial ruin.

In the rude days of society, trade was simple barter. Grain was given for shoes, a firkin of butter for a suit of clothes, a load of wood was delivered on account of the minister's salary. The claim is made that all trade to-day is barter. The claim would be as true that every machine is a lever, because all mechanical appliances can be reduced to the lever in the last analysis. Trade has grown out of barter. But in the wide range of commerce direct exchange of merchandise rarely occurs. Even in local traffic the producer of one article is seldom brought into contact with the producer of another. Exchange has passed into other hands, and has become an occupation by itself. Even the keeping of the papers which are used in the processes of commerce has become one of the most lucrative and honorable of vocations. You do not pay the farmer in shoes, or clothing, or books, for his grain, or his butter, or his poultry. He has long ago delivered his products and received credit for them. He has perhaps deposited the proceeds in the bank and applied them in the reduction of the mortgage on his farm, or he has invested them in stocks or bonds, or in the purchase of new lands. He has contributed to a church, he has assisted to establish an academy, he has rounded out a sum which he has set aside for his maintenance in old age. If he has debts, he has applied his money upon them; if he has not, he has used it for buying necessaries or luxuries, or he has put it aside in savings. This is the process of all classes. The mechanic pursues the same course. The merchant uses his profits to enlarge his business, and thus keeps his capital rolling and increasing. The sum of a nation's transactions is the sum of these individual experiences: it sends away that which it can sell; if it wants merchandise it buys it; perhaps it has previously bought more than it could pay for, then it leaves the price of its exports, in whole or in part, to cancel the indebtedness; it may desire much more than it has to sell, then it runs into debt; but it may neither have debts to pay, nor want merchandise to offset its sales, then it creates a credit on which it may draw for future use.

Thus an individual may keep on selling more than he buys, and he will have a large credit to his account with the purchaser or with the banker. Such a man we call rich. He may sell less than he buys, and, after exhausting previous savings, he runs into debt. If this process is long continued he exhausts his credit. Such a person we call poor. He may keep his sales and purchases closely balanced; he will then be living fully up to his income. Such a person may be thrifty, but he is not increasing his wealth; any misfortune will force him to run into debt. If the best he can do in prosperous times is to keep even with the world, adversity signifies ruin to him. The sum of such experiences of many individuals is the experience of the nation which they compose.

In order to know from his sales and purchases whether an individual is growing rich or poor, we must be informed of other conditions with reference to him. It is essential to learn whether he has a credit balance to begin with, or whether he is in debt at the start of the transactions which we are to examine. We must be told also whether he has other operations besides those expressly submitted to us; is he engaged in work which must be taken into account, or is the dealer on the other side running up other charges against him? With all of these data presented, it is not hard to tell whether a man is making money or losing it. Neither is it hard to tell in the vastly broader fields of national commerce, whether the profit or the loss is in excess on the one side or the other.

The balance of trade is not a mystery. It involves many items, as may the account between a number of persons. When all of the details are gathered, the sums are only a matter of footing and comparison. No aggregation of persons, such as we call a nation, can violate the laws which apply to the trade of individuals, without paying the penalties which the individuals separately must pay. It is the individuals who suffer in adverse commerce as it is the individuals who gain when commerce is profitable. The operations of the farmer are not mere barter. The operations of the manufacturer are not mere barter. The transactions of the merchant at retail or wholesale are not barter. Commerce is as varied as the necessities of mankind, and as the devices for ministering to human luxury. Its devices are as curious and changeable as the tricks of men for getting rich, and as the machinery of communication and transportation.

Commerce itself confers value. It carries the corn which may be burned as fuel in Iowa to the markets, which will pay for it in diamonds for the maidens of the Western fields, or in teas from China or coffee from Brazil. The tables and the parlors of all lands are adorned with Oriental colors which the merchant exchanges, after many processes, for the petroleum of our wells or the rifles of our arsenals. The carrying of the diamonds from South Africa is a part of their price to us, and the transfer of our grains to Liverpool enters into the cost to the consumer there. The share of transportation in the value of all merchandise becomes an item in the balance of trade. The nation which receives pay for the carrying trade can expend such earnings for imports and not run in debt. The people who have been long the world's bankers must get much merchandise to pay for the loans which they have made, for the banking facilities which they have afforded. Such a nation may also continue for a long period to buy goods from all lands on credit, before it can be charged with poverty.

Except for these considerations, the nation which sells more than it buys is getting rich. The nation which continually sells less than it buys is getting poor. Measure the growth of a nation's exports, and you can determine its material progress. Offset against them its imports and any service it may render in carrying or in banking, and the balance is as inevitably a true statement of the condition of the nation as are like figures expressive of the condition of the individuals, who are in this case the nation itself.

Eliminating, for simplicity, the matter of transportation, the equation of exports and imports is the true statement of a nation's commerce not only, but of its progress or decadence in wealth.

Let us not fail to do justice to the carrying trade. The producer is more useful than the porter. It is true that merchandise may be comparatively useless in one place and of extreme value elsewhere. But the first element in the value is the creation of the merchandise. The porter will have nothing to carry in the absence of the producer. In due time the producer can secure some one to carry his goods, if he has any to be transported. A rough estimate is that one tenth of the foreign commerce of the world is to be credited to transportation. Naturally those who are first in production may not be first in the carrying trade. Holland at one time, notwithstanding her small territory and her comparatively small contribution to the world's merchandise, controlled a large share of the ocean carrying trade. The same distinction has now fallen to Great Britain.

The accumulation of wealth is going on all the while before our eyes. The farmer lays up money from his labor and his products. The mechanic makes gain from the work which he does and the wares which he turns out. Even the merchant reckons his business on what he sells and not on what he purchases. In every case the wealth is gathered from that which goes out. From the farm or the workshop or the store it is the export which brings profit, and the excess of it over that which comes in, over the import, is the credit balance. A nation's trade and business is only the sum of that of the individuals of which it is composed. It is governed by the same laws and must be subject to the same principles. Then the nation which exports more than it imports is adding to its wealth, if it gets pay for its exports.

The individual may accept for the products of his farm, for his wares or his merchandise, either other products or wares, or he may deliver his goods in return for debts before incurred, or he may sell them on credit. These are for the individual the only forms of trade. They are also for nations the only forms of traffic.

The capital which the individual has in hand is not to be reckoned in the profits of any transaction. It must be accounted for separately. The debts which he incurs can even less be taken into account as a share of gain. If in any trade he uses up his capital or runs in debt, he in both cases cripples himself. Either process, persisted in, involves complete failure for the person. The like experience must be that of the aggregated person which is styled a nation. Nation or individual can pay for commodities in services, but if the sum of the commodities received, including services, constantly falls below the sum of the commodities and services given out, the drain must fall on accrued capital or pass into debts; in either case the adverse balance is damaging. The individual and the nation may waste inheritance and savings; the nation and the individual may run into bankruptcy.

In the case of individuals we do not always know whether the adjustment is to be made from past savings or from future credits; from payments out of capital or to take the form of debts; but the purchase of more than one earns or produces brands the spendthrift. The adverse balance of trade with individuals is understood by everybody. Examples of it are frequent in the community. Spend more than you earn, and you enter the path to ruin. Whether you are nation or man, the law is absolute. In the case of nations, the aggregation of capital may permit the process to go on for years, for a generation; and established credit may add another generation, for trade permits the payments of yesterday's purchases to create credit for to-day and to-morrow and perhaps for the next day. The fluctuations of trade may enable the debtor of yesterday to become the creditor of to-morrow; the demand for services may enable individual or nation to offset the indebtedness of to-day by the services of another day.

The balance of trade between nations does not differ from the balance of trade between persons and communities. When a man buys beyond his means, and keeps on doing it, his fate is sure. Every season the process of trade between the farming districts and the trade centres goes on. The farmer may sell his hops, his grain, his cattle, and he may take back commodities equal to his sales. Then he saves nothing and creates no obligation. Or he may buy less than his products bring, and then, in some form, he will get a balance to his credit, available for settling up the mortgage on his lands, or for investment in some form. When farmers buy beyond their production, or when they cannot get pay for their products, there befalls the land the worst form of panic and distress. Then the farmers as a class have created a balance of trade adverse to themselves. When, on the other hand, they sell their crops and pay for what they get, and leave no debts, they prevent that adverse balance; and when as a class they lay up money, they establish a balance in their own favor. Then the country is rich, where, with an adverse balance, it felt the pressure of poverty. The law is identical for manufacturers and for capitalists. If the producing classes anywhere buy more than they can pay for, they are punished by financial stress. If the capitalist lays out more than his income, the adverse balance of trade catches him in its clutch, and may even crush him into utter poverty.

Now, between individuals the government has nothing to say. Every man can buy all he can get credit for. Every part of the country can adjust its purchases to its own desires and the temper of the dealers. So can the individuals in this land, in their relations with those of every other nation. The sole question which concerns us is whether imposts should be so adjusted as to encourage purchases beyond the means of our people to pay for; whether it is a good thing to be sought by governmental policy, for our citizens to be squandering their patrimony on foreign commodities, or running into ruinous indebtedness to foreign merchants. If between individuals an adverse balance is not desirable, if he who spends more than he produces is condemned by the common sense of mankind, then the policy of the government ought not to encourage such waste and prodigality on the part of the nation as a whole.

Explanation is possible of large purchases for the nation or the individual, but of itself an adverse balance of trade is damaging for both the one and the other. It means drain upon capital or debt, or both. The revenue system which aims at such results, or accepts them willingly, must be false.

THE AMERICAN WAR LOANS.

The very broadest illustration of the manner in which an adverse balance of trade may be created was afforded just after our civil war. The United States had afloat over $2,200,000,000 in interest-bearing securities. They had been sold at home, but foreign capital was sought by those who were dealing in these bonds. Before 1870, from one half to one third of this vast debt was transferred to foreign holders. The operation involved the transfer of some money, but in far greater part this country took commodities for its bonds. Through the machinery of commerce the merchant was induced to buy goods and transfer his bills of exchange to holders of bonds, who shipped them instead of money. Our railroads bought very largely of rails and other supplies in the same way. The debt existed, and it was a convenience for our capitalists to sell the tokens of it to foreign investors. This series of transactions concentrates the experience which generally covers a long period of time. The nation had in its official capacity run into debt to its own people, and therefore we are able to trace the movement of capital much more clearly than would be possible if the debtors were individuals. But the principle is identical. If individuals had incurred the obligations to the same extent, the consequences would have been precisely the same. The country took commodities of every kind: those which contributed to the vast railroad inflation which precipitated the panic of 1873, the luxuries which impoverished families, the wares which came into competition with the labor of our mechanics. At one time, it was estimated that Europe and Britain held $750,000,000 of the bonds of the American government, and $450,000,000 of state and railroad securities.[1] For these representatives of our indebtedness we had received less than $100,000,000 in money. For all the rest the country had taken commodities. Commerce revels in such transactions. This is not barter; it is exchange, with all of its diversities and problems. The vast debt had to be met. For-

[1] It is stated by Mr. Wilson in his volumes on the *Resources of Modern Countries*, that in the interval between 1866-1875, 37,000 miles of railway were constructed in the United States, at a nominal cost of several hundred millions sterling. From £70,000,000 to £100,000,000 were raised in Europe by the sale of bonds. — Brassey's *Foreign Work and English Wages*, p. 22.

tunately, while we have had precious metals to ship in part pay, the Old World has needed our provisions and other products. The monstrous debt, which might well lead our financiers to tremble, has been canceled.

At this time less than $100,000,000 of our government bonds is held abroad, and this sum could be returned in any year without detriment to our business prosperity.

Such experiences enable us to judge of the arbitrary assumptions of certain writers. Say insists that nations pay for products only with products. Even Mill says that the produce of a country exchanges for the produce of other countries at such values as are required, in order that the whole of her exports may exactly pay for the whole of her imports.[1] In the generations, this may prove true. The savings which we call capital have resulted from products, but at any period they have taken this other form, and certainly nations can pay for products in capital. Britain is doing this very thing to-day, and is able to do it for a long time. A debt is not a product, and yet nations may incur immense debts for products. The public debts of European powers will probably never be canceled. It is conceivable that without utter bankruptcy indebtedness may take the shape of long obligations, on which interest only will be paid. In this case nations will not pay for products with products. The constant

[1] *Political Economy*, b. iii. ch. xviii.

danger exists in all traffic on credit that the indebtedness will never be canceled. Against that danger of utter bankruptcy and disgrace Say and Mill have taken no precaution. A wise theorist will not neglect such a contingency. A system of revenue which invites it cannot be too severely condemned.

COIN AND BULLION.

Blanqui expresses a common allegation that superstitious regard for the precious metals lies at the bottom of the apprehensions of an adverse balance of trade.[1] Coin and bullion are like other commodities in many respects, and a nation like our own which produces gold and silver can afford to include them in its exports. Yet a marked difference may assert itself. The export of any other commodity creates no serious pressure and no general distress. Wheat or cotton or iron or grain may be exported, and the price can never reach the point at which ruin will be threatened to industry, and commerce be paralyzed. Yet these results do follow from the excessive shipment of gold and silver. The story of the aggregate of debtors is summed up in that of the individual. While the creditor is content to take for his products what the debtor can turn out from his farm or his

[1] Paper money has driven out coin wherever its presence has diminished the value of coin, in spite of the penalty of death inflicted on the smugglers. The fear of paying for foreign commodities with the precious metals is a vain fear; the precious metals never go from one country to another to pay pretended balances, but to seek the market where they will bring the most. — Blanqui, p. 311.

factory or his furnace, there is no distress for the debtor. On the contrary, the process is regarded as a sign of prosperity. The sales which cancel his obligations are healthy trade. But the instant that the creditor insists upon money, upon an adjustment of the account in coin, the stress occurs. If the money can be raised bankruptcy is avoided, but the means for carrying on production may be taken away, and the channels of trade be dried up. The sum of all debtors is identical with the aggregate of such experiences. The means of production are taken away, and the channels of trade dried up.

This is the reason why an adverse balance of trade is dangerous for man or country. Gold and silver are not wealth, nor are they more precious than other commodities. But they represent more than anything else savings, capital, and they are the medium in which, on demand of the creditor, debts must be paid. Therefore it is waste to ship an excess of gold and silver, and it is ruin to base trade on the promise to pay them in the future, beyond the prospect of prompt production.[1]

[1] The indebtedness of nations results from the relative totals of all the amounts expended by each upon the other, whether in payment of produce and manufactures, or for the purchase of shares and public securities, or for the settlement of profits, commissions, or tributes of any kind, or for the discharge of the expenses incurred in foreign residence or travel: in fact, from the entire payments or promises to pay which pass between the respective countries. The liability is identical in effect, whatever its origin may be. — Goschen, *Foreign Exchanges*, c. ii.

Sidgwick, p. 227, says: "Every such liability has to be liquidated

THE ATTITUDE OF THE NATIONS.

The French author Blanqui declares that "No enlightened man in Europe believes in the marvels of the balance of trade."[1] He leaves us to understand that he means that no enlightened man believes that it is dangerous for a country to run on in commerce so that its imports shall continue to exceed its exports. With that understanding his statement is radically at variance with the truth. The school of free trade protests that it is of no consequence how long such an adverse balance is kept up, indeed that the volume of imports is the measure of wealth. But the legislation of every country in Europe, except Britain and Holland, proceeds on the conviction that it is not well to spend your capital or to run in debt, as a continuous process. When capital is great, when a country is the banker of the world, when vast profits are collected out of the carrying trade, the evils of the process may be diminished or postponed. But the laws of mathematics are not changed to please any school of theorists. The experience of mankind controls the action of men and of nations. When exports in the average of years equal or exceed the imports with the services rendered, then commerce contributes to national prosperity. When purchases

---

by the transmission either of money, or of an order to receive money, payable in the foreign country."

[1] Page 312.

abroad are for a long period of time greater than the sales abroad, then the scales of industry and of trade must show the consequences, and poverty must take the place of wealth.

Buckle, with a half-wisdom not uncommon with him, declares that " it would be as absurd to attempt to impoverish a people with whom we trade, as it would be in a tradesman to wish for the insolvency of a rich and frequent customer."[1] The fallacy here is in the assumption of a wish to impoverish anybody. Blanqui borrows the same thought in implying that by the protective system nations try to injure one another.[2] A tradesman, to return to Buckle's illustration, does not try to impoverish a customer, when he refuses to buy himself more than he can pay for. Neither does a country try to injure another, when it seeks to prevent an adverse balance of trade. The best customer is he who buys no more than he can promptly settle for, and keeps himself in a position to continue his purchases. The worst customer is the spendthrift, who squanders his patrimony and then asks for credit to which he is not entitled. The worst injury which a great nation can inflict upon its neighbors and the world is to waste its capital, and to incur indebtedness which it cannot pay. The very best service which one people can render to another people, and to mankind as a whole, is to add to the common production, to buy only what can be promptly paid for, and to avoid debts which may

[1] *History of Civilization*, vol. i. p. 157.   [2] Page 316.

bring disaster upon the entire commercial and industrial interests of all nations.

One of the anomalies of revenue discussion is that those who insist that our legislation must not be adjusted to foster our own industries, plead strongly that we should legislate in a spirit of broad humanity, and seek to help all mankind. They denounce statutes which favor our own people as conceived in hostility to other nations. Now there is a very good rule that charity begins at home. The first duty of a nation is to take care of itself, and of them all not one has yet exhausted all of the resources for elevating and developing its own people. Until a government has provided all of the conditions essential to the prosperity of its own people, to the fullest development of production at home, it has no right to trouble itself about the welfare of other countries.

PROFITS OF COMMERCE.

The plea is urged that profit accrues to individuals from imports, and therefore this is an addition to the general wealth. For example, a cargo valued for duties, and stated in the records at $50,000, may be sold in detail for $70,000. Is not the wealth of the country augmented by the sum of the increase? In figures, as between the inhabitants of this country, there is a distribution on this basis. But the power to pay debts abroad is not enforced; the treasure of the country is not augmented. In the settlement with the foreign manufacturer or his agent, the aggregate population of this country is not any better off by the nominal increment, either for canceling past obligations or for obtaining new commodities. Simply for convenience the body of purchasers in this country is spoken of as a unit, as the country itself. It is clear that the distribution of imports on the one basis or the other between the individuals does not change the problem as it relates to the entire body of them. This is not a case to juggle with statistics. If the people of the United States as a body buy more abroad than they sell abroad, the difference must be paid for. The sum of what they have to sell abroad is the credit column from which all adjustments must come. At home, profits may be great or small, and may come from imports or from home production. If a debt is to be paid abroad, the resources must be derived from the common fund, and while individuals may be benefited by the nominal profits on imports, the people as a body can settle obligations only by the exports, past, present, or future. In other words, the case is again identical with that of a person. If the people buy abroad more than they sell, they must pay from past savings or from current productions, or must run in debt. This item of profits in trade within our own territory does not change the elements of the real problem, and surely does not create any new resources by which the nation can settle adverse balances.

BALANCE OF TRADE AGAINST BRITAIN.

An adverse balance of trade has not brought ruin to Great Britain. Such a balance has continued for more than a quarter of a century. In 1882 it had reached a round hundred million pounds, or five hundred million dollars. If that country can go on creating such a balance, and increasing it steadily, then the example may be safely followed, urges some zealous advocate of free trade. This is the staple argument of the school. But notice, first of all, that wise statesmen in Britain are greatly depressed at the industrial condition of the entire realm, and not of Ireland only. They are asking, almost with dread, whether influences are not busy which are full of danger. But let us assume that British commerce is very prosperous, and brings in every element of profit which is claimed for it.

Surely no country any more than an individual can keep on buying commodities without paying for them. How then does Britain pay for the imports in excess of its exports? One claim is often urged that the sum of the apparent balance stands for the profits of the British capitalist. But no mathematician can reckon any such results in trade. On an aggregate of £306,660,714 of exports, no such sum as thirty-three per cent. of profit can be supposed to be received. It is to be admitted that the exports are stated in official documents at the price without addition of transportation, and the imports are brought in with all charges paid. But the relation of these two sums is not that of profit and loss directly. For all of these transfers imply many operations which involve expenses not entering into the custom-house reports. As well might a merchant insist that when he had reckoned the original price of his purchases, and the sum of his sales, he had struck his balance and determined his profits. His details of expenses for administration, for destruction, for a thousand incidentals, must be included.

Britain has for the present the carrying trade of the ocean. For this service it is earning money. It can afford to take commodities in exchange for it. No other nation performs any such service in extent or value; and consequently no other can buy so much in excess of its imports. This service is a commodity which fails to be reckoned in the exports. Just what this service is, statisticians widely differ. Suppose it amounts to five per cent. of the total commerce of Britain, it is then £35,000,000 a year, a little more than one third of the adverse balance.

But of the British imports not less than nearly one fourth comes from the United States. The commodities thus represented are in many cases produced from British capital, and are in part a return for its earnings. British capital is in the ranches of Colorado, in' the sheep ranges of Texas, in the iron works of Ohio and Pennsylvania, in the banks of New York, in varied manufactures and enterprises of all parts of our land. The sum of this capital invested here is not known, but all can see that it is increasing. Estimates of its amount range as high as £200,000,000. Five per cent. on that sum will give £10,000,000 annually, for which Britain can afford to take our products without expecting to return us commodities.

Another adjustment of this adverse balance of trade is found in the sums which emigrants send back to family and friends. Sir Thomas Brassey in "Foreign Work and English Wages,"[1] estimates these returns at £19,800,000 from 1848 to 1876, or £1,100,000 a year. These figures take no account of the fortunes earned and taken home by those who return from Australia and India to die on their native soil.

Still in addition Britain is the banker of the world, even more than Holland ever was. Capital belonging in all lands may receive its dividends in London. The London banker may be willing to receive goods instead of money in the course of international exchange, settling with his principals as may be satisfactory. From these four sources, and these alone, can Britain repay the balance which its commerce shows against it, except as it trenches directly on its hoarded capital, or creates debt to be hereafter adjusted.

The problem of British prosperity depends largely upon the degree to which these latter processes are going on. British statesmen must discuss these questions for themselves. Britain may stand the appar-

[1] Page 261.

ent drain upon its resources. No other country in the world could endure this drain for the generation which has passed. Certain it is that our country has no such carrying trade, no such reserve of capital invested elsewhere, no such world-wide system of banking, to enable it to create an immense balance of trade against itself. For Americans the only safe rule is not to buy abroad any more commodities than they can pay for with commodities as they are produced year by year.

Any system of revenue which invites an adverse balance of trade is therefore dangerous for us, however it may prove for Britain. The theory of free trade aims at just that result. The boast of its advocates is that they seek to increase the volume of foreign trade, and, to begin with, an increase of imports. That is the obvious significance of reducing duties to favor commerce.

FRANCE.

Let us admit that a reduction of duties will, as a rule, increase the importation of the article relieved from imposts. As a matter of fact that is the teaching of experience. But seldom do exports find that they are adjusted to any new equation. They are seldom increased. They are often diminished. France under the second empire sought to augment its commerce by abandoning the traditional and historical policy of Colbert and Sully. Cobden succeeded in securing the reciprocity treaty for Britain in 1860. The credit balance was over five hundred million francs for France in 1861, before the effect of the treaty was felt. But it was changed to the other side, and was five hundred million francs against France in 1864, increasing to six hundred million francs in 1866.

Immediately on the fall of the empire in 1871 the exports began again to exceed the imports, and in 1875 they were nearly four hundred million francs in excess.

Since that year the exports have never risen to such magnitude, while the imports have increased, and the adverse balance in 1881 was over 1,300,000,-000 francs. No wonder that France is complaining grievously of poverty in spite of the thrift of its people and the greatness of its master-spirits.

AMERICAN COMMERCE.

Our own foreign commerce has been cited as disproving the principles which have been announced. For in many years of our history we have imported larger volumes of merchandise than we have exported. One element in the calculation is omitted from the official statements, and it has been of continuous and very important effect. The tide of immigration has added year by year to our material wealth, reckoning only the money and not the human value of the new-comers. The most careful estimates substantially agree that counting the personal property which they bring, the immigrants add on an average at least one thousand dollars for each person to our wealth. Abraham Lincoln gave the weight of his authority to this standard. Mr. Graham, a British authority cited in Brassey's "Foreign Work and English Wages,"[1] accounts this money value of immigrants at £175 a head, or $875. In order to be beyond question within the truth, let us place the estimate at the very lowest, $500 for each person. This is an importation which does not need to be paid for. It becomes at once an addition to our capital. It has enabled us in the past to adjust adverse balances with the Old World. It has contributed to our producing power, and multiplied our riches. In 1820, for example, this movement brought us 8,385 persons. Our imports exceeded our exports by $4,758,331, but the immigrants were worth to us over $4,192,500, and thus we found no difficulty in paying the debt. In 1840 our immigration was 84,066. Our foreign trade showed a balance in our favor of $25,410,226. The increase of capital by immigration is to be reckoned at over $42,000,000. There is no wonder that our prosperity advanced by rapid strides. By 1860 the immigrants numbered 150,237. The balance of trade had been steadily against us since the adoption of the Walker tariff of 1846, with the exception of only two years. It was in 1860, $20,040,062. That sum is not the measure of our foreign relations, for the wealth brought by the immigrants amounted to $75,000,000, and kept us solvent and

---

[1] Page 260.

strong. By 1880 the volume of immigration had reached 457,257, and its addition to our wealth attained the magnitude of $228,000,000. At the same time while our imports of merchandise had become $667,954,746, our exports had mounted to $823,946,-353, showing a balance in our favor of $167,683,912. In 1882 our imports were $724,639,574, while our exports of domestic merchandise were $733,239,732. Our favorable balance thus fell to $25,902,683. But it was enforced by immigration of 788,992. These people, equaling some states in numbers as well as in productive power, brought us $394,000,000 in money value. They enable us to meet demands upon us from abroad; but still more they require that our legislation shall consider production as deserving of its favor beyond any claims of commerce.

A CONTRAST BETWEEN THE UNITED STATES AND BRITAIN.

British trade itself constitutes a complete warning for every other country, in which capital is not in excess, to beware of favoring other interests at the cost of home production. The corn laws were passed in 1846. It is the practice to take the trade of 1840 as a fair exhibition of the situation before Peel's legislation, and 1854 as the first typical year succeeding it. In 1840 the excess of imports over exports of British produce was £8,695,260, and was 8s. 9d. for each person of the population. In 1854 the excess of imports became £55,204,327, or £2 for each person.

When we reach 1860 this excess had become £74,639,646, or per head £2 12s. 5d. By 1870 the excess of imports over exports reached £103,670,671, or per head £2 6s. 5d. In 1881 it was £162,999,811, or £4 13s. 4d. per head. The exports have grown in forty-one years by £182,613,938, but the imports in the mean time have run up by the sum of £335,018,489, or by very nearly twice the amount.

We are concerning ourselves all the while with the effect of a revenue system. On that account our comparison must be made with Britain. We are forced to follow this course, but in no unfriendly spirit; but first, because that nation confessedly leads the world in commerce; second, because no other country exceeds our records either in exports or imports; and third, because it is the only important representative of nominal free trade. We are told that the development of British commerce should compel us to adopt the British system of collecting moneys for government purposes. The argument to that end relies wholly upon the extension of British commerce. Let us inquire what we have to gain. Since 1840 Britain has multipled its imports by more than six times. That is a good result, and has led to great boasting. In the mean time the United States has also increased its imports more than six times. Since 1840 Britain has multiplied its exports by more than four and a half times; in the same period the United States has multiplied its exports by eight times.

During this interval of forty-two years the United States has borne the brunt of a terrible civil war. Yet in foreign commerce our growth has been equal in imports to that of Britain, and in exports we have grown twice as rapidly.

Compare the movement of foreign commerce in both of these great nations since 1865. During these years Britain has multiplied its imports by one and four tenths; the United States has multiplied its imports within the interval by nearly two times. Britain has increased its exports by less than one third, while the United States has multiplied its exports by six and four tenths. Since 1865 the increase in British imports has been $629,751,020, and our increase has been in imports $403,919,108, less absolutely than that of Britain, but a much larger percentage. In exports our increase in this period has been $746,985,699; while the British increase has been $340,934,765. In other words, we have gained in exports nearly twice as much absolutely as Britain has gained, and over twenty times as great a percentage.

The official figures upon which these comparisons are based are taken from the "Statistical Abstract" of Britain and a document bearing a like title from the Bureau of Statistics of the United States. By these reports it will be seen that in the years stated imports and exports were as follows:—

UNITED STATES.

Exports: 1840, $111,660,561; 1881, $883,925,947; increase very nearly eight times.

Imports: 1840, $98,258,706; 1881, $642,664,628; increase more than six times.

Exports: 1865, $136,940,248; increase to 1881, $746,985,699; 6.4 times.

Imports: 1865, $238,745,580; increase to 1881, $403,919,048; increase nearly two times.[1]

GREAT BRITAIN.

Exports: 1840, £51,308,740; 1881, £234,022,678; increase by 4.5 times.

Imports: 1840, £62,004,000; 1881, £397,022,489; increase by over six times.

Exports: 1865, £165,835,725; increase to 1881, £68,186,953, or $340,934,765; a little more than one third.

Imports: 1865, £271,072,285; increase to 1881, £125,950,204, or $629,751,020; or an increase of less than one half.

SOME BRITISH AUTHORITIES.

Sir Thomas Brassey, in the work already cited,[2] makes this admission: "If we test the comparative efficiency of British labor by the amount of exports, we shall see that we have lost ground chiefly in our trade with the great manufacturing countries, where the supply of capital and labor has been abundant, and where we have to encounter a serious protective

---

[1] If the imports of 1882 be taken for comparison the increase is $485,893,994, or more than two times.

[2] Page 157.

tariff." And again : [1] "Excluded from the principal manufacturing countries by a protectionist policy, it is to the colonies and to the half-civilized countries that we must look for new openings for the expansion of our trade." On the other hand, Lyon Playfair, in "MacMillan's Magazine" for February, 1882, concedes that in addition to cheap food, "the general conditions for productive industry, I would even say for productive supremacy, prevail in the United States."[2] But he adds, with a mistaken narrowness: "The conditions of prosperity in the United States are internal and not external." Is it not proved that out of internal prosperity external prosperity must be developed?

These must be the types of facts which led the present British premier to acknowledge in his article, Kin beyond Sea,[3] the "menace which, in the prospective development of her resources, America offers to the commercial preëminence of England. On this subject" — these are his words — "I will only say that it is she alone who at a coming time can, and probably will, wrest from us that commercial supremacy. If she acquires it, she will make the acquisition by the right of the strongest; but in this instance, the strongest means the best."

Accordingly we have no reason for changing our revenue system to that of Britain. We have main-

[1] Page 258.
[2] *MacMillan's Magazine,* February, 1882, p. 329.
[3] *North American Review,* October, 1878, p. 180.

tained the highest ratio of growth in our agriculture which any statistician ever estimated. At the same time we have far surpassed every other land in the extent and variety of our manufactures. But more than this is true. Even in foreign commerce we are running a winning race with our only rival. Our rate of increase in imports since 1865 has been far greater than that of Britain, and in exports we have gained over twenty times as rapidly as Britain and twice as much in absolute volume.

In every way Britain is proving that a revenue system which aims to favor commerce at the expense of production does not even promote commerce.

CHAPTER VIII.

FALLACIES ABOUT MARKETS.

The Place to sell and the Place to buy. — Commerce Complex and Continuous. — Creating Foreign Markets. — The Trade with Brazil. — The Trade with China. — Great Britain and the United States. — The Home and the Foreign Market. — McCulloch's Fallacy. — Two Deposits. — The Whole Apple, or only a Part. — Markets and Government Charges. — Revenue collected at Home. — Aggregate of Taxation. — Shall Labor or Trade support Markets? — Britain and its Revenue System. — Mr. Gladstone's Statement about Manufactures. — Sir Eardley Wilmot. — Nineteenth Century. — Raw Materials. — Wool. — Germany. — Protected Industries. — Boots and Shoes. — Our own Markets the Best for us.

EVERYBODY has heard the cant assumption, that we must buy in the cheapest market and sell in the dearest. It is one of those phrases which pass for wisdom, and yet simply conceal the problem which is presented for solution. It is announced as one of the axioms of political economy. For that reason it deserves to be analyzed. Commerce has become one of the most complex affairs, involving considerations so various, and often so conflicting, that it appeals to every faculty of the mind, and to every energy of the muscles. The truth has many times been brought very close home to the most enterprising and most diligent, that one must sell where he finds a purchaser, while he is forced to buy in the market which offers. Experience embodies the rule: Sell where you must, and buy where you can.

If you have the cash in hand, you can seek out your market and force the seller to accept your terms, if his stress is greater than your own. You can then go to the cheapest market. But this is seldom the case. Really, you want to sell more than you want to buy. You are willing to lay out a part of the results of your sales in purchases, if the sale is satisfactory. But you cannot buy at all, unless you can first sell. In the course of trade, the time comes when you must sell in order to meet your obligations. You desire to get the best price possible. The crisis arrives when only a week or a day separates you from bankruptcy. You must sell to save your credit, to keep your manufactory in operation, to prevent utter ruin. The market is most desirable for you in which you can dispose of your commodities. As a matter of experience, this is the market in which you must buy. You must buy in the same market in which you sell. It is the equation between sales and purchases which determines for you whether the market is the best one for your purposes. You can better pay ten dollars in grain or potatoes or wood or cotton or tobacco or shoes or woolens or iron, for these you have, than you can pay one half that sum in gold and silver, which you do not possess. It will prove much more economical to pursue this policy; for unless you can sell your own commodities, the price, whatever it may be, will be too great for you. In the desert, or on shipboard in a wreck, all treasure is cheap. That will be the best place to buy the merchandise which may be at hand. But it cannot be put to use. The cheapness is no advantage. The commodity elsewhere precious ceases to be valuable for the very reasons which make it cheap at that spot. That market is desirable where commodities are not only to be paid for by such articles as you have to give in exchange, but also where they can be turned to use.

On the other hand, the fallacy is only less complete that you should sell in the dearest market. If commerce were a single transaction, the rule would be simple. But it is a continuous process. The profits come not from a single sale, but from a constant flow of commodities outward, and returns which are remunerative. The merchant who establishes the reputation of maintaining high prices loses his customers. A market, however broad, becomes disadvantageous by the like policy. The attempt to extort the last farthing in a sale is not the wisdom of commerce. The highest price in a given transaction may be the ruin of what might have proved a steady source of healthful profit. You should sell where you can, to develop a reciprocal trade. If by selling your cloths or machines to a farmer you can get him to buy other wares, and enable him to earn the means to maintain a regular trade with you, a lower price will well reward you, while if the exchange were to stand by itself the return would be wholly inadequate.

The very dearest market to buy in, in the long run, is that in which you cannot hope for regular sales of the commodities from which you must secure the means of buying at all. The worst market to sell in, whatever the nominal price, is that from which you cannot expect regular traffic.

Profits come from the steady flow of a trade which may be determined by neither the greatest cheapness of purchase nor dearness of sale, but by community of interests, and by its influence on the increase of production.

Great Britain finds the United States its best customer, although it is notorious that by reason of competition here British commodities are sold in our markets at much lower prices than in India or China, and in many instances lower than within a mile of their manufacture. But by very large production it is possible to make profit from the sale of great quantities of fabrics or general merchandise, and the certainty and quickness of the returns render a small margin satisfactory.

In addition, Great Britain is forced to buy from us a great deal of its food and a large share of its raw cotton. It can most conveniently pay us by shipping its surplus of manufactures and accepting the very lowest profits upon it; while it is true that in buying in the cheapest market, it is beyond question that British manufacturers are often accepting the United States as the cheapest market also for selling their wares. Often their surplus is sold here at less than the cost of production. But this is when the surplus is in excess of any demand here or elsewhere at the natural standard of prices.

CREATING FOREIGN MARKETS.

The American advocates of favoritism for commerce tell us that we must buy freely abroad in order to create a market for our own products. This is a like suggestion with one that an individual must buy more than he wants, or where he does not care to buy, in order to sell something in which he deals. This is neither political economy nor common sense. Neither a people nor a person should buy more than he needs or more than he can pay for. If he needs an article, it is wise to purchase it where advantage will return to him by the sale of his own commodities, so that the true rule is to try and buy where you sell. But experience will demonstrate that the best market to sell is not always where you buy.

Brazil affords a very striking example. In 1882 we bought from Brazil $29,540,151 worth of coffee, $1,445,541 worth of hides, and $8,193,878 worth of india-rubber, and all of these articles came in duty free. Our total imports from Brazil in that year were $48,801,878, and that was below the sum of the preceding years. But our total exports to that country in that year were only $9,152,562, and that was fully up to the average for the past decade.

China is quite as striking a refutation of this plea, that if we buy abroad we make a market for our own wares; for in 1882 our imports from that country amounted to $20,250,346, of which no less than three fourths, or $15,899,607, were free of duty, in the form of tea and raw silk and other non-dutiable articles. Our exports to China at the same time were only $6,429,783.[1]

With both of these countries we have established relations much more liberal than any other nation in the world offers them. We collect no duties on their chief products, while Great Britain makes tea and coffee the objects of very heavy charges. Yet Britain, in 1882, imported from Brazil $34,410,720 of value, and exported to that country $36,626,595. Our cousins, while buying rather more than two thirds as much as we did, sold there four times as much. Surely it is not by buying that we can create a foreign market for our products. The lesson is the same in China. There Britain bought $46,680,460 worth in 1882, and sold only $24,458,070 worth. The British trade there is much greater than our own. Its imports from China are more than double our own, but it is unable to sell to the Chinese more than about one half as much as it buys. We sell to China less than one third as much as we buy; but we transact our business with that country far more cheaply, for we are at no such cost for naval display and influence or for diplomatic control.

Great Britain buys from us more than from any other people. This result is achieved in the face of

[1] Bureau of Statistics.

the constant friction caused by the British demand for the reduction of our customs duties. The purchases are frequently made, not in good will, but simply because they are here secured at the lowest rates or on the best terms. Thus in 1882 we exported to Great Britain, of our own productions, $404,248,031 worth. According to the theory of the doctrinaires, who tell us that a nation must buy in order to sell its own commodities, Britain ought to have sent to us commodities of equal or approximate value. But with all the efforts to crowd its wares upon us, by disposing of its surplus at prices less than the cost of production, and the attempt to destroy some of the growing rivals in new branches of competition, Britain sold to us in 1882 only $154,850,735 worth of British and Irish produce. We are, nevertheless, the best customer that Britain has in the world; but we are so because our own production enables our people to buy more commodities than any other equal number of persons on the globe. This is a good market for Britain, and British commodities are thrust upon us, because our people produce in larger ratio than any other population. The best service that we can render to Britain is to go on with our own policy. We can buy more just in the degree that we produce more. Our markets are the best for Britain, while British markets are still better for us. But in neither case is the axiom verified enjoining that one must buy in the cheapest market and sell in the dearest market; for in the case of Britain, it buys from us because it cannot get what it wants so promptly and so well elsewhere. Its grain and cotton merchants allege that they make the prices for the world. Just to the extent that their boast is true prices are equal for them from all producers. The British demand here is then not determined by price, but by other considerations. Certainly British commodities are sold here at less price than they are sold, reckoning transportation, either at home or in any other market of the world. But this is a vast field for traffic. The British producer and merchant seek to occupy this market at any cost. The vastness of transactions, the illimitable demand for commodities from our people, impel the British manufacturer and trader to look with wistful eyes in this direction, and to desire, before any or all other markets in the world, to enter in and possess that of the United States.

In 1882 Britain exported to the United States nearly twice as much as to France or Germany, and three times as much as to Holland, while no other country came within much more than one fifth of the values. In the same year Britain bought from the United States more than twice as much as from any other country, and only eleven per cent. less than the total imports from all of the British possessions.[1]

[1] Britain exported of British and Irish produce, in 1882, to the United States, £30,970,147; to France, £17,421,212; to Germany, £18,518,024; to Holland, £9,379,737. Britain imported in 1882, from the United States, £88,352,613; from France, £39,090,381; from Germany, £25,570,985; through Holland, £25,320,709. From

If any increase of trade with Britain could be effected by any change in our revenue system, it could only be by offering such premiums as would make up to British producers the losses which they might incur by an aggravated endeavor to compete with our manufacturers, while already we provide for whatever deficiency occurs in the British food supply, except as India is now trained to raise grain. For the European competition diminishes just in the degree that the general condition of Russia and Austria improves, and the people at home are able to eat the wheat and flour which they raise. In other words, Britain takes from us now, on the average, as large a ratio of our commodities as any fiscal policy on our part could force upon her people. It is clear that we buy as much as it is for our interest to take of manufactures which we can provide for ourselves, of quite as good quality and at as low a price, considering the mode of payment.

Yet the attempt of those who call themselves free traders is to increase our trade with Britain. The missionary efforts of the Cobden Club have in view that patriotic end. Why should we offer a bounty to have our cotton shipped to Lancashire or Normandy to be weaved, when we can do the work ourselves, and largely with labor which otherwise will not be employed at all? Why should we neglect our iron ore and seek to take the manufactures of iron and

all the British possessions the imports were £99,430,897. — *Statistical Abstract of the United Kingdom.* 1883.

steel from Sheffield and from Birmingham, when men who else would be idle can add to our national wealth by transforming the ores of Pennsylvania, Tennessee, and Georgia into the highest expressions of mechanism? Why should we fail to gather our own clothing from the backs of the sheep which roam in the ranges of Texas and California, simply in order to keep up factories in the North of England, in France, and Germany?

THE HOME AND THE FOREIGN MARKET.

McCulloch puts into distinct phrase a fallacy which underlies much of the discussion in favor of free trade. He declares that "the individual who uses only Polish wheat, Saxon cloth, and French silks, gives, by occasioning the exportation of an equivalent amount of British produce, precisely the same encourragement to industry here that he would give were he to consume nothing not directly produced among us."[1] It is difficult to account for such blindness on the part of any student who understands the simple rules of arithmetic; for, in the case supposed, the buyer of Polish wheat and Saxon cloth and French silk pays for something made abroad, and sends out of the country, to Poland, Saxony, or France, the equivalent of these commodities. If, on the other hand, he bought home products, his own labor with that of the producers of the wheat and cloth and silk would remain to be added to the general wealth.

[1] *Principles of Political Economy*, p. 104.

But this is only one element. There is the cost of transportation both ways to be deducted from the value which he receives for his outlay made abroad.

When one buys foreign produce, he gives to his country simply what he has himself wrought. If by buying domestic produce he develops any industry, he not only keeps at home his own labor, but adds to it that required for the products which he buys. It is a plain mathematical proposition. He who buys abroad casts into the common fund only his own labor. If he buys at home, he adds to his own labor in the common fund the value of the materials and labor in the commodities which he buys, and the freight charges both ways.

The champions of foreign commerce assert that traffic always includes two profits. Hence they allege that the opposition to an adverse balance of trade must be based on a fallacy. In the first place, traffic, while it aims at profits for both sides, may result in loss to both sides, and all gain may be swallowed up by the carrier and the banker. Commerce is only an effort to get profit, and is not always successful. In the event when success crowns it at all points, foreign commerce gives only one profit to the domestic participant, while the transportation and the other end of the account confers benefit on foreign producers and dealers. Domestic trade is an apple, all of which belongs here at home. In the case of foreign commerce the apple must be cut up, and often by far the largest part must be surrendered to aliens on foreign soil.

MARKETS AND GOVERNMENT CHARGES.

Our immediate concern with these fallacies about markets is only to insist that a revenue system should not be based upon them. It is obvious from national experience as well as from individual parallels, that it is folly to try to build up trade by making purchases in order to tempt others to buy our commodities. Our purchases must be dictated by our own desires and tastes and measured by our means of payment. No reason exists on this ground why our duties should be adjusted in order to expand our imports. Since it is not broad economy to say that we must buy in the cheapest markets, unless they are also the markets in which we can sell, our revenue laws should not seek to tempt us to buy abroad. The best service legislation can do is to contribute as well as it may to production, and the buyer will look out for himself. Only when our own is the dearest market to sell in is the dearest market the best for the seller; for British example is continuous that by selling, even in very cheap markets, the home prices can be maintained. Our own producers have thus far found that at home they have been able to sell at remunerative rates, and they have not been often forced to discharge their surplus on rival countries. When that time comes our exports will be increased to just the extent of that excessive surplus.

Instead of buying in order to sell, the true rule is to sell in order to buy. The price is secondary, either

FALLACIES ABOUT MARKETS. 247

in purchasing or selling, in any single transaction, to the effect upon the whole current of industry and trade. To sell in China may be well, but remote trade is always unstable. To sell at home, if you can get your pay, is to rest upon as secure a basis as traffic can present. Buyer and seller have mutual interests. They must expect to prosper or fail together. But the rock-bottom of all trade is production, and government performs its full share when it adjusts all of its machinery to develop production in all of its phases, and lets commerce take care of itself.

Every article made at home is burdened with its share of the taxes levied and collected here. The land tax and the charges on food and the common comforts of life attach to all commodities of domestic product. These become an element in the cost of production, and the effort of all trade is to recover them. In markets like ours the prices are determined in great part by the volume of home production. Every commodity of foreign origin is put upon our markets with the aim to secure the highest price possible. That is the general law of trade, and it has full application with imported goods, as well as with all others. If the imported article is suffered to escape all domestic imposts, the benefit will not accrue, as a rule, to the consumer, but will be pocketed by the importer, by the maker abroad, or by some intermediary agent. To exempt foreign goods from all government charges is to open our markets without charge to competition of foreign labor, to the benefit of the latter. The bounty thus offered to foreign competitors is equal to the average of the domestic taxes.

The domestic imposts enter into the prices of commodities in our markets in very unequal degree. As has been shown, the land tax is multiplied by just the ratio that a manufacture becomes complex, and includes many operations. On the average, a well-to-do mechanic must allow about one fourth of his wages for rent, and about one fifth of this sum goes for taxes. This is a rough statement, but it includes the average of many inquiries. This would place the land tax at about one twentieth of the receipts for wages. But this land tax appears in this way in every operation of mechanical production. It must be supplemented by the imposts upon articles of prime necessity. In gross, the total imposts paid by our people in 1880 were very nearly seven and a half per cent. on the total annual product of our agriculture and manufactures; for they were, including state, local, and national charges, $646,277,221. The sum of our agriculture and manufactures was $8,869,579,191. If these imposts were not multiplied at all, therefore, any imported commodity ought to bear a charge of at least seven and a half per cent., to stand upon the same basis as American wares in our own markets.

But if you will take your watch in your hand and follow out the many manipulations which the material must undergo in order to record the seconds and minutes and hours with absolute accuracy, you will find that the industries involved are very numerous. The same is the case with cotton fabrics, from the boll to the delicate stuff which passes for lace or silk, or even to the standard cottons of trade. The calculation contains many elements. Now no charge is paid by the manufacturer, as we have seen, that he does not try to collect with a profit from the wholesale merchant, who again repeats the process with the retailer, and he seeks to get his money back with a profit from the purchaser, who very likely buys in order that he may employ the commodity in some new manufacture.

This process of repetition varies in different commodities. It may occur only two or three times in some articles; it may run up to a dozen times in the more complex manufactures. No skill in mathematics will present all the elements of the problem in all cases. But see: where the process of repetition mounts up to seven times, the government charge equals more than one half the actual original value of the product. The average multiplication of domestic taxes must be at least threefold. The compensating duties on this account ought to be then twenty-two and a half per cent.

In this estimate the profits of commerce, domestic or foreign, are not included. For while imposts are in part paid from the profits of commerce, in the long run they must be recovered from production. This is one of the real problems in the demand for free trade, as the modern phrase runs : Shall the labor and industry, the agriculture and manufactures of this country, pay the charges which are necessary to maintain American institutions, and relieve all foreign importations from every like burden ?

The pretense is that the relief of importations from imposts is in the interest of consumers. But bear in mind that consumption adds nothing to the resources of the people; it only takes away from their ability to pay any charges. Just in so far as our markets are opened freely to foreign producers, our own production must pay the cost. Fair play requires that any foreign commodity brought to our markets shall pay its share of the expense of maintaining the institutions which render that market desirable. No simpler or more effective way has been adopted, or even suggested, than that of levying customs duties. The fact that some of our own products are burdened with imposts to one half of their original value does not enter the mind of theorists. They do not study the equation of taxes. They plead for free commerce; the burdens of trade afflict them. Free markets are impossible. The only question is, who shall pay the burdens? Shall commerce be relieved from its due share of imposts, and labor be forced to pay additional charges?

Since production is the first condition of any commerce, shall we not rather adjust our revenue system to favor industry and to develop our natural resources? For just in so far as we let in foreign commodities without paying charges in due ratio to those levied upon home products, we offer a bounty for importations.

It is a common and cheap response to say that if we adopt this policy, then other countries will collect from our exports like charges. The first question for us is to determine what is wise for us, and what is practical sense. If we place all producers upon an equal footing in our own markets, we can do no more in justice to our own industries. But as a matter of fact, every nation does seek, and will seek, its own advantage in its adjustment of imposts.

If a nation cannot feed itself, it is forced to favor the introduction of food even by such a bounty as exemption from imposts. When the nation reaches the point that it cannot clothe itself, it must also admit fabrics on a like footing. If a nation devotes itself to enterprise outside of its own borders and secures a large share of earnings on the sea, and its home production falls below its consumption, it cannot do less than offer a premium to the world, to give it something to carry, and to bring it commodities of all kinds for its support.

GREAT BRITAIN AND ITS REVENUE SYSTEM.

Let us be specific. Britain never struck off her protective duties until the proof was brought home by a famine in Ireland,[1] and her own inability to

[1] Fawcett, *Protection and Free Trade.*

afford adequate relief, that the British islands do not produce provisions sufficient for the support of their inhabitants.[1] With that demonstration came the farther lesson that in clothing and household comforts the production on the islands was not, and is not, equal to the requirements of the people. Ocean carrying may be profitable. It depends upon the will and the wealth of other nations in large part. A country which must seek its returns in considerable degree from such an occupation naturally offers premiums for its development. The markets of Britain are free, so far as they are free, because the necessities of the British people cannot be supplied without constant appeal to other lands. But these markets are rendered free by imposts upon the people, especially on some articles of prime necessity, and by excise charges, which have become very nearly *per capita* burdens. The poor of Britain pay by far more than their share of the imposts of the government. The cry is loud and long that the capital of the realm, and particularly its land, does not meet its due part of the imposts.

At the same time the invitation to foreign competition has struck British production blows of the

---

[1] See the speeches of Richard Cobden and John Bright from 1842 to 1846. At a conference between Mr. Bright and Sir Thomas Acland, February 22, 1843, the latter said: "In ten years, perhaps, the people might amount to three or four millions, more, and then no science, no skill, no industry, applied to agriculture, would be capable of enabling it to supply a sufficiency of food for the country." — *Life and Times of John Bright*, p. 139.

most serious character. Mr. Gladstone at Leeds, in 1881,[1] declared that the United Kingdom was paying every year $225,000,000 for manufactures which it ought itself to furnish. The official statistical abstract enforces the declaration. From 1854 to 1880, the imports of manufactured articles have increased by 406 per cent., while the exports of such articles have increased by only 123 per cent. The imports of articles partly manufactured have increased in the same period by only 90 per cent., of raw materials by only 84 per cent. And even of food materials the imports have in the interval increased by only 213 per cent. In other words, the dependence of Britain on other countries for manufactures has grown within this period nearly twice as rapidly as its power to buy food abroad. Sir Eardley Wilmot, a member of Parliament, has put forth some startling statistics[2] showing how the British markets are passing out of British control. He shows that in ten years Britain has paid $1,400,000,000 for ten articles of manufacture. As a consequence production by the people in the realm is diminishing in many branches.

A notable article in the "Nineteenth Century" for June, 1883,[3] demonstrates that in the flax industry since 1861, in England and Scotland, 203,500 spindles have been stopped, and within six years 85,000

---

[1] Speech at Leeds, October 8, 1881.
[2] In a recent pamphlet.
[3] *Falling Trade and Factory Legislation*, by A. W. Finlayson.

have been stopped in Ireland, making a decrease of 290,500 spindles, or 18.05 per cent. These stoppages have thrown 20,000 hands out of employment. In woolens the exports have within fifteen years fallen off 26.05 per cent., while the imports have increased within twenty years nearly seven fold. In silk the British manufacture is less to-day than it was in 1871, and the imports of raw silk have fallen in ten years from 8,000,000 to 3,000,000 pounds. Sugar refining has become almost a lost art, and only one refinery stands on the Thames where at least twenty formerly were active. The iron and steel industries are commonly taken as the type and measure of British prosperity, and the exports as the test of their extent and growth. In 1871, the total British exports of iron and steel were 3,169,219 tons, and in 1881 they were 3,820,225 tons, no marked advance; in 1882 the exports rose to 4,350,297 tons, an increase so slight as only to emphasize the lesson.

That lesson is that in the name of commerce British production is sacrificed to foreign competitors, and the development of the industries natural to the soil is stunted. The British markets may contribute to foreign trade, may lead aliens to glut supply by the surplus of other lands; but the result is deadly to all the interests which constitute national wealth, and especially such as promote individual progress and the elevation of the body of the people. Mr. Gladstone was right at Leeds in urging that Britain ought to make more of the manufactures which it uses. Sir Eardley Wilmot is right in demonstrating that production is hampered by shackles which check the energies and vigor of the great people whom he addresses. In the attempt to force trade abroad, the British policy has trodden under foot the muscle and the thrift and the producing power upon which alone a nation can permanently rear the structure of prosperity. The markets which are best are those which rest upon home interests, and are extended by the push and flow of home production.

We want to employ our labor in agriculture and manufactures, and to sell our products. Thus far we have found by far the best markets at home. The example of Great Britain proves to us that by abolishing customs duties, instead of extending our export trade in its ratio to importations we should certainly bring in foreign commodities to compete with our own labor, and should sacrifice our production to the chance of getting a share of the ocean carrying trade.

Thus far in human history no nation has ever won and long held the mastery of the seas for commerce, except at the price of war and the maintenance of a very costly navy. The story of foreign markets has always been a record of strife and of diplomacy, with armies and navies to sustain them. We seek commerce only upon the basis of peace. Our domestic trade exceeds the traffic of five times the same number of people anywhere else in the world. We offer the best markets to everybody else, and therefore also the best markets to our own producers. The nations which in all ages have sought the prizes of commerce have gone as Jason went to seek the golden fleece, at the sacrifice of home attractions and rewards. The American policy has wisely been to foster production, and to seek foreign trade only through the strong currents which may flow beyond our shores because of abundant prosperity at home. We sell because we produce more than we can use; and then we buy, because while our necessities can be supplied at our own doors, we are able to indulge in our tastes, and even our whims, from the surplus of our earnings.

RAW MATERIALS.

A suggestion just now pressed with vigor applies to this matter of markets in relation to the revenue. The proposition is that to gratify the desire to get raw materials more cheaply we ought to reduce the customs duties upon them. But the radical question is whether that is the best way to render all such materials more accessible at practicable prices. For example, is the way to get cheap wool to reduce the duties on that commodity? to get cheaper iron ought we to let foreign iron in free of duty? Let us take these articles for tests. Where will you look for the cheapest iron? Is it not at the mouth of the ore-bed, at the door of the blast-furnace? Can you ever get wool on better terms than directly off the sheep's back?

We have already illustrated how under low duties the production of pig iron kept at the minimum, while under fair rates of customs the increase has been large and continuous, and has outrun the development of that industry in any other land. We have not begun to open the ore-beds of the oldest states, and in the newer regions the ore lies almost on the surface, ready to work. The maximum rate of growth has not even been approached. In the cities labor is lying idle which can be turned at once into this occupation; why should it not be put to use? All over the land capital is tempted into speculation simply because regular employment for it is not brought home with sufficient directness to the persons who hold it. Bring the labor and the capital together under favorable circumstances, and we can make every kind of iron as cheaply as it is made anywhere else in the world, with the single allowance of rates of wages. Hence no reason exists why we should not greatly multiply our production in this line, and contribute to the building up of many new branches of mechanism among our people. The way to bring down the price of iron is to increase the production of it right here on our own soil. Certainly we ought not to offer a premium in the reduction of duties for foreign producers to pour their surplus into our markets. Beyond any question iron is cheaper here than it could ever have been rendered by any other method than by vast mining and blasting enterprises by our own people.

Another strong appeal is addressed to Congress, to abolish the duties on wool, on the plea that manufacturers will thus be assisted. Notwithstanding the extension of the use of this staple in garments, and the demand for it created by the improvement in the condition of artisans and laborers, during the past sixty years the price of the raw material has not advanced, but has on the finer grades shown a decided falling off, from sixty to sixty-eight cents a pound in 1824 to forty-two to forty-four cents a pound in 1883. On the other hand, the coarse grades have kept fully steady or tended to advance. We need now cheaper wool. To-day, with Australia, the United States is the largest producer of wool on the globe. Great Britain handles the largest quantity of the staple, but it is only as middle-man. Any reduction of duties would tend, as it has tended before, to lead to the killing off of sheep in this country, to the purchase of foreign wool, and to the advance at an early day of the charge made by foreign merchants for the raw material. At the same time, the disposition to raise the prices of foreign wools has been checked and overcome, and the river Plate and Australia have been unable, even with the aid of British middle-men, to dictate terms to our factories.

The growth of the wool production in this country has been very encouraging. Already from Vermont fine breeds of animals are shipped to other lands, and from that state all over this continent the production of fine wools has extended. In southeast Ohio the finest wools are obtained by the most successful of our manufacturers. Instead of discouraging this

FALLACIES ABOUT MARKETS. 259

source of wealth we should strive to extend it. Our own experience teaches us how to extend it and how to get cheap wool. That experience also presents a warning what course to avoid.

From 1850 to 1860 was the period of the Walker tariff and its successor, avowedly free trade projects. The increase in the production of wool in this country was from 52,516,959 pounds in 1850 to 60,264,913 pounds in 1860, — an increase of fifteen per cent. From 1860 to 1870 the production ran up to 100,102,387 pounds, an increase of over sixty per cent. Again from 1870 to 1880 the wool clip was increased, according to the figures of the census tables, to 155,681,751, or fifty-five per cent. But the estimates of the expert who examined the whole field reach the total of 240,000,000 pounds, or two and a half times the product of 1870, and four times that of 1860. The first effect of the tariff of 1846 was to carry down the prices of wool, but as soon as the foreign dealers were able to get control of the market they raised the price against our manufacturers. On the other hand, since the war closed, under the present rates of duties, wool has ruled lower than during the free trade period, and the tendencies are not now upwards.

The proposition is a very plain one: Is there any possible plan by which wool can be brought down in price more effectually and permanently than by multiplying its production by four within twenty years? Is not that by far more sure and trustworthy than a policy which added only fifteen per cent. to the clip within an entire decade? In coarse wools especially is there need of very rapid extension. No one questions our ability to raise this sort of the staple. By continuing the present policy of developing our wool clip, in another decade we will establish prices such as will dictate the rates to the world.

Germany pursues the system of admitting its raw materials free of duty, and thus fosters the manufactures of the last and highest stages. As we have already urged, it is wise to collect the government charges at as great a distance as possible from labor, upon the last form of production. In that way the charge is repeated to the minimum extent. But we can produce all of our own iron, and no reason exists why we should seek the golden fleece anywhere away from our own domain. For these reasons, the example of Germany is not applicable to our case. The place for us to look for the cheapest iron is in our own ores, and for the cheapest wool, on the backs of our own sheep.

PROTECTED INDUSTRIES.

An adroit attempt is made by the advocates of foreign commerce, the theoretical free-traders, of whom David A. Wells is a conspicuous example, to draw a line between what they style "protected industries," and those which are not protected. They count as "protected" those of which the products appear in the tariff schedules. They assume that all industries not included directly, and by name, in the imposts, do not secure protection through the tariff. This is the plea just made before the Ways and Means Committee. Let us see. You establish a new manufacture under the stimulation of the protective policy. That, these theorists would call a " protected industry." But it has set at work masons and carpenters to put up buildings; it has required the rudest laborers to dig cellars and to make mortar and carry the hod. New homes are demanded in the neighborhood. Every building interest has been stimulated. The new homes must be supplied with furniture, with decorations extending with improved wages. Every mechanical occupation has shared in the advantage. The operatives have been drawn from the farm, from other industries. The standard of pay has been raised along the whole line of labor. Everybody can live better. The competition with the farmer has been reduced, while the demand for his products has been augmented. The farmer gets a share, constant and large, of the advantage. The effect of a given duty is to stimulate production in all its branches, to protect industry in every one of its phases.

When you seek to raise a chain of which the links are all connected, and to raise it for a considerable height, you need not fasten your hook to every link. If you grip closely a single link, you lift the whole chain as far as that link is raised.

Here is a lake which you desire to flood over the

whole surface. Can it be necessary to pour so much water over every square yard separately, and will you raise the level only where your stream enters or falls? Let the current touch the lake where it may, let the point of entry be only one, the surface will rise equally, the level will be maintained, and the smooth beauty of the increased depths will adjust itself with a mirror which will tempt the sun and reflect the clouds.

Thus under the American policy all industries are protected, and often most those which are not represented in the tariff schedules. The petty pleas based on a classification which assumes that the ocean of our industry is made up of painted cards, piled up by fancy, and lacking cohesion and vitality, are not worthy of the authors or our subject. Our production is one like the deep, over which winds may sweep, and for the moment terrible depths may appear, and monstrous waves may rise; but its true surface is more level than earth presents. Whatever benefits American labor at any point confers blessings on every part of its efforts and its products. While any industries are protected by our legislation, our production is, as a whole, stimulated and encouraged.

Take boots and shoes as a test. These are not included in any tariff schedule. Yet in no case is the effect of protection more manifest. For by the high wages in this country, by the standard of comfort and of luxury here maintained, the style and quality of such commodities required by our working-people are better than in any other land. Here are no clogs, no wooden shoes of any pattern; but serving maids and apprentices wear on their feet as good material and work as in the Old World any caste or class will demand. This requirement of quality and of frequent change are the impetus to a manufacture which has become so extensive. These conditions are established and promoted by the protective policy. In the same way the whole level of labor and of employed capital is lifted up.

We shall therefore get the best markets to buy in as well as to sell in, by fostering our own industries. Even our raw materials will be brought soonest to the lowest standard of price practicable, by producing them from the gifts which a generous Providence has bestowed upon our territory, and contributes in the variety of our climate.

Why and how our markets are the best, it will not be difficult to show in a consideration of duties, wages, and prices. For the present enough has been shown to forbid any declaration that any improvement in our markets can be secured by a change in our tariff laws.

CHAPTER IX.

DUTIES, WAGES, AND PRICES.

Many Causes of the Material Development of the United States. — Condition of American Labor. — Benefits of High Wages. — Happiness in the United States. — Industrial Activity and Progress. — Robert P. Porter on Wages. — John Bright on English Wages. — A Cotton Mill in Bolton, England, compared with a Cotton Mill in the State of New York. — A Woolen Mill in Scotland and one in New York. — The Consular Reports. — Report of the Peabody Trust in London. — "Chambers' Journal." — Ratio of Capital, Labor, and Imposts. — Testimony before the Tariff Commission. — Logic of Immigration. — Savings Banks. — Railroad Charges. — Expenses of Government. — Prices of Commodities. — New York and Liverpool Markets. — Details. — Summary. — Cost of Living. — Figures from Consul-General Merritt. — The Charity Organization in England.— Classes of Expenses. — Living in the State of New York. — How Wages are expended. — Retail Prices in the Country. — Clothing from One Tenth to One Fifth of Expenses of a Family. — Purchasing Power of Money tends to Equilibrium. — Efficiency of Labor. — Example in Cotton. — Wages in Britain and on the Continent. — British Production. — American Results. — A Revenue Policy which will strike down Wages cannot be tolerated.

THE people of the United States have had many allies in attaining their present elevation of material development. The freshness of the soil has favored agriculture. The gifts of nature in mines, water, climate, have afforded admirable conditions for manufactures of the most diverse kinds. The quickness of intellect and the facility of hand have developed invention to an extent unparalleled elsewhere, and have enlisted curious and effective machinery in all branches of industry. To all of these blessings the government has added security and peace and encouragement by the general current of its legislation, and by the spirit which has almost uniformly prevailed.

Thus the condition of those who depend upon their daily labor is better here to-day than in any other part of the world, not only in the political equality insured to them, and in the moral privileges which surround them, but also in the pecuniary advantages which they can command by industry and thrift. So far as our fiscal legislation bears upon their condition, our theme requires us to consider the causes and the effects.

BENEFITS OF HIGH WAGES.

We propose to inquire how customs duties which protect American industry affect wages and prices. For if a governmental policy tends to the lowering of the condition of labor, no humanitarian can excuse it, and very grave considerations of necessity must be shown to justify even its temporary maintenance. You will often hear that the only problem to be investigated is the ratio of wages to prices, and the purchasing power of money. As a mere material proposition this is in part true. But the scale of wages has reference to many things besides the prices of commodities in the market. Notably the relation of wages to the cost of a homestead is an element which the prices current will not always illustrate. The ability of the workman to secure his own home and to keep it, is one of the incidents in his progress and elevation. As a rule, no one will deny that the selling value of land is lower in this country than in any of the nations of the Old World, and is to be paralleled only in the British colonies and the adjacent states of America. If it were conceded then that prices of commodities in the markets were higher in the United States than they are in other countries, while land is much lower, so that many more persons dependent upon their daily labor own their own homes here than elsewhere, the demonstration would be complete that the higher wages here are a real benefit. This is one of the incontestible facts in our civilization. Americans not only raise and maintain homes, but they are, beyond any other people in the world, the landlords of their own homes. This advantage is not simply one of property; but it has a moral basis, and contributes to political security. It enables Professor Seeley[1] to declare: "There has never been in any community so much happiness, or happiness of a kind so little demoralizing, as in the United States." Citizens who from their own homes control their own government afford the most favored spectacle which political institutions can present. This condition certainly exists in the United States. The ownership of their own homes is the demonstration of the superiority of the material and moral circumstances of our industrial classes.

[1] *Expansion of England*, p. 155.

In other ways high wages, independently of the prices current, mean more comforts and broader opportunities. Schools are not much affected by the markets. Travel is not, as a rule, more costly in countries of high wages. Social relations are determined in part by the leisure to enjoy them, but many of them in all countries are costly, and must be met by some expenditure. It is therefore true that many conveniences and enjoyments go with high wages, even if the prices of commodities are carried up in much greater ratio. But when the equation of wages and prices is kept upon the same level, high wages signify the advance of those who labor with their hands in all the elements which make up the conditions of happiness and prosperity. Comfortable homes tend to diminish at least the brutal crimes. Education lifts the individual up to the possibilities of a riper and more fruitful life. Wealth is certainly one of the powers for the elevation of society as a whole, and the development of cities and states. High wages furnish the lever for lifting up the whole social and political fabric.

In a period sufficiently long to allow the results to appear, high wages will produce an amelioration in the moral and social condition of the industrial classes which will affect taxation and the cost of government. Industry will become more skillful and more productive. It will be facile in invention. It will strike out into new fields. It will borrow whatever other lands have discovered, and will make useful all the devices of past ages. It will force its way to the front in variety and extent of production. All of this has happened in the United States. The time has not yet gone by when intelligent persons speak of this republic as an agricultural country, and treat its manufactures as a secondary interest. Yet the truth is that the American people have already rushed so far ahead of all competitors, that their manufactures exceed those of Great Britain in annual product by at least fifty per cent. They are more than double those of France. They are twice and a half as great as those of Germany. They are four times those of Russia, and more than five times those of Austria. Within a hundred years, from nothing our industrial progress has brought us to the head of nations in the value of our mechanical productions, and certainly in their variety and usefulness. We employ more hands in manufactures than Great Britain employs. We bring from the ore-beds and work more iron than any other nation except Britain, and our increase in this industry is far more rapid than that of any rival. In finished iron our product is already about equal to that of Britain. In steel we surpass Britain in rails, and just fall below it in Bessemer ingots; in some other forms we are yet behind.[1] In wooden commodities no land can compete with us, as the homes of our people demonstrate. In wool, only Australia surpasses us in its clip; our growth is more rapid, and in manufactures

---

[1] *Report of American Iron and Steel Association*, 1883.

of this staple we are challenging some of the best fabrics of the older countries. In cheaper qualities, the retail prices here are as low as they are abroad. In silks we stand next to France in extent of manufactures, and supply an increasing share of our own consumption, nor needs the quality shun comparison with rivals in many styles. In glass, we are on a par with either France or England in value of product; in many articles prices are lower here, and the question of excellence one of dispute. In cotton fabrics our manufacturers equal any competitors, and enter on equal terms the markets of the globe. If in linens we fail to attain the prominence which invites us, in copper and lead, and many minor materials and manufactures, our people need not yield on any field. In the textile industries, in twenty years the number of operatives in England fell off, while in the United States there was an increase of more than one hundred per cent.

We add in annual value $5,369,579,171 to the national production in manufactures, or, some authorities insist, as much as $8,000,000,000.[1] While so much is produced, no reason can be adduced why even in larger measure we cannot meet every demand of our growing population, and by multiplying production cheapen every comfort and most of the luxuries which civilization has provided for mankind.

Thus the blessings are combined here of higher wages and cheaper living, on the same grade of com-

[1] C. S. Hill before Tariff Commission.

forts, than in any other land. Many circumstances contribute to produce this happy combination, and all of our experience proves that our revenue system favors both the high rewards of labor and its most fruitful efficiency.

STATISTICS OF WAGES.

We have tried to deal with the broadest lessons of history, with the most radical considerations of national life. Let me now illustrate the demonstrations of statistics. Robert P. Porter, who has been making this subject a special study, concludes, in an elaborate address before the Fair Trade Congress at Leamington, England,[1] that wages are from sixty to one hundred per cent. higher in the United States than in Great Britain, and from one hundred to one hundred and fifty per cent. higher than in Germany, France, Belgium, and Holland. These results can be tested often by individual experience. As a result of inquiry among many persons, mechanics from Great Britain, recently immigrated, testify that their wages here are just double what they were at their old home in the same trade, and that they save here a sum precisely equal to their total wages there.[2]

---

[1] November 10, 1883.

[2] Before the Ways and Means Committee at Washington, in March, 1884, among the witnesses was Thomas Williams, an iron puddler, born in England. He had worked five years, he stated, in the iron mills of England, before emigrating to America. His wages there amounted to $1.25 a day, puddling iron, and he did not have steady work, either. "It is said that in England it costs much less

DUTIES, WAGES, AND PRICES. 271

John Bright, in a speech in Birmingham, March 29, 1880, gave very strong testimony indirectly with reference to the general standard of wages in Britain. In criticising the Disraeli administration, he denounced it for taking up its time with things far remote from the true interests of England, and neglecting "artisans such as you are," speaking to his auditors, "with your twenty shillings, or thirty shillings, or forty shillings a week." No public speaker in the United States would address workingmen as the recipients of five, or six, or eight dollars a week; he would naturally set his standard at ten, fifteen, and twenty dollars a week.

This question of wages is vital to this whole subject. Let me present some recent comparisons, based upon figures for which I am willing to be personally

---

to live," remarked Mr. Williams. "I deny that most positively, and I speak from actual experience. My board there cost from $3 to $3.50 a week, and we did not live as the laborers of this country do. For breakfast the English laborers get bread and butter and a cup of tea. Dinner is composed of bread and meat, and if they get an egg with their tea in the evening, they consider it extravagance. There are many women at work in the mills of England, also. They do the unloading of coal, and are kept at other unskilled labor. Their wages are nineteen cents a day." He feared there would be many women doing the work of men in this country ere long if free trade was adopted, because the male laborers could not more than support themselves. He contrasted the different wages paid laborers in this country with those of free-trade England. At Youngstown the puddlers made $5.50 out of the same amount of work English laborers were paid $1.25 for. The laborers at Youngstown, he stated, got at least three times as much money for their work as those in England, and their living cost them about the same.

responsible. In the latest report submitted by Consul-General Merritt, he embodies the statement of A. D. Shaw, United States Consul at Manchester, giving the wages in a cotton factory in Bolton, England. By the side of those figures are placed the actual wages paid in the month of February, 1884, in a representative cotton mill in the State of New York, as given to me by the superintendent: —

	Bolton.	State of New York.
Card-grinders, men, a week	$5.59	$8.28
Card-strippers, men	5.59	7.25
Slubber-tenders, girls	4.36	6.00
Mule-spinners, men	5.95	10.50
Frame-spinners, girls	2.31	4.50
Warpers, girls	4.22	6.00
Weavers, men, per loom	1.30	
Weavers, girls, per loom		$3 or $9 a week.
Loom-jobbers, men, per week	9.00	12.25
Mule overlookers, men	10.22	18.00
Mechanics, average	7.54	13.00
Engine-drivers	10.22	18.00
Firemen, average	5.00	8.40

Notice that the American rates are seldom less than fifty per cent. above the British standard, and sometimes, as for weavers, are nearly one hundred and fifty per cent. in advance.

Even more striking is the contrast in woolens. Let me present side by side the wages now paid in a typical woolen mill in the State of New York, given from the pay rolls for February, and the wages of a woolen mill, in many respects similar, in Aberdeen, Scotland: —

Wool-Sorters.

	Scotland.	New York.
Overseer	$7.50	$18.00
Men	5.50	12.00
Dyers, men	3.75	7.00

Carding.

	Scotland.	New York.
Overseer	16.50	30.00
Card-cleaners	4.50	7.26
Card-tenders, girls	2.00	4.00

Spinning.

	Scotland.	New York.
Overseer	7.00	18.00
Men		12.00
Boys	1.50	4.00

Warping and Drawing.

	Scotland.	New York.
Overseer	7.50	18.00
Dresser-tenders, women	4.50	men, 10.50
Children	1.50	3.50 to 4.00

Weaving.

	Scotland.	New York.
Overseers	16.50	30.00
Section hands	7.50	13.50
Weavers	3.75	10.00
Pattern weavers	5.50	10.00

Finishing.

	Scotland.	New York.
Overseer	15.00	35.00
Shearers	3.75	7.50
Pressmen	3.75	8.00
Burlers, girls	1.75	4.00
Fine drawers, girls	3.75	6.00
Giggers and fullers	3.75	7.50

Observe that the New York wages are much more than double those of Scotland, in many cases are two and a half times, and will average not far from one hundred per cent. greater.

While comparisons in other trades are not so easy, the cotton and woolen industries fairly illustrate the whole field of industry.

The most recent investigations fully sustain the results of the exhaustive comparison made by our consuls abroad, and published by the State Department in 1879. Mr. Evarts then presented a summary of the conclusions, which showed that the rates of wages in the United States were then more than twice those of Belgium, three times those in Denmark, Germany, and France, once and a half those in England and Scotland, and more than three times those in Italy and Spain. At the same time the prices of the necessaries of life are lower in the United States than in any of the foregoing countries. While the details have changed in some respects, our consuls abroad still cite these figures as substantially a fair statement of the conditions in the several countries at the present time.

Incidental confirmations can be deduced from unquestionable authority. Thus, in the houses of the Peabody Trust in London, which take in the most thrifty and tidy working people, 3,525 heads of families engaged in seventy-four different occupations with 101 persons unclassified, earn, according to the official report of the trustees for 1882, an average of £1 3s. 6¼d., or $5.68½. These are picked instances in the chief city of the country. They establish the figures of the consular reports.

"Chambers' Journal" for January, 1884,[1] gives a

[1] Page 831.

condensation of important statistics, which from that source deserves especial notice. That authority says, —

"Assuming the produce of labor to be one hundred: —

"In Great Britain, fifty-six parts go to the laborer, twenty-one to capital, and twenty-three to government.

"In France, forty-one parts go to the laborer, thirty-six to capital, and twenty-three to government.

"In the United States, seventy-two parts go to the laborer, twenty-three to capital, and five to government." [1]

This comparison, remember, is not invented to help our argument. It is the unwilling testimony of the world's experience to the superiority of our methods, and not least of our revenue system.

The prolonged and exhaustive investigation of the Tariff Commission in 1882 brought out a great variety of facts under circumstances which led to careful criticism and adjustment. By that test the comparison of wages was made more complete and satisfactory than is possible by any unofficial attempt. The result is on record. It is that in industrial pursuits generally the standard of wages is at least sixty per cent. higher here than in Britain, and the difference is still greater against every continental country.[2]

---

[1] The London *Times* gives the same figures.

[2] In the prolonged hearings before the Tariff Commission of 1882,

276   AMERICAN SYSTEM OF REVENUE.

Europe maintains a protective policy, so that the comparison with any part of the continent does not witnesses often gave statistics of wages in this country and abroad. This testimony is in large part condensed here.

FLAX.

At Troy, N. Y., hacklers, men, in 1861, received $1 per hundred for dressing.

Hacklers, men, in 1882, received $2 per hundred.
Skilled spinners, women, 1861, received 50 cents a day.
Skilled spinners, women, 1882, received $1 a day.
Boys and girls, 1861, received 50 cents a week.
Boys and girls, 1882, received $2.40 a week.
Unskilled men, 1861, received 50 to 62½ cents a day.
Unskilled men, 1882, received $1 a day, p. 273.

In New York (p. 279), we pay from $6 to $8 for spinners, while Scotch and Irish spinners receive the same number of shillings for precisely the same labor.

Thomas Barbour, Paterson, N. J. (p. 289), also manufactures in Ireland. Average wages, $5.50 a week, including girls from twelve years to forty; some make $10 a week; children $3 to $4 a week; a man can make $1.50 to $2 a day. In Ireland or France we pay twice as much wages.

IRON.

In saddlery hardware, p. 381, we have men who earn $27 to $30 a week.

In barbed wire, Des Moines, Iowa, average $1.75 a day, p. 1138.

In cutlery, in United States, $2 a day; in Germany, 50 cents, or up to $1 and $1.25, p. 1940.

Pig iron, wages in United States double those in England, p. 838.

Iron ore, labor in Lake Superior mines, $2 a day, or from 30 to 150 per cent. above Spanish and Canadian rates, p. 845.

In ore and iron and stone and brick, cost of labor, 60 per cent. less in England, France, and Germany, than here, p. 1912.

In Sweden, wages in ore-beds and furnaces, 25 cents a day, and here $1.25 to $1.50, p. 2067.

bear on the question of revenue, but on other social problems.

On tin plate, difference in cost of labor between United States and England, about 40 per cent., pp. 2083–84.

Witness does not think there is 25 per cent. difference in wages of miners between this country and England, and 20 per cent. in pursuits where much machinery is used, p. 1886.

Coal and ore miners here earn $1.75 to $2 a day; in England, 75 cents to $1, p. 2214.

Wages in iron and other mills, 50 per cent. higher here than in England and Europe, and in some lines even 100 per cent., p. 2389.

SUGAR.

In sugar, in Louisiana, field-laborers, 85 cents to $1 a day; second class, 75 to 85 cents; ditching, building levees, etc., $1.25 to $1.50; sugar-house work, $1.25 to $2.50, p. 549.

GLASS.

In glass we pay (New Albany, Ind.) from two to four times as much as is paid in Europe for the same labor, p. 938.

Tables, p. 1190, compare Europe, England, and United States showing this difference.

Tables, p. 1532, confirm statement.

In glass, our wages average 50 per cent. higher than in Belgium, p. 2001. The actual rate is 50 to 60 per cent. higher, p. 2513.

POTTERIES.

In potteries, tables for wages in Staffordshire, Eng., and Trenton, N. J., show the English average, $8.69, and the American average, $18.50, latter about 113 per cent. higher, pp. 615–17.

Wages in Staffordshire have advanced 40 per cent. in thirty years. In Trenton, lower than before the war, p. 762.

This statement denied, p. 872.

Tables, pp. 866–68, show fully 100 per cent. average difference between English and American potteries.

In Cincinnati, we paid $1.25 before the war; now we pay $2.25 to $2.50, p. 872.

IMMIGRATION.

We can appeal to the nations in a body to declare whether it is not true that the material condition of

Tables, p. 1980–33, compare foreign and American wages, showing difference sometimes as high as 275 per cent.

Tables, p. 2129-31, show American wages 126¾ per cent. over English.

Clay-pipe makers, $8 a week here and in England, p. 1533.

Wages in potteries much higher here than before the war, p. 2405.

LUMBER.

In lumber (East Saginaw, Mich.), average wages in saw-mills, $2 a day; in forests, $1.75, pp. 956, 959.

SILK.

In silk, wages in Basle, Switzerland, not one fourth those paid in this country, p. 2174.

Tables, p. 2297, show wages 100 per cent. more here than in England; 200 per cent. more than in France; 300 per cent. more than in Italy, and still more as compared with Germany.

COTTON.

For cotton, highest wages of a spinner here range from $10.08 to $13.36, while in England they are $7.20 to $12, with a reduction of 10 per cent., pp. 1699-70.

MISCELLANEOUS.

Leather dressers are paid here 35½ per cent. more than in Britain, 66⅔ more than in France, and 93¾ more than in Germany, p. 384.

In photograph albums, price of labor in Germany only about one half that in this country, p. 2445.

In alkalies, skilled workingmen receive not exceeding $1 a day in England, while the average here is over $2, p. 2495.

Watchmakers, Providence, $8.89 to $12 a week.

Gold leaf, $12 to $18 a week, in Boston, p. 660.

In England, men work for 45 to 50 per cent. of our wages, and in Germany they get only 35 cents for our dollar, p. 1053.

the industrial classes is better here than in any other land. Political liberty counts for something, doubtless, in their estimate. But when there is a pressure for the necessities of life, it is not in human nature to exaggerate any considerations above those of getting food and shelter for one's self and family. Upon this point the movement of peoples bears unimpeachable testimony. Against every assertion that the American laborer does not get better wages, whether measured in money or in commodities, the grand army of immigrants from all lands flocking to our shores is the eloquent protest. These immigrants come from the countries which are our rivals in manufactures, which have bent every energy to restrict our foreign trade. These immigrants go into manufacturing, mining, and the mechanic arts in larger numbers than into any other occupation. While in all occupations the percentage of persons, natives of

Gold beaters earn $13.50 a week in Philadelphia, p. 431.

Biscuitmakers would require fifty per cent. more wages than in England or Europe, p. 538.

Ropemakers, wages in United States 50 to 70 per cent. higher than in England, p. 649.

Papermakers, wages in England not more than half rate here, p. 852. See tables, p. 991, showing increase here of 50 to 100 per cent. since 1860, and difference of much more than double here over England in 1882.

Filemakers, wages here 50 to 100 per cent. higher than in British factories, p. 862.

Unskilled labor, $1.75 a day in towns and factories, Des Moines, Iowa, p. 1158.

In rice (Charleston, S. C.), after war, wages 40 cents a day, now $1.

all foreign countries, is only twenty, and in agriculture is only ten, in the branches of manufactures, mechanics, and mining, the percentage rises to nearly thirty-two.[1] Our immigrants come in largest numbers for wages and not for land.

These are our imports; these are our constant additions to our wealth, and they add each year to our production. These are the millions who during ten years, during a generation, have testified to the excellence of the American system. Count them and question them. They numbered in 1882 over three quarters of a million persons, — 788,992. Of these, 179,423 came from the United Kingdom. Out of every 195 of the population in the British Isles one came to the United States, to live and to seek a better condition. This migration is generally of picked men and women, of those who have life and hope before them. It fell off for a while after our panic of 1873, from which we suffered with all the world. During this period Professor Fawcett found a pretext for arguing that our depression was to be cited against our revenue system. He turned the circumstance adroitly. But again the tide of migration constitutes an overwhelming proof that the men and women who labor with their hands find America, and not Canada but the United States, the most attractive of homes, and the land of most unquestioned prosperity. The immigrants come, and they bid

[1] *Report on Statistics of Manufactures, Tenth Census*, vol. ii. p. xxxvi.

father and brother and son to hasten hither. They can measure wages and prices, and the equation which renders saving and improvement possible. Against any theory, any special plea from any quarter, I cite these witnesses who have from the British Isles, between 1872 and 1882, been 1,175,155, or more than one thirty-fifth of their entire population. From the continent of Europe they have numbered 1,996,406. From the whole world the vast army has within ten years reached the multitude of 3,949,264, more than our total population when we asserted our independence. The aggregate is greater than the population of the state of New York in 1865, and greater than that of any state in the Union in 1882, with the exceptions of New York and Pennsylvania. These are the forerunners sent before to spy out the land, and they testify in every form possible to all the world, that for workingmen, for those who depend upon their own labor, that is to say for producers and production, no other land compares with the United States.

SAVINGS BANKS.

One of many methods of comparison of the condition of the industrial classes is by the measure of their savings. Both in Britain and in this country the statistics are quite full on this subject. The post-office savings banks in Britain have been highly commended, because they have invited and encouraged savings in large degree. In 1882 the total capital or deposits at rest in all the savings banks of the United Kingdom, including the post-office institutions, was £83,750,402, according to the official "Statistical Abstract;" that is $418,752,010. The increase in these deposits was £2,269,297 for the year from 1881 to 1882; in dollars this is $11,346,485. From 1880 to 1881 the increase was £2,513,182, or $12,565,910. In no previous year did the increase ever amount to $10,000,000.

In his annual report for the year 1882 the comptroller of the currency presents the summary of the returns of the savings banks of the United States. They show that the aggregate deposits in these institutions in 1882 were $1,003,500,000, and the increase from the preceding year was from May to May, $28,800,000.

By deposits greater by more than double, as ten to four, and increasing by nearly three times the swiftness, or as ten or eleven to twenty-eight or twenty-nine, the savings banks of the United States testify that in the equation of wages to prices, in the adjustment of production to the cost of living, this country is better off than Britain.

This is one demonstration that our revenue system favors our laboring classes.

RAILROAD CHARGES.

Another group of facts affords excellent ground for comparison of the general relations of wages and production on the one hand, and of prices and the cost of living on the other, between the United States and other countries. Into the railroads enter all the considerations which affect cost and prices. In this country our distances are vast, and our population scattered as compared with the states of Europe, except Russia. The audacity of enterprise has pushed these iron ways often far beyond the demands of population and trade. They have been built with more regard to rapidity than to economy. They have cost more than they ought in many cases. Speculation has added still more to the capital upon which dividends must be earned. It would not therefore be strange, if, in order to get returns on all of the outlay, the charges for freight and travel were made much higher than in the Old World, where many of these incidental evils have been avoided. Keep in mind that the railroad represents labor in the roadway, in the iron of its tracks, in all of its equipments the highest style of mechanical skill. Keep in mind also that in the management of our railroads high priced labor is constantly required. The wages of all the persons employed about our railroads will average as high as in any other occupations. They may fairly be taken as a just standard of all wages in all occupations, for the ratio of unskilled labor is not less than it is in vocations generally.

The rates of passenger fare are adjusted to the estimate of the railroad managers of the due equation of the charge to all costs of construction and management. They afford an opportunity to reach some conclusion on a very large scale of prices here in their relation to wages, and to place them alongside those of the Old World. Now on first-class passengers it is found that the rates are lower in the United States than in any country in Europe, as a general rule. The exceptions are rare, and the comparison is so strikingly in favor of this country as to disarm criticism or doubt.

Our census exhibits the average first-class fares in this country at $2.33 for a hundred miles, or that number of cents for one mile on the average. Even in Belgium, with its limited territory and dense population and very low wages, the rates are $2.34. They are the same in Norway, where also labor is very cheap. Russia stands next in order of fares, at $2.45 to $3.10, but there the government stands behind the roads and the fares are probably unremunerative. In Britain and Switzerland and Germany the fares are from $3.11 to $5 for a hundred miles; in Sweden, they are $3.04; in Holland and Denmark they stand at $3.30; in Italy and Portugal, $3.50; in Austria-Hungary $3.69; in France $3.88; in Spain, $4.08; in Turkey $5.66, and in Roumania $7.

It is necessary to make allowance for the element of government control in railroads in some countries. But the authorities seek to place the fares at a just standard, and therefore the comparison cannot be much out of the way.

Second-class rates are not common in this country, because our people exhibit their sense of equality in traveling as in other practices; and every man likes to ride in as good style as his neighbor. But taking these second-class rates and placing them side by side with European charges, we find that the only countries in which the second-class fares are lower than here are South Germany, parts of Russia, Sweden, Belgium, Norway, and Greece.

We have no third-class fares on railroads in the United States, because we have no people who are willing to travel as third-class passengers.

In a different sphere, and yet in no less degree, labor and prices enter into all the conditions of freight transportation by railroad. In Britain population is more dense than here, and for that reason freight is concentrated into larger volumes for a given distance. The cost of moving every ton a single mile ought, therefore, to be less under conditions otherwise similar. But the reverse is true. The cost of railroad transportation of merchandise is lower here than in Britain, according to the testimony of railroad experts. The manner in which statistics are kept in Britain prevents comparison in detail by figures. But the radical fact is conceded by those who have studied the problem most thoroughly. The cost in Britain is less than in any European country, unless perhaps Belgium.

The latest statistics at hand are quite worth studying. They show the following rates per ton per mile: —

	Cents.
New England States in 1882	1.7
Middle States in 1882	1.0
Southern States in 1882	1.8
Western States in 1882	1.2
Pacific States in 1882	3.1
Average for the whole country in 1882	1.2
Average rate for France in 1881	1.66
Average rate for Germany in 1877	1.685
Average rate in Belgium	1.5

This demonstration is that in spite of our vast distances and scattered population, the average cost of transportation is less than even in Belgium, as shown by figures, and less by about the same difference, than in Britain. These railroad statistics include many of the elements which enter into all prices, and go far to sustain the conclusions which are attained by other paths.

In our coastwise trade, a like illustration of wages and prices can be found. While it is difficult to present statistics on the subject, it is conceded that in our coastwise marine the freight charges are lower than those of the home fleet of any other nation.[1]

GOVERNMENT EXPENDITURES.

A very broad group of expenditures connect themselves with the government. If we confine ourselves to the central administration, to the national government, to use the American phrase, injustice might be done, because royal institutions are so much more

[1] See article in *North American Review* for April, 1884, by Hon. N. Dingley, Jr.

costly than our republican system. But if we include all the local charges in two countries, taking those which affect cities and counties, or shires and parishes, everything which concerns every department of government, we shall get one of the most complete grounds for comparison. Now in the United States in 1880, the total government charges for the national, state, and local authorities, so far as they could be collected by the census-takers, were $647,277,221, and out of them was paid on the national debt $84,425,350, leaving, as the cost of government in every department in this republic, $562,851,871, and this was exactly $11.22 for every person enumerated.

In Great Britain in the same year the total of national and local taxes was £145,280,234, and this was *per capita* £4 1*s*. 8*d*., or $19.84.

So many considerations enter into administration that this comparison is not altogether a just measure of prices. But it has an important bearing upon it. In the old country fewer improvements are called for year by year, and in the cities extravagance is greater here probably than in Britain. The burden of taxes becomes a part of the cost of every article, and in that way, at least, this statement of government charges may be taken as indicating that the cost of living here on a similar level of comfort cannot be greater than in the land in which taxes are so much heavier.

PRICES OF COMMODITIES.

If we descend to a comparison of prices by commodities we shall come to the like conclusion. In all articles of food, first of bread, of wheat, and corn, and oatmeal, the markets in this country always rule below the British markets, taking the latter as the lowest in the world external to our own. Beef and pork and poultry are also cheaper here than in Britain or on the continent. The rates on the sea-coasts with us are generally, but not always, higher than inland by the cost of transportation. Taking the average rates for the whole Union we find the prices of food, whether flour or meats, or tea and coffee, and even sugar, at retail, are lower here than in Europe. The claim is made that Liverpool fixes the prices of grain; it determines the rates at which the surplus will be taken. But the home demand decides whether or not any surplus shall be offered abroad at any price. It is certain that the rates here cannot be above those which foreign consumers will pay.

Let us bring together the New York and Liverpool prices of staple articles at wholesale, as reported during the current month of February: —

	New York.			Liverpool.		
White wheat, hundred lbs.		$1.73			$2.08	
Beef, extra India mess, bbl.	$24.00	to	26.00		27.00	
Beef, mess, extra, bbl.	19.50	to	20.00		23.00	
Fresh beef, lb.	.1025	to	.11	$0.11	to	.12
Pork, prime mess, bbl.	14.50	to	17.00	15.62	to	18.61
Mutton, lb.	.06	to	.07	.18	to	.19
Eggs, dozen	.35	to	.37	.38	to	.43
Butter, lb.	.32	to	.35	.36	to	.42
Cheese, lb.	.13	to	.14		.15	
Tea, Congou, lb.		.205			.2516	
Coffee, lb.	.1075	to	.1090	.11	to	.117
Petroleum, gallon		.0825			.1525	
Sugar, refined, lb.		.0710		.062	to	.07

American prices are sometimes twenty per cent. lower, often fifteen per cent. lower, and on the average on these articles more than ten per cent. below the British standard.

In cotton fabrics of every grade the American buys as low as anybody in the world. As the large producers of the raw material we exercise a measure of control over all markets. While cotton is not king, it is an important factor in the comforts of mankind and in the trade of all lands. We export shirtings and sheetings to Britain, and in the far East we prove that we can adjust prices as low as any competitors.

The commodities which are made of wood, except articles which take value from their age or as curiosities, can be bought in the United States as cheaply as in any other country. If we import anything in this class, it is because it is costly and outside of the range of common demand.

No other land can furnish more cheaply the grades of leather in most ordinary use. Boots and shoes and harness, and the miscellaneous wares in which leather enters, are therefore sold here at figures quite as low as anywhere else. We are constantly exporting leather, and many of its products.[1]

---

[1] As some controversy exists relative to leather, the following paragraph from the *Trade Circular* of Boutcher, Mortimore & Co., under date of January 4, 1884, deserves to be cited:—

AMERICAN LEATHER.—At no time during the past year was there any very active demand for hemlock sides, and at one time the large failures in the States and Canada induced holders to sell at very low

In many of the products of iron we excel other nations, and in steel we are already in the forefront. In iron our progress is most rapid. Thus we are exporting agricultural implements, which we can sell in competition with any rivals. In the London newspaper called "Iron," in August, 1881, testimony is given relative to an advanced stage of metal production. The "Iron" recognizes "the superiority of the tools which are now so largely imported into Britain from America, and which, while remarkable for their quality and finish, are much less costly than the English production." Sir Thomas Brassey concedes that we are formidable competitors in edged tools and some kinds of machinery.[1] This testimony deserves to be extended to cutlery of the kinds in every-day use in the household and for personal convenience. Such utensils as frying-pans, sold in this

prices, but generally the market was steady, though dull, and the tendency during the first half of the year was to lower prices; damaged of all classes and low-priced sides at all times met most inquiry, and for really prime sides there was always a steady trade, but consumers found that many tannages of English sole leather were relatively quite as cheap, and gave them the preference; and as a result the quotations for hemlock sides were at the close of December fully one halfpenny per pound lower than at the corresponding period in 1882. Curried splits have been received in considerable quantities throughout the year, and during the past two or three months there has been more inquiry and rates are steady, without much change from those ruling in January last. Rough upper is not represented here, neither are curried skins, both being relatively dearer in the States.

[1] *Foreign Work and English Wages*, p. 84. This is attributed to the superior ingenuity of American manufacturers in producing light and well-shaped tools, at a cheap rate, by machinery. (Page 85.)

country at $4.25 a dozen, bring $4.48 in England. Enameled kettles, sold here at fifty cents, bring sixty cents there. Tools, like masons' trowels, sold in this country for $7.50 a dozen, cost $8.24 a dozen in England. These are illustrations of the broad statement of the London newspaper.

Tea and coffee are sold in this country more cheaply than in any part of Europe, and certainly at lower prices than under the heavy British duties. Sugar pays a very high duty in the United States, and yet, such are the facilities for refining here, that our people find the retail prices as low even as in Britain. Our land is especially rich in petroleum, and it is offered in our markets as cheaply as in any part of the world.

Official figures show that the value of coal at the mines in Britain was, in 1881, the latest year reported, $1.78 a ton. Sir Thomas Brassey places it, two years earlier, at $2.25.[1] This coal was in very large part bituminous. The average value of coal of this kind at the mines in Pennsylvania last year ranged from $1 to $1.75 a ton. The value of anthracite, which is in general use in this country, was not far from $2 to $2.25. At equal distances from the mines, coal was sold last year as cheaply in this country as in Britain. The price, for example, in Bradford, England, was $3.89 a ton, with twenty-five cents a ton extra for every mile of drawing. This price is higher than at a like distance from the mines

[1] *Foreign Work, and English Wages*, p. 30.

here. For example, at Scranton, anthracite coal is sold at retail at $2.50 a ton, the purchaser paying for hauling.

The most careful study will prove that all articles of prime necessity, including food in its essential varieties and the comforts of life, are cheaper here, not only in their relation to wages but in money, than in any other country. Any difference in the cost of living will proceed from the desire, and in an important sense the demand, that the person who depends upon his manual labor shall possess more and enjoy more of the comforts and even the luxuries which civilization has produced. By actual statistics it is demonstrated that, except silks, linens, and woolens, and novelties and commodities which derive their value in large part from fashion, prices rule here as low or lower than in Britain or in Europe.

COST OF LIVING.

The demonstration relative to prices and the cost of living can also be rendered absolute mathematically. Consul-General Merritt gives the following as a representative schedule of the expenditures of a carpenter in a colliery district, who has a wife and three children, four, five, and seven years of age. He earns five dollars a week, and he spends it all for these items: —

Rent	$0.72
Poor rate and school rate	.09
Club	.16

Coal	$0.48
Cheese, 16 cents a pound	.32
Butter	.32
Potatoes, one half peck	.16
Bacon, 16 cents a pound	.32
Butcher's meat, 15 cents a pound	.72
Clothes	.48
Tea, 48 cents a pound	.36
Sugar, 7 cents a pound	.28
Soap, 6 cents a pound	.12
Flour, 4 cents a pound	.12
Candles eight for 12 cents, sixteen to pound	.06
Milk, one quart	.07
Tobacco	.12
Beer	.12
Total	$5.02

These expenses may be classified, for convenience, into these items: —

For rent and rates	$0.81
For flour and butcher's meat	.84
Other provisions, with soap and candles	2.01
Coal	.48
Club, beer, and tobacco	.40
Clothes	.48
Total	$5.02

Observe that the rent and rates are less than one sixth, the flour, meat, and other provisions are much more than one half, the fuel is one tenth nearly, while, for the family of five, only two shillings a week, or less than thirteen dollars a year, is allowed for clothing. Let the expenditure for beer, tobacco, and club pass without comment. But you cannot resist the conclusion that for every item except that of clothing, the articles are such as can be bought in the United States more cheaply than in Britain. That item of clothing is just one tenth of the total outlay, and it must include shoes and cotton goods, which also are cheaper in the United States than in the United Kingdom.

These figures are confirmed by investigations made under the auspices of the Charity Organization Society in England. We do not go down to the slums of London, to the dens where families huddle in a single room.[1] We take the expenses of living of per-

[1] In a sermon in Bloomsbury Chapel, delivered on Sunday, December 9, 1883, Rev. Stopford Brooks compared London with the House of Pride, in Spenser's *Faëry Queen*, and said: "When the Red Cross Knight escapes by the Priory postern, and sees the outcast London of that place, —

> Scarce could he footing find in the foulle way,
> For many corses, like a great hay stall
> Of murdered men, which, therein strewed, lay
> Without remorse or decent funerall.

London is this palace of Lucifera. No words, as you have heard of late, can exaggerate that which lies behind the stately edifice of our wealth and pride. Here, close at hand to this chapel, there are dens where decent folk live, nine in a cellar scarcely larger than six of the pews in this church, for which they pay five shillings a week. It is the picture of thousands of rooms dwelt in all over this city, the filth and vermin and nameless horrors of which deepen, year after miserable year; and every improvement made in this town for the sake of the greater comfort and pleasure of the upper classes, without previous provision for housing those whose dens are pulled down, increases this overcrowding, and raises the rent on those whose life is already crushed out of them by overwork, and whose wages for this overwork are starvation wages; and work is almost as much overcrowded as the dwellings. There are thousands who cannot get any work at all, and whose lives are spent in daily despair, and while their souls are eaten

sons earning twenty shillings a week, or a trifle less than $5, with a wife and three children to support. Upon a very large group of facts, the summary is that the allowance for meat, "if any," ranges from three shillings, or seventy-five cents, to nine shillings or $2.25. The rent and bread each cost a little more than one fifth of the assumed wages, $1.04 for rent and $1.08 for bread. Only fifty cents a week is allowed for clothing the entire family. For school expenses eight cents a week is appropriated; and for club, that is for the privilege of sitting in a public

<blockquote>
away by this vulture their bodies are burnt up with famine. Famine is common in this town, and especially the famine of children, and the fact speaks well for the brutality of the first city in the world. Then those who do earn wages, say twenty shillings a week, with a wife and children, and a room costing them seven shillings, are eagerly supplied, by the theory that all trade is to be free from interference; a temptation to which they are peculiarly prone, which it is almost impossible for them to resist, so that a third of their wages never reaches their homes at all. We are preëminent in London in these matters. There is nothing so terrible in any other great civilized city, — no, not Paris or New York; there is nowhere else in the Christian world such a mass of wretchedness, squalor, and degradation as in England; in no other country is there such complete and satisfied belief that all that is necessary is done for the poor, or such quiet shoving aside in Parliament of measures necessary for their elevation; and except in countries under wholly irresponsible government, there is no place where for many, many years the law has so unmistakably taken the side of wealth and rank and power as against poverty and weakness and ignorance. The insolent wealth and flaunting folly of a London season, recorded day by day in the journals of what is called society, have as their background, before which they play their careless comedy, the fires and the woe, the blackness and the crimes of hell."
</blockquote>

house, and for drink and tobacco, a shilling. Other items exhaust the full wages, week by week.

Like comparisons, carefully extended as far as has been practicable, bring to me, from workingmen in the state of New York in many vocations, and earning wages from $8 to $25 a week, many instructive statements. The sum of many of them shows that they save more or less money, and of their expenses for living, the division ranges thus, for families of from four to ten persons: —

Rent	12.5 to 25 per cent.
Bread	6 to 10 per cent.
Meat	10 to 25 per cent.
Other provisions	18 to 40 per cent.
Shoes and cottons	7 to 12 per cent.
Fuel	7 to 15 per cent.
Church and charity	0 to 8 per cent.
Tobacco and miscellaneous	small percentage.
Silks and woolens	10 to 20 per cent.

Retail prices here and abroad will show the relation of the important articles in this list. The authority for the prices is the latest consular reports and the regular quotations in the daily papers. Comparison is made between rural towns in Britain and Utica: —

	Utica. Cents.	Rural Britain. Cents.
Bacon, a pound	14	16 †
Beef, fresh	12–20	14–31 †
Butter	30–38	37–42 *
Coffee	20	28 †

* *Aberdeen Journal*, January 5, 1884.

† Consul General Merritt's report, November 30, 1883.

Cheese	14	16 *
Eggs, a dozen	38–40	44–50 *
Flour, a pound	035	4 *
Lamb	16–18	20–26 *
Milk, quart	6	8 †
Mutton, pound	14–18	16–24 †
Pork	11	16–20 *
Potatoes, a peck	15	32 †
Sugar, a pound	5–8	5–8 *
Tea, a pound	40	48 †

Careful analysis proves that the average family among working people in Britain, when the ability to do so exists, expends for rent about one quarter of its total outlay. In this country this charge is from twelve and a half to twenty-five per cent. When the rate of expenditure rises, the share allotted for rent becomes larger, and upon a total of $1,500 a year may be here as much as one third. For bread and meat abroad rather more than one half goes, while in this country only from sixteen to thirty-five per cent. For groceries in England forty per cent.; in this country that share is seldom reached. For articles of cotton and for boots and shoes not much less than one eighth is spent here; and for silks, woolens, and other clothing, from ten to twenty per cent. These ratios vary, but the outlay for provisions tends to increase rather than diminish. In England the allowance for clothing must always be much less than it is in this country. Here the share for shoes and cottons will be about ten per cent. and for other clothing from ten to twenty per cent. of the total expenditures.

When, therefore, a family starts to set up its own home in this country, it will find that for furniture and cutlery, for the miscellaneous articles necessary, it will be charged for those essential to comfort as low rates as in any part of Britain or Europe. Plain pottery and glass ware are as cheap, and the latter is at least twenty per cent. cheaper here than in England. The coarser carpets, in which now some hair is introduced, and blankets of like quality, cost no more here than elsewhere. But when luxury is approached, when crockery is of a higher grade, and French and Asiatic carpets are demanded, our people must pay a little more for the commodity.

But reckoning the saving in furniture and in common articles the total outlay will not necessarily exceed the like preparations in Britain. Naturally the American wants more, and on that account he will expend more. But for the like comforts the outlay here will not exceed the outlay in Britain.

A careful calculation will prove that since food requires about half of the expenditure of the average working family, it will save on these items alone quite enough to make up for the added cost of woolens and silks; for the share of income apportioned to these latter is only a small percentage of the whole.

Under like conditions rent in this country is not more than in Britain or Europe. Our people demand better accommodations and are willing to pay for them. But if we place rent on the same footing of cost we concede all that is fair to the old countries.

Our studies show that for at least three fourths of the usual expenditures of a family, large or small, the prices of articles are in favor of the United States. Upon the same scale of comforts the money cost is less here than in the lands of lower wages. If we concede that in woolens and linens and silks the balance is against us, these articles never amount to one fourth, and as a rule only to from one tenth to one fifth, of the expenditures of a family to which economy is a necessity. The addition to the prices of these classes of commodities cannot counterbalance the savings on food and the other necessaries of life.

In no land do the prices of even these exceptional articles tend downwards as they do in the United States. The fall in woolens and in silk is the standard complaint on the one hand and boast on the other hand of the manufacturer and merchant. It is only in the novelties, in the fabrics sought for fashion and display, that prices are maintained at the standard of a quarter of a century ago.

These are the classes of facts which compelled the commissioners to our Centennial Exhibition to bear testimony such as is on record. The French commissioners declared after their elaborate investigations: "Under the shelter of a prohibitory system" the people of the United States "have organized a powerful industry which rivals England in cheapness." The president of the German commission testified that "the present condition of American manufactures shows the fallacy of the free trade doctrine, that the productions of a country are raised in price by protective duties."

By reason of this American equation of wages and prices, in no other country that the sun shines upon is there so steady a movement from the ranks of labor to the ranks of capital, from the shop to the college and the professional chair, from poverty to wealth and culture. With fair health there is no excuse in this land for any person to suffer from want.

Pauperism increases, but in a less ratio than the population. Not only are large fortunes multiplying, but the number of small fortunes is multiplying in far greater degree. In every manufacturing village you will find families who are laying up from their daily wages sums which become the beginnings of wealth, which insure education for their children and competence for themselves in old age.

Nor is that all. The tendency of wages in long periods is upwards, while the tendency of the cost of living on the same scale is falling.[1] The civil war carried wages to an abnormal standard, and a fall came soon after peace. But in every vocation wages are to-day higher than they were before the Rebellion; in some occupations they are fifty per cent.

[1] J. S. Mill, in an article published in the *Fortnightly Review*, says it is yet to be proved that there is any country in the civilized world where the ordinary wages of labor, estimated either in money or in articles of consumption, are declining; while in many they are, on the whole, on the increase.

higher; in many they are at least twenty per cent. higher.

With the spirit which now prevails, and with the development of production in this country, the process must go on. It is a great deal for a nation to absorb three fourths of a million people in a single year and not find its wages fall and its cost of living advance.

EQUILIBRIUM OF PURCHASING POWER OF MONEY.

Let us turn to another group of considerations. By the constant and close intercommunication between nations, the purchasing power of money approaches an equilibrium all over the world. The broad differences in the prices of commodities no longer exist. The makers of shawls in the provinces of India and Turkey feel at once the impulse of demand in Europe and America. Even in the heart of Africa the gewgaws which formerly could buy kingdoms are only rated as bits of glass or hollow shams. In all lands commerce has penetrated, and the cost of transportation and the hazards of trade serve largely to fix the price which can be secured anywhere among men. This tendency to equilibrium of prices affects directly the cost of living. Even in Asiatic countries, where people exist on the merest necessaries, the cost of those necessaries has advanced according to the rates existing elsewhere. In the rural districts of France and in Switzerland, where economy attains its maximum, the price of bread is as high as it can be in Russia or Australia, or in any part of Europe. The articles with reference to which the prices vary seriously in different countries are quite few. They are commonly luxuries, and are affected by fashion rather than by cost of production or actual substance of value. Thus it follows that the cost of living on anything like the same scale becomes a matter of close comparison rather than of contrast in different lands.

On the same plane with the same comforts and the same regard to style, the people of the United States live as cheaply as can the inhabitants of any country. The American wants more of what goes to make up the material attractions of life. He wants a neat house, with pretty decorations, and with bright fires and glowing lamps or gas. He wants schools and books for his children, and piano for his daughter, and perhaps painting and other artistic accomplishments. The children of the operatives and mechanics are the leaders of society, and of the movements which elevate mankind in this land. All the preparation which this career implies costs money. The homes which in every comfort would vie with the palaces of Queen Elizabeth or of the great Louis of France, involve expenditures such as the wages of Europe do not allow. But these comforts cost no more here than they cost in European markets. Only here money is better distributed, and reaches in larger measure the hands of the producing classes. Possibly extravagance has penetrated into the hamlets and even to the farms of our country, as well as into the villages and cities. Our people spend more money than their cousins in other lands. But they have more to spend, and they get quite as much for every dollar which they do lay out.

To some extent this tendency to equilibrium affects the wages of the world. It is beyond question that the pay of all classes, even in the remote districts of Asia, has been raised by the example of America and by the demand for Asiatic products. The standard of wages of European countries has been still more advanced by the emigration of skilled workmen, and by the intelligence received from America of the returns which labor receives here. Under Elizabeth, Hume says the wages of ordinary labor in England were eight pence a day. Not all of the advance is due to American influence. Human labor is less easily removed than is its product; commodities can be transferred as the demand varies. Prices are adjusted by the relation of the supply to the demand. Labor becomes more or less attached to the soil. It requires deliberation and effort to transfer families and every incumbrance which time gathers about them. Thus while the index points towards equality all over the world, the obstructions to advance are many and grave. In the United States wages have been long maintained at their maximum for the world. They have in some vocations fallen somewhat as those in European countries have advanced in some degree. But in every department, except those of art and pleasure, and possibly of high literature, the returns in the United States continue far above the standards which any other country has established.

EFFICIENCY OF LABOR.

Nor is it necessary, as some allege, to reduce wages in order to secure a share of foreign commerce. The other alternative is to increase the efficiency of labor. The advocates of free trade do not deny that the money rate of wages must be reduced if their policy is to prevail. It is confessed in every quarter that American labor is more intelligent and more efficient than that of any other land. It has been brought up to this point by reason of the great prizes offered here to production. The comparison of the cotton manufacture of Great Britain and the United States shows that in the former country the product secured from each spindle per year was $12.01; in this country it was, in 1880, $18.03, or fifty per cent. greater.[1] From 1865 to 1875 the improvement in England was twenty-three per cent., and in Massachusetts one hundred per cent.[2] In other departments this superiority of American labor is admitted, and it is proved by actual comparison of results. Upon this superior efficiency we must rely to win for the United States the supremacy in commerce which this republic has already won in manufactures as well

---

[1] United States Census, 1880, the Factory System, p. 9.
[2] Brassey, p. 54.

as in agriculture. The aim and purpose, as well as the direct consequence, of the protective policy is to maintain and develop this superior efficiency through education and adequate rewards.

GREAT BRITAIN AND THE CONTINENT.

Wages in Britain are beyond question higher than on the continent of Europe. Our comparisons have been adjusted to British standards. The plea is urged that in spite of free trade, Britain pays its working people better than the countries on the continent which maintain a protective policy. This is true. Britain continues to reap the harvests of the strong policy of promoting manufactures, which, from the time of Elizabeth into the reign of Victoria, was the distinction of its legislation and administration. The foundations which were laid in courage and maintained by persistence have served to keep the structure solid against the competition of the world. The colonial system, which has brought so much of the globe to the feet of the British throne, has not ceased to bear fruit. By arms and diplomacy, markets are yet held in India and Turkey and Egypt and the islands of the sea. Constitutional freedom crowns Britain with many of its enduring laurels, and the rewards of the British workingmen are among its prizes.

But the advance in wages on the continent during the past forty years has been far greater than in any part of the United Kingdom. The development of manufactures has shown a larger per cent. of progress in the continental countries than in the British islands. Relatively the producing interests of the continent gain more every decade than under all the strain of British energy can be won for the textile or metal or miscellaneous manufactures of Britain, with all the incitement of the control of the markets of the world. Time was when British statesmen could boast that their islands were the master workshop of the world. That era has passed away. Germany and Belgium lead in iron, France in silks, our own and other countries in leather, the United States in cotton and sugar-refining, and in many sorts of metal-working, and in no single industry does the United Kingdom keep up the rate of growth of half a century ago. Thirty years ago Britain had 850,000 flax spindles, and the continent 190,000, four and a half times more than the continent; now the United Kingdom has 1,292,000, and the continent 1,705,600, or thirty-two per cent. of excess for the latter. Yet "Britannia rules the waves." She holds the ocean carrying trade. In the streets of Liverpool you may hear the constant complaint that foreign sailors are hired to man her ships because they will serve for lower pay. Even in the land where three centuries of strong protection had fortified manufactures you may see the evils which have come from prostrating every interest to commerce as the engrossing and engulfing idol.

AMERICAN RESULTS.

Can foreign commerce offer any prize adequate to justify the check of the progress of this republic? High wages, tending to advance even with shorter hours, are one of the chief incitements to industrial achievements here, to the elevation of the working classes, to the continual merging of the hand-worker into the inventor, and the student into the teacher and the leader of men. Let me be far from claiming for my countrymen superiority over all mankind. But here we find to-day the conditions which, better than anywhere else on earth, may serve to lift up the whole body of citizens, to present the field for individual growth and training, to break down the barriers which shut the unfortunate into outer darkness, to incite to tasks which ally the brain with muscle, and set heart and soul to dominate over all.

A revenue policy which, by the confession of its advocates, will strike down the money wages of producers, must be the foe of the progress which has been the glory of our republic, and must tend to destroy the diversity and the efficiency of labor which have been the chief instruments of our development as a nation, and our improvement as a people.

CHAPTER X.

ALTERNATIVES OF PROTECTION.

Sciences of Administration. — Political Economy an Applied Science. — Cairnes' Classification. — A Professor before the Tariff Commission. — Senior. — The Teachings of Experience. — Political Economy Everybody's Business. — If not by Protective Duties, how shall Government be supported? — The British System and the American System. — Appeal for Fair Trade in England. — The Cobden Club. — Demand to abolish all Customs and Excise. — Financial Reform Association. — Direct Taxation asked for. — Opposition here to any Tariff at all. — British Taxes burden Labor. — American Imposts fall on Wealth and Waste. — Duties should be adjusted to protect American Industry at Fair Prices. — The Equation of Wages. — Cotton. — Iron. — Stability the First Need. — German Action. — Exaggeration. — The Chancellor and the Army. — Lasker. — Three Schools of Political Economy. — Incidental Protection: repudiated by John C. Calhoun. — Legislation must affect Production. — Should be Deliberate and Intelligent. — Duties should be Adequate. — Free Trade and Labor. — Free Trade compels Specializing. — We must provide for Growth of Population. — Free Production enlists Idle Capital and Labor. — Enlarges Competition. — Patents give Monopolies. — Complaints of British Workmen. — Complaint in London "Quarterly" on behalf of Property and Land. — London "Spectator" on Free Trade. — The Choice between the American and the British System.

THE Germans maintain in their higher institutions of learning chairs of what they call bureau sciences, or, as we should say, sciences of administration. In this department they class political economy, and under it would stand the principles of revenue systems. In it are illustrious such teachers and authors as Roscher and Wagner are, and as List, Rau, and Hoffmann and Hermann were in their day. The Germans rightly think that sensible men will seek to get direct benefit from their investigations and studies. Branches there are in which pure reason revels, and which are only remotely connected with the tasks and burdens of daily life. They have their sphere and purpose. But in all of the applied sciences the ultimate object is to discover and put to use the knowledge which can be acquired. That is especially true of the natural sciences of which our times have made so much, and which they have brought to such extent and grandeur. It is no less true of political economy, and of that branch with which we have been concerning ourselves.[1] The value of our studies may indeed be measured by the degree to which they can be applied to the solution of the problems which confront us as citizens, and which

---

[1] Now political economy seems in this respect plainly to belong to the same class of sciences with mechanics, astronomy, optics, chemistry, electricity, and, in general, all those physical sciences which have reached the deductive stage. Its premises are not arbitrary figments of the mind, formed without reference to concrete existences, like those of mathematics; nor are its conclusions mere generalized statements of observed facts, like those of the purely inductive natural sciences, but like mechanics or astronomy, its premises represent positive facts; while its conclusions, like the conclusions of these sciences, may or may not correspond to the realities of external nature, and therefore must be considered as representing only hypothetical truth. — Cairnes' *Political Economy*, p. 62.

can be rendered of use in legislation and administration.

In the prolonged hearings before the Tariff Commission in 1882, Professor Sumner, of Yale College, who is not the most reserved of the advocates of nominal free trade, presented an elaborate paper in which he demanded the repeal of all protective duties. One of the commissioners asked him the very natural question, "What system would you advise us to adopt" in their place? Mr. Sumner's answer was blunt and positive: "I am not a statesman at all; I cannot formulate a revenue system for the country. I have never taken such a matter upon me; it is quite out of my line." Senior had said long ago: "The economist is not to give a single syllable of advice. His business is neither to recommend nor dissuade, but to state general principles." Professor Sumner expanded the thought by declaring: "It is the business of congressmen and statesmen to provide a revenue, not the business of professors."

In this country congressmen and statesmen must come from the ranks of the people. It will be well if they can be selected in no small part from among those who have the advantage of instruction from professors, and who enjoy all the facilities of our great institutions. Instruction which fails to teach men how to meet the questions of citizenship is by that very fact insufficient and *prima facie* wrong and misleading. Education can have no better aim than to train men for the responsibilities of life; and in a republic no obligation is more important than to know how to frame statutes, and certainly to be able to judge them fairly, and to show how to correct any evils which may exist. Under any government inequalities will arise; under any system there will be friction; under any principle there will be difficulty of just application; under any legislation there will be complaint. Political science has for its mission to compare the methods which mankind has invented and tried, and to deduce from them the plans which will bring results at the least cost of money and annoyance. Critics of a revenue system, who can propose no remedy for ills, confess that these ills exist unavoidably. With all the experience of mankind it must be possible to point out methods which embody the greatest advantages with the minimum of discomforts and burdens; and professors who cannot tell investigators what is the lesson of experience, and what are the teachings of patient study of this experience, compel prudent citizens to seek enlightenment elsewhere.

TEACHINGS OF EXPERIENCE.

In no other matter concerning legislation and administration has there been such general agreement in all ages and in all lands among men, as with reference to the controlling methods of a revenue system. We have aimed, in the studies in which we have been engaged, to furnish the foundations upon which every student can examine statutes and methods, and apply for himself the hoarded wisdom of the world and the current criticism of experts. Our object has not been to demonstrate that by curious devices it is possible to come very near to perpetual motion. Our task has been to show how governments can secure the money necessary for their highest existence with the least grievance to their people, and with the broadest benefits to every interest. Our privilege has been to prove that industrial freedom demands the first consideration for production, and the second place, certainly in this country, for commerce. Our purpose has been to enable every citizen to answer to any commission of the government, that revenue should be raised on certain principles, and these principles should be applied according to certain rules. For beyond all question the subject is not confined to congressmen and statesmen, but it concerns very intimately every citizen of every land. It is, as Say declared long ago, *l'affaire de tout le monde*, — everybody's business.

We have found that the uniform experience of mankind has pursued well-defined paths, and that the wisest and most successful rulers in all times have aimed by their systems of revenue to develop their home resources, and to cast its share of burdens upon commerce. The founders of the American republic, with a fullness of scholarship, and an acquaintance with the practices of nations, never found elsewhere among an equal number of persons charged with vast national interests, deliberately adopted the same principles. They began by seeking to develop home industry, and by requiring foreign traffic to render its account, and make its contributions to the public funds. In the century in which our institutions have grown and our nation assumed its rank in the forefront of civilization, this policy has been maintained with a steadiness which rebukes the distrust which some feel of the stability of popular convictions. In all of the Old World, except Britain and Holland, not a single nation refuses to act upon the rule of protecting its own production and assessing commerce for its part of government charges, and in both of those countries agitation threatens the policy of free trade. On the contrary, Germany in its reconstruction, Austria, France, and Russia, have recently increased the rates of protective duties collected within their domain. Japan, in seeking to introduce the most recent achievements of science and state craft from all of the western nations, has established a protective system of breadth and consistence. While Britain pleads for free trade, its colonies, from the West Indies and Canada to the far Australasian islands, insist upon protective duties, and refuse to listen to appeals and arguments from Cobden Clubs and Chambers of Commerce in London and Liverpool. India, receiving all of its inspiration and direction from Downing Street, and governed in the interest of Britain, until 1882 adhered to protective duties even on such articles as cotton from

Lancashire. The colonies yet protect themselves against the home country. As Alexander Forbes, in the "Economist" for October, 1883, puts it pithily: "The Australian taxes alike imports from Britain and from Batavia." Professor Fawcett, in admitting the existence of protection in India against the home manufacturers, pleads, in "Protection and Free Trade,"[1] that "there is no article of general consumption except salt, which it is possible to tax, and the duty on salt in India has been strained to the utmost. The proposal to abolish the existing import duties on cotton goods cannot be dissociated from the question: What new taxation is to be imposed to fill the void in the revenue which the repeal of these import duties would create?"

This is the real problem of the revenue system: if not by protective duties, how shall government be supported? Britain has tried to answer the question in its statutes. For India Professor Fawcett quails before enforcing the British methods. The colonies generally refuse to accept them. But however the response is evaded, the comparison is direct between the British system and the American system. The radical difference between them is apparent, and cannot be explained away: the British system casts the whole burden upon home production, seeking to relieve foreign trade absolutely. The American system tries to levy upon commerce the imposts which, distributed in part upon the foreign producer and in

[1] Page 172.

part on luxuries brought in to our people, and in less measure on necessaries of life, render the charges upon production as light as possible. Now we allege that no system can be more unjust than the plan of our transatlantic cousins. Because they have just at present the ocean carrying trade, they are not yet crushed by the burdens. For any people which has not vast aggregated capital and this profit from service on the high seas, the British methods would be quickly destructive.

DEMAND FOR A CHANGE IN BRITAIN.

The appeal for fair trade, for the salvation of manufactures from the despotism of commerce, is growing louder and more vigorous before the people and in Parliament. The popular advocates speak in no doubtful tones. The Duke of Portland and the Earl of Salisbury represent their cause in the House of Lords. The clamor on the other side is still louder. At the last annual meeting of the Cobden Club the secession of several members was reported. The chairman declared, "It is useless to disguise the fact that protection is not dead in England." He predicted that "certain politicians may endeavor to restore protection under one guise or another." It was at this meeting that a formal motion was made to abolish all customs and excise.

This is the radical logic of the British system. There are thinkers and they have followers who accept the tendency and the conclusion. These are the advanced apostles of "financial reform," who in formidable publications demand the abandonment of the "wretched sham which now assumes the name of free trade," and, by the substitution of direct for all indirect taxation, seek to secure, instead of "partial freedom of trade," the blessed reality. The Financial Reform Association,[1] which formulates this programme, has among its officers not less than twenty-nine members of Parliament, and its denunciations of the present policy will bear comparison with any assaults on our tariff for virulence and sweeping generality. This association aims at raising all revenues from direct taxation on land and incomes. This is the fundamental distinction: Shall we collect revenue by indirect taxation or by direct levies? American practice and American doctrine favor indirect taxation, with its absence of friction and with its protection to home industry.

NO TARIFF AT ALL.

Some Americans do not hesitate to accept the alternative. The Brooklyn Revenue Reform Club recently held[2] an annual meeting and celebrated its position by a supper, at which frank speech was indulged in. Henry Ward Beecher presided, and he pronounced first, for the removal of all duties from raw materials, and concluded by declaring that he does not want any tariff at all. He asserted with force and positiveness that he does not want any in-

[1] See *Financial Reform Almanack* for 1883. [2] December 7, 1883.

direct taxation.[1] Another speaker, who has published a book on the tariff, insisted that there should be no tariff, and that it should be wiped out absolutely and immediately. These gentlemen carry their convictions to their logical conclusions. Free trade is a delusion and a snare while any duties are collected on importations. The controversy is well defined: it must come between free production on the one hand, casting duties on importations, and free trade on the other side, with the revenue collected from the homes and labor and food of the land.

BRITISH TAXES REDUCE LABOR.

Already the British taxes bear upon the laboring classes with undue severity. The stamps and the income taxes brought in, in 1882, £24,054,000, and this sum fell upon those able to pay it; but all of the customs, amounting to £19,275,668, came from tea, coffee, spirits, tobacco, which are consumed by all in nearly like ratios, and therefore are collected almost *per capita*. The same is true of the excise charges, amounting to £27,170,798. Hence, by the British practice, fully two thirds of the revenue is collected almost as a poll tax in its effect, for it falls not upon persons according to their wealth or general expenditures, but upon them according to their use of articles of prime necessity, like tea and coffee; and Laing[2] calls the duty on tea one of the worst

---

[1] See Brooklyn papers of December 8, 1883.
[2] *Fortnightly Review*, February, 1884.

taxes possible; or of such common use as beer and spirits, which unfortunately are consumed by the working people certainly in as large ratio as by their rich neighbors.

Richard Cobden declared, in 1865, after his policy of free trade had gone into full effect, that he believed " the income of the government is derived in Britain, in a greater proportion than in any other country, from the taxation of the humblest classes." [1]

John Bright testified that every workingman in Britain " gives at least two hours extra per day of toil and of sweat to support the government." [2]

This is the obvious injustice of the plan which is recommended to us as a substitute for our system. It imposes the charges upon industry and poverty, and checks production. It becomes almost a tax *per capita*. It favors property at the cost of labor. It sacrifices everything for the benefit of foreign trade. In spite of the prophecy of Cobden, that other nations would be compelled to follow the example which was set when the corn laws were repealed and the protective duties abolished, no other land has believed that the practice of Britain deserves adoption. Its own colonies and its Indian dependencies refuse to accept it.

[1] The statement occurs in Mr. Cobden's letter of February 12, 1865, to Mr. Gladstone, declining the office of chairman of the Board of Audit.

[2] Speech in Leeds, December 11, 1860.

AMERICAN IMPOSTS FALL ON WEALTH AND WASTE.

While the British system is thus very nearly a poll tax in effect, the American system operates to collect the revenue from those who consume most and the greatest variety of articles. By imposing a duty which in fact raises the price of any single commodity, gross inequality is inevitable. Either it will fall upon a single class, and therefore be unjust, as, for example, a duty raising the cost of a mason's tools would do, or, if it is upon tea, it will reach the poor even in larger ratio than the rich, and prove a grievous burden, as the British duty is in fact. But the standard of general expenditure may be taken as at once the measure of wealth and of that waste which is fair subject for imposts. By a broad schedule of duties, therefore, just in the degree that the incidence is upon the consumer will the revenue be collected from the wealth and the surplus of the community. Such schedules may be rendered so complex as to involve undue expense and friction in collection. Until that border is reached, a levy upon general commodities disperses the charges most equitably upon the rich and the wasteful.

This has been the experience derived from the American methods. By a tariff which has covered many commodities, the revenue has been collected without grievance in any quarter, and the distribution has been such as to reach those who have spent the most money. In the instances where the duties have been thrown back upon the foreign producer the relation has not been changed, for then the labor of this country has been benefited by development without incurring any impost at all.

The advantage of imposts upon finished commodities over a tax on land or on property is, that the opportunity for multiplication is brought down to the minimum. Especially if the commodities subjected to duties are not those of first necessity, the multiplication is prevented, if the collection falls upon the article after it has passed finally out of the area of production. Food and perhaps fuel are the only articles of first necessity, for clothing may be reduced to great scantiness and shabbiness without real suffering, such as hunger and intense cold will involve. Our tariffs impose duties only in very exceptional cases on any article of food, unless sugar may be so regarded, and always with a view to increase production.

In so far as duties are levied upon raw materials, or on commodities which serve for any additional processes of manufacture, there is opportunity for multiplication, unless the duties can be thrown back upon the foreign producer. Here the effect of the creation of home production must be rapid and marked to counteract the disadvantage of this multiplication. In this country we rely upon our vast resources and growing population to correct any evil which may ensue from duties on the materials used in manufactures. Our iron ore is lying in such quantities, our opportunity for raising wool is so abundant, our prospect for development in many phases is so unbounded, that our statesmen have not deemed it wise to sacrifice to the apparent gain of the moment the immense attainments of the future. In Germany and France the policy has been adopted of bringing in most raw materials free of duty. In such old countries where the natural resources have been fully tested, and the chance for vast increase of such materials cannot be rapid and assured, the argument for such free introduction stands apart from the general policy of protection. Their example, however, does not become wisdom for us. With our iron ore lying almost upon the surface, with our sheep-ranches needing only time and care for untold increase, where our metals of all sorts are unlimited, and where only patience and industry are needed to guarantee us all materials at the lowest rates, in very little time, it is far from clear that we should invite competition from abroad to delay the development which is the pressing requirement of our industrial condition.

ADJUSTMENT OF DUTIES.

Under any principle of legislation details will involve many considerations. When we have established the doctrine that protective duties are wise and the best attainable plan for raising revenue, we reach the questions of rates, both absolutely and in their relation with each other. In Britain, internal taxes are collected on spirits and certain chemicals. Customs duties are levied to countervail these taxes. The rule is the same here. To offset the taxes which we collect on spirits and tobacco, we levy duties on imports of the like articles. The adjustment is obviously just and right. When customs duties are levied on materials which enter into other commodities, it is only equally proper that additional duties should be collected upon the finished manufacture, in such cases as from the conditions it is probable that on the average the first duty must be paid even in part here. That is the ground of the adjustment which has prevailed upon woolens. Since a duty is levied upon raw wool, that rate is collected upon the finished fabric, with a separate rate deemed necessary for the fabric apart from the wool in its first cost.

Generally, customs duties under the protective system should be placed at the standard which, while guarding the treasury from unhealthy surplus, will prevent foreign commodities from destroying our industries in any branch, and yet will forbid American producers from charging excessive prices for their wares. This is generally the equation of difference between wages here and abroad, although, by reason of the greater facility and efficiency of American workmen, the real rate may be even less than this difference implies. Thus in cotton fabrics the duties are below any relation of the equation of wages. Capital has ceased to have an interest in duties on cotton; and as home competition would be reduced if the protection were removed, established factories would command the market. But labor employed in cotton is especially interested in maintaining and extending home competition. Therefore the duty remains to serve its protective purpose, but even in larger measure as a source of revenue, pure and simple. In cottons, however, the protective purpose cannot be wholly subserved until we manufacture the crops which the South produces, and send them abroad in the shape in which the world will use them. It is one of the shames of our industrial progress that the cotton which we produce is yet sent to Lancashire and to Normandy to be wrought into fabrics for sale. When we can spin and weave all of our own cotton, the duties on cotton goods can be dispensed with, but not until then. We ought not to complain of our growth, for we have increased our annual product from $115,681,774 in 1860 to $210,950,383 in 1880, nearly double.

In our iron industries the opportunities for extension impose grave obligations upon the American statesman and the American citizen. Our ore-beds cry aloud for the work and the enterprise which will transform them into looms and locomotives and steamships. Not one burden of tax should be imposed upon the ore until it has come forth to do battle for us in the markets of the world, and to carry our flag on the sea. Not one favor should be extended to commerce at the cost of our own production, until we have done very much more than has yet been accomplished to bring out the wealth which nature has put under our feet.

Every duty should be moderate in order that it may be permanent. Stability is the first need of our industries. Our labor has become organized, and it would be a vastly more difficult task to scatter the operatives of our factories and mills, than it was to disperse the vast armies which put down the Rebellion. For the latter passed at once into the grand array of production. The destruction of the iron industry in this country would turn loose on every other trade thousands of men competing for employment. Even the unsettling of industry shakes the whole structure of our society. Changes will be necessary in any series of schedules for revenue, but they should be made only in the calmest spirit, and only for the gravest public reasons.

Germany is dealing with the matter of revenue very radically. Prince Bismarck is laboring with vigor to relieve the states of the empire from the burden of collecting moneys for the maintenance of the imperial establishments. He finds that dependence upon the several states for revenue tends to disintegration. In this country the attempt to collect a direct tax through the state machinery for national purposes has been three times tried, and never with good results. Such a plan came to us from the old confederation, but it was abandoned in 1802 as soon as the system of Hamilton was perfected. For the

War of 1812 it was again resorted to as a temporary expedient, but its unpopularity led to its early repeal. During the Rebellion it was the only device for raising revenue which failed signally. Bismarck finds like difficulty, and he relies upon American methods in large degree for raising funds. He carries theories of governmental intervention to an extent which our people would regard as savoring of communism. But with reference to customs duties he adopts the American theory and practice as far as he can. In establishing a monopoly for tobacco he goes back to mediæval arts. But his anxiety is to separate the revenues of the central government from those of the states, or perhaps rather to render the empire superior to the states in all financial measures. For our purposes the lesson to be drawn is that United Germany, without the complications of old methods to hamper it, has deliberately chosen a strong protective policy as essential for its own profit and strength in Europe. In this course, it is not too much to say that the great chancellor is sustained by the leading scholars of his country, and by the ablest thinkers and writers who have rendered the German name illustrious during this century.

Exaggeration is possible under any system, and all extreme is bad. The course of the German as well as French authorities in excluding American pork, on the pretense that it is diseased, is such an exaggeration of a desire to protect the farmers of those countries. But the injury to our producers will be slight, if the incident shall teach us self-reliance and self-development. The German chancellor fears the drain upon the brain and sinew of Germany, as he beholds the young men whom he wants for his armies hastening to the farms and shops and general enterprise of America. His return of the resolution of our House of Representatives is based on his dread of the attractions of our institutions and of our industries, in quite as large degree as on his disapproval of the career and teachings of Lasker.

THE RIVAL SCHOOLS.

Three schools of political economy have claimed the attention of mankind at different intervals. They have been styled, according to their theories, the physiocratic or agricultural, the mercantile, and the industrial schools. They may be regarded as depending in large degree on the estimates which are made by their advocates, of land and its uses, of commerce and its scope, and of labor and its operations in the sphere of human effort and achievement. It is to be noted, however, that the title mercantile was accorded to the school which sought in zealous energy to lift production above commerce. In like manner Adam Smith, who is the chief apostle of the industrial school, has been cited as the scientific founder of the free trade theory. But Quesnay, in urging his physiocratic creed, grasped a half truth. The mercantile school claims Sully and Colbert as its masters, and its general doctrines have prevailed in all lands, with various expansions and illustrations, for it has maintained the harmony of agriculture with trade. It was left for Adam Smith to exalt labor, and to become the teacher of the great fact that labor underlies all human prosperity and creates all the wealth which the world can possess. When this labor is employed on the land, it develops agriculture, and deserves consideration in that sphere. When it is enlisted in manufactures, which is by far the chief field of modern industry, it attains to a magnitude which compels the notice of statesmen. In commerce no less it is an element of vast moment. But labor is the master consideration in all of these departments.

This is the point to which all schools of political economy lead the student of revenue. Agriculture, as the earliest and most vital of human interests, should never be burdened by a feather which can be kept from its shoulders. Next to the production of food, which must be preserved free, on any just theory of legislation, and yet is burdened in all lands, comes the general production which has created civilization. Commerce, the minister of exchange, is the natural collector of imposts, and its competition is the best distributor of the imposts. For this country, certainly, commerce is the agent of luxury, or at least of taste and convenience. We need hardly go abroad for one article essential to our necessities. We need not in our poverty pay one cent to the support of our government in its national character.

When we begin to enjoy comforts and luxuries, and to revel in superfluities, we can contribute in the same ratio to the charges of legislation and administration.

INCIDENTAL PROTECTION.

Certain statesmen in these days appear as the champions of what they call "incidental protection." Mr. Calhoun long ago showed very conclusively that this phrase is misleading and deceptive. The schedules of a tariff may include accidental protection, as he well said, but unless the aim is direct and intelligent this accident may fall like other accidents where the mischief may be great or even fatal. The vast concerns of our domestic industries are entitled to the most deliberate and careful attention. The very best and most skilled intelligence cannot serve them too well, cannot assist them in their contributions to the progress and prosperity of the country more than wisdom and patriotism require.

Every revenue system must bear upon production either with friendly or hostile hand. Can it be wise to leave the effects of the heavy charges which government must make to be the result of chance, to be either the incident or the accident of reckless legislation? The very least which can be demanded is that intelligence shall rule, and that whatever policy is adopted it shall be directed by the highest prudence and the most careful deliberation of its bearings on the interest of the greatest numbers of our people, on the concerns which are vital to every element of civilization and growth, on active production.

Our revenue legislation, then, should be intelligent, and its bearing upon production should be deliberate and carefully studied, directed by purpose and by reason. If we aim at protecting our industries, the methods employed should be adequate to that end; the tariff should be sufficient for the object; the duties should be enough to help American labor. Even if these duties first enhance prices, they will soon develop such home competition as will carry down the prices, and the danger of duties of too high a rate is, that they will advance competition to a point beyond the healthy standard. But this equation is soon determined by experience. Every new industry or extension of manufactures draws upon capital either idle or employed in less intimate relation to labor, and it enlists fresh hands either from other employments or from the ranks of idlers. It must add to the sum of production, and thus to the fund from which expenditure must come. It tends immediately to increase wages by augmenting the volume of work. It sets the currents of trade into greater activity, and contributes to the material amelioration of all classes.[1]

[1] It is an economic disadvantage that any commodity should be produced at a distance from the market in which it is nominally sold, and if in any case this disadvantage can be got rid of, without incurring any equally serious drawback through the production at home of some commodity hitherto exported from abroad, the resulting diminution of trade would be obviously a mark of industrial improvement and not of retrogression. — Sidgwick, p. 214.

ADMISSIONS ABOUT FREE TRADE.

Sidgwick admits that, "under a system of free trade, if any important class of producers in one of the trading countries is undersold by similar producers elsewhere, it may be impossible for some time to find employment for all of them at home nearly as remunerative as that in which they were previously engaged, — even leaving out of account the loss of acquired skill, which, in some cases, would constitute an important inducement to emigration."[1] The stability of employment is one of the advantages which domestic trade secures, and this affects directly the markets, and contributes to the welfare and to the profits of both the seller and the buyer.

In a very thoughtful work which comes from Cambridge University, on the "Growth of English Industry and Commerce," Professor Cunningham declares that "with a perfectly free trade, it would probably be impossible for any country to refrain from specializing.[2] . . . No nation would be likely to consist permanently of a mingled population, of whom a large part were engaged in tillage, and another large part were in manufacturing." He, however, explains that, by reason of government interference to protect laborers by reducing hours of labor, and to enforce education and apply moral restrictions, England does not fully exemplify free trade. But the principle remains that the British policy is to create special

---

[1] *Political Economy*, p. 495.   [2] Page 410.

industries. The result is, that while foreign commerce is the chief boast of the realm, every domestic industry has justified the declaration of this author that "the guiding power of private enterprise in seeking out and developing the most profitable industries is on the wane." At its best, this tendency to sink out of general and diversified production is not the aim of the American people. This republic is broad enough to maintain every sort of employment to which human ingenuity and skill can possibly be turned. We need to-day, not the exclusion of any branch by tendencies towards free trade, not a diminution of the mingling of vocations and occupations, but rather the multiplication of industries, so as to afford to every man employment in that field in which his tastes and talents and energies can earn the largest rewards.

But further: In this country population is constantly increasing. In the lifetime of many now adults the census will show not less than two hundred million persons seeking for occupation and food within the territory of the United States. They must consist of a mingled population; they must combine manufacturing with tillage and pasturage. They must, while they foster special industries, also diversify their productions. They must not simply buy, but they must raise and produce everything essential to the comfort and even the luxury of mankind. With such a future, it would be a crime for American legislation to contribute to the narrowing of our field of production, and to adopt a revenue policy which, by consent of its advocates, seeks to favor foreign commerce rather than diversified industry on our own soil.

FREE PRODUCTION. — CAPITAL AND LABOR.

The whole effect of a revenue system which protects home industry is to extend the employment of labor and capital here within our own borders. By drawing from agriculture some of the surplus workmen, it advances wages in that department. By increasing occupations, and thus the demand for labor, it carries up the standard of wages in every sphere. In the same way it affords returns to capital. It transforms the funds of speculation or of wastefulness or of idleness into productive capital, putting them into factories and furnaces and shops, and expending them for materials and for wages. The protective clauses of a tariff serve to recruit the armies of labor out of the ranks of the listless and careless, and to make the streams which have been lazily humming the melodies of drowsiness vocal with the glad choruses of iron and steel and woolen and cotton and silk. The idle naiads are changed into the ministers of progress and the creators of every blessing of civilization.

The allegation is urged that protection does not increase the volume of capital or of labor in any land. It possesses a shadow of truth, but the conclusion is far from just that capital and labor are not enlisted in new vocations and rendered manifold more fruitful. I know a brook which springs in the far-off hills, and comes leaping down their sides, beautifying its banks and enriching the meadows all along its course. Before any tariff, this brook sang its song and served its mission of beauty. Only a few farms ran down to its waters, and the cattle idly ruminated as they were reflected from its bright surface. The homesteads of thrifty families were decorated by its meanderings. But, long ago, prudent manufacturers saw that this beauty could be rendered helpful, and they built factories, and cotton and woolen are weaved by the force of the musical waters, and the smoke of furnaces rises above them, and millions of money are coined along the stream which nature gave and enterprise has made its handmaid. In just this way the protective policy has often lifted idle capital and unemployed labor into activity and fruitfulness.

The tendency of other methods is, as Cunningham illustrates, to narrow the basis of industry. It would be unjust to charge that this is in the direction of monopoly. The word is much abused. It is certain that a system of revenue which offers premiums for additions to production in every field cannot be justly put under the imputation of developing such influences. Complaint is frequent in Britain that the government is meddling more and more with the factories, with the hours of labor, with the regulations of mills and mines, with the homes and the conditions of the laboring people. The pressure of their necessities and sufferings may compel this course. But it is not freedom either of production or trade.

Freedom here has increased the industries included under the tariff schedules, so that the establishments which were 123,025 in 1850 were, in 1880, 253,840; and the persons employed have grown from 957,059 in 1850 to 2,738,950 in 1880. The annual wages which were $236,755,464 in 1850 were, in 1880, $947,919,674, and the total production has become greater than can be shown in any other land.

Such a development inevitably tends to broaden competition. Yet we hear critics complain of monopoly in our manufactures. The whole field is open for all. In no other land is there such complete liberty, and in no other sphere is there less of the evil of combination. Outcry is raised because copper, which is protected, is largely in the control of a few persons who manipulate prices. Something of this is true, but the remedy is in conceding for a while such inducements as will develop our copper mines in all parts of the Union, and thus break down combinations. It is not in manufactures or in mining products that "corners" are most frequent, and certainly it is not in such commodities that "corners" are most pernicious. Unless patents interfere, production will receive such an impetus by attempted combinations, that abundant remedy will soon be provided for the evil. The curse of "corners" falls on food and like articles of prime necessity, which are not included in the tariff schedules. It has been in wheat and corn and barley, in beef and pork and lard, that combinations have been formed, which have oppressed the community, and ruined many of the operators. Such markets have rivaled Wall Street in speculation. The tariff has rarely served as even a pretext for "corners."

Both in Britain and in the United States special privileges are conferred under the patent laws. These are not part of the revenue system, although that is often held responsible for the exactions which patents permit. The right of an inventor to reward for his ingenuity deserves to be recognized. Whether abuses are not consequent upon the unlimited control accorded to devices for applying the powers of nature is worth investigation. Often a simple mechanical invention affixes charges upon articles of common use which add in undue ratio to their price. The very cheapening of processes of manufacture is diverted to establish mastery over the making and the sale of the commodity. Thus it has been charged that certain patents relative to the making of screws have concentrated the manufacture and the trade into few hands, and have enabled the owners to maintain prices which are exorbitant. In the case of barbed wire the same charge is urged. Patents on making steel are held to keep the benefits in few hands. The country understands how, by reason of the patents upon the telephone and other electrical appliances, the charges which have to be endured have served to confer suddenly vast fortunes upon a few persons. In various processes of manufactures patents have operated in the same way. In several instances patents have affected commodities which have also been subject to protective duties. This double charge is not defensible. But it would be difficult often to exclude articles from the schedules of a tariff simply because some inventor had discovered methods for bringing down to a low figure the cost of production. The life of a patent is not over seventeen or twenty-one years. After the privilege expires the whole benefit accrues to the community. No revenue system is to be confounded with the rewards which legislation provides for inventors. In the latter class will be found every instance of monopoly which has ever been asserted against American manufactures. In not a single case can that term be applied to the effect of any tariff which our statute books have ever contained.

COMPLAINTS OF THE BRITISH PEOPLE.

British workmen feel their burdens, and their complaints are loud and threatening. A circular signed "Fair Trade and Justice," distributed in the manufacturing towns of Britain, is fraught with the whole argument against the policy of the empire. It exposes the hollowness of boastings over commerce while the mills and factories are idle, of the assertion that food is cheap while there is no employment to provide it. This circular denounces the " devilish system which goes under the name of free trade" as "unlicensed swindling." It speaks of dangers ahead, and declares that "the working classes are beginning to rally, and woe be to law and order if their rising is not prevented by a timely interference of the legislature to sweep away this curse of one-sided robbery." The whole policy, the circular asserts, is "a pernicious system which is fraught with danger to the empire." Surely this is not the inducement which can be held out to the American people to abandon the policy by which they have marched to the forefront of nations in manufactures as well as in general prosperity.

Another complaint arises in behalf of property and land. You will find it in the London "Quarterly" for January, 1884.[1] The writer, speaking as an Englishman, says: —

"While we have been enduring an added income tax of one or two pennies in the pound to reduce our national debt, our total indebtedness has increased in ten years from about 840 to above 900 millions; our total taxation has increased from about 83 to about 106 millions. This has occurred, moreover, in a period of depressed or slowly reviving trade; so that beyond question both our debt and taxation have risen much more rapidly than our wealth, and have become a heavier burden on the national income."

The entire article is a severe criticism on the falling off of the excise, and the tendency to cast additional imposts on income and land.

[1] Page 91.

Another significant utterance relative to the British revenue system comes from the London "Spectator." This language indicates that free trade is not fortified beyond assault, and that its wisdom is challenged in high quarters. The "Spectator" speaks as a partisan, opposing the return of the conservatives to power, and this is its argument: —

"The return of the conservatives to power would certainly mean a raising of various indefinite but passionate hopes that the policy of free trade was to be abandoned for a policy of retaliatory tariffs. We do not deny that Sir Stafford Northcote has carefully avoided committing himself to any policy so insane. But Lord Salisbury has declared again and again that inquiry into the operation of what is generally known as free trade is only reasonable; Mr. James Lowther has gone in boldly for protection; Lord Randolph Churchill has spoken of a system of free imports with the utmost contempt, and has declared his belief that the free trade policy is an utter failure; and such views as Mr. Ecroyd's are widely diffused through the conservative party. Every one knows how malleable Sir Stafford Northcote has often proved in the hands of his go-ahead followers. And no one with the smallest political sagacity can deny that a change of government now would lead to a very general hope of the partial restoration of a system of protection. It would be the first great blow at the policy of free trade to restore the conservatives to power at the present time."

THE CHOICE.

Practically, the contest is between the British system on the one hand, and the American system on the other. Yet in Britain the assault upon custom houses and the excise lacks no feature of the aggressiveness which inspires the advocates of free trade in the United States. There the contest is clear and bold over a plan for imposing all charges upon the land, upon homes and farms and plants of industry, and their earnings and savings. Commerce is not content with the favoritism which has enriched it. It is quite as zealous in trying to cast upon production every charge of the government. In all discussion, this advanced guard of the logic underlying legislation must be taken into account.

In this country, on the other hand, the policy has been from the beginning to favor industry here on our own soil. To that end duties have been levied upon commerce, deliberately, and with studious adherence to principle. The design has been to draw from commerce its due share of the revenue. Even if this share should come out of our own people, that would be quite as easy for them as imposts upon land or other property, or on consumption or vocations. But as a matter of experience, it has been demonstrated that always a very large part of customs duties is thrown upon the foreign producer or his agent. In every instance, after a period varying with the character of the commodity, for every industry established in this country lower prices have been established than prevailed before the duty was imposed. We look for foreign trade through the triumphs of our industry. Just as our grain and our meats and our cotton, and our tobacco, our leather, and our petroleum have entered the markets of the Old World, so our watches and our cutlery, our agricultural implements and machinery, our calicoes and our carriages, our musical instruments, our paper, our drugs and chemicals have won their foothold.

Foreign commerce must always be the concern of a few; production enlists the many. The British system claims a monopoly of favor for trade by sea; the American system places foreign trade on the same level with other occupations, but gives it a rank after domestic industry. It casts upon trade by sea a share of the burdens involved in maintaining the government. Seeking freedom for every interest, it begins by insisting upon freedom for the handiwork of the multitude, for the production which lies at the beginning of all wealth.

CHAPTER XI.

THE RIVALRIES OF COMMERCE.

The Protective System interferes with Commerce, but asserts Industrial Freedom. — The War of 1812 and the Rebellion hurt our Carrying Trade. — The Price of British Commerce. — John Bright on Wars waged by Britain. — Professor Seeley's Expansion of England. — The Spanish War and English Foreign Trade. — Three Centuries of Conflict. — Pitt. — Carlyle. — £100,000,000 spent in Thirty Years in Avoidable Wars. — Turkey and Egypt. — Greater Britain. — Trade of the Colonies. — Protection of Colonies against the Home Country. — The Home Country collects Duties on the Tea of India. — Imports and Exports of Britain, Germany, France, the United States. — Turkey and Egypt a Part of the British Possessions in Fact. — The Colonial Trade not Foreign Commerce. — Duration of Nations. — War and Commerce. — State Interference in Britain. — George J. Goschen. — Herbert Spencer. — Freedom at Home.

THE crucial point of criticism against the protective system is that it interferes with commerce. But it asserts industrial freedom in the whole range of production. The appeal is urged to abolish protective duties, especially in order that we may find a foreign market for our wares. In addition to this plea is a demand that we shall by removing duties restore our flag to the ocean. The assumption that we can secure the carrying trade by sacrificing our manufactures is not sustained by anything but phrases. We lost a share of the ocean carrying first by the War of 1812, which was waged directly to drive our vessels from the waters, and succeeded in checking our maritime progress. We had made vast gains, when again the War of the Rebellion enabled foreign powers, under the flag of the Confederacy, to strike a deadly blow at our merchant navy. The introduction of iron for ships contributed to supplant our wooden clippers by steam-vessels, and we have not yet recovered the lost ground. Nor is it the first or the most important task which devolves upon American enterprise. Until we have still further extended our home production, and carried still further the net-work of our railroads, we have labors quite as imperative as any foreign rivalry can prompt. Capital and industry are getting better returns in these home enterprises than ocean service can now promise. When these fields are fully tilled, American courage and foresight will tempt the seas once more. There are those who believe that we are wandering unprofitably in these home domains. It is a fact that we are devoting all our energies here. When shall the movement begin to the ocean traffic? We can wait. By and by the march will commence, and by and by our enterprise, after a delay and struggle as trying as those of Xenophon in his retreat, will shout: Thalassa, Thalassa; the sea, the sea. But for the present the ocean carrying trade is held by Britain. It is a source of wealth and power to that country; so is its commerce.

THE PRICE OF BRITISH COMMERCE.

How has Britain secured its position on the ocean? What has been the price which has been paid for preëminence in foreign trade? No nation has ever yet secured the control of commerce by a change in revenue systems, by any adjustment of its government charges. We want no commerce which we do not win on the fields of fair competition. We refuse to maintain a costly navy to force our commodities on unwilling peoples. We have always declined every suggestion to conduct our diplomacy in the interest of foreign trade, except as it is welcomed by the peoples whom we go to seek. The course which we are pursuing has never before been pursued by any great nation. The story of commerce has been a story of violence and grasping greed. The wars of the world have been in large part incited by the purpose to extort treasure and commodities, and to thrust the products of the aggressive power upon reluctant peoples.

John Bright has more than once presented the terrible summary of British wars. He has not indeed traced them to commerce, as Professor Seeley has so effectively done. But he has shown the exhaustive outlay of blood and treasure which Britain has so long suffered from, and which drains her resources at this hour. At Birmingham, in 1880, he said: "I believe if we could have an accurate account of all the governments of England have done

— the ministers, the cabinets — during the last hundred years or more, we should find that nine tenths of that time, thought, and labor had been devoted to matters abroad, connected with wars, conquests, annexation, gunpowder, and glory, and perhaps not more than one tenth had been expended upon the true interests of England." [1] In Glasgow, in the same year, in his address as Lord Rector of the University, he declared: "Since the beginning of the century less than one fifth of all our expenditure has been in civil government; more than four fifths have been expended in wars past or wars prepared for the future." [2] In London, in 1883, he summed up British history by saying: "We have had two centuries, — I will say nothing of the time beyond that, — we have had two centuries of almost incessant wars; and during these wars we have spent thousands of millions of treasure, produced by the toil and the sweat and often by the misery of millions of our countrymen, and sacrificed hundreds of thousands of lives, with an amount of agony which no imagination can picture, and with a sacrifice of blood which it would be impossible to gauge." [3] The great orator was impressing his hearers with the enormity of war. His eloquence is no less instructive as pointing out the cost to Britain of the commerce upon which the realm now depends for its prosperity.

For all the history of the world the example of

[1] Robertson's *Life and Times of John Bright*, p. 504.
[2] *Ib.* p. 533. [3] *Ib.* p. 540.

England is a summary and a condensation. Our cousins have been no worse than their rivals. They have sought their own interests regardless of the welfare of others or of the demands of humanity. They have followed in the footsteps of all commercial nations. Nor has commerce been worse than other causes which have tempted to aggression and expansion. But since trade has engrossed in such large degree the energies and ambitions of mankind, it has proved, in the later centuries especially, the occasion and incitement to the movements of governments and the determining influence in diplomacy and national policies.

Professor Seeley, of Cambridge, has condensed the spirit of English history for centuries in a short volume, recently from the press, entitled "The Expansion of England." He declares with Ranke that it was trade which brought on the War of the Spanish Succession, for France was trying, through Spain, to acquire power in the New World. It was for trade that Europe sought this New World, and for trade the nations struggled to possess and to hold colonies here. It has been for trade also that England and France have been putting forth their hands into Asia and Africa to open pathways for speculation and for enterprise. The imposing spectacle which Professor Seeley presents is the grouping of the wars, from the Commonwealth in the seventeenth century to the fall of Napoleon, as a century of conflict between France and England for America and India, — that is directly for foreign commerce.

But much farther back than the Commonwealth goes the struggle of England by arms to establish foreign trade. The Spanish Armada, which frightened Elizabeth, was a gigantic effort to hold the New World and its traffic for Spain. When the Armada went to pieces and to the bottom, British commerce received an impulse which has been enduring. Professor Seeley says, "that Spanish war was the infancy of English foreign trade." That was in 1588, — three centuries ago. Trade-rivalry prompted the war of the Commonwealth against Holland. English statesmen asked for the destruction of that Protestant power, in the age of strong religious feeling, to aggrandize commerce. The restored Stuarts followed the policy of Cromwell and the Commonwealth. The English navy was founded then. Cromwell took Jamaica from Spain; and Charles the Second acquired Bombay from Portugal and New York from the Dutch.

Thus in world-strife British commerce was cradled. In 1745 the French ambassador at St. Petersburg complained of the maritime despotism of England. Out of that alleged despotism have followed whatever wars England has been engaged in. During the Seven Years' War on the Continent, William Pitt declared: "If I send an army to Germany, it is because in Germany I conquer America." Carlyle, in his "History of Frederick," uttered the same refrain: "The soul of all these controversies and the one meaning they have," he found in the struggle for the New World. Napoleon sought to strike England in India, as Louis XIV had tried to check its progress in America. Over its trade policy ostensibly at least came the revolution which created the United States. The War of 1812 was directly a commercial strife. The advance of Russia towards India led the allied armies into the Crimea. Laing says that within the last thirty years Britain has spent £100,000,000 in avoidable wars.[1] For the sake of its commerce England has maintained its costly navy, as well as waged these continental and bloody struggles. What has it cost Britain to establish the commerce which it to-day possesses? In the aggregate of its monstrous debt, in the weight of its crushing taxes, in the records of battles won and lives lost, the lesson is written in plainer teachings than words or figures can convey.

It has been for trade also, in part for the defense of the path to India, that England has expended its means and exhausted its diplomacy upon Egypt and Turkey. The massacre of Sinkat and the surrender of Tokar are only a part of the price paid for the trade of Egypt and the path to India. For trade England has devoted so much attention to China, before and since the opium war. In a word, Professor Seeley's suggestive studies may be supplemented by the declaration that British arms are used and British diplomacy is maintained with all of its expenditures and complications, to sustain and ex-

[1] *Fortnightly Review*, January, 1884, p. 80.

tend British commerce. In its wars and its foreign offices of all kinds Britain has paid, and is paying, a high price for its commercial supremacy.

Just what is that supremacy to rival which we are asked to change our revenue system and our traditional policy? What is this structure of commerce, based on centuries of conflict, and sustained by diplomatic establishments in every nation? In the very suggestive work which has already furnished us with texts, Professor Seeley dwells upon Greater Britain, which has been created by the expansion of England. It includes the colonies in America and Australasia, and the possessions in India. These are the elements of Greater Britain,— these are the parts of the British empire. Is it a united nation,—is it to be treated in fairness as a single power? Germany is made up of separate states. It is considered as one nation. Austria-Hungary is divided in many interests; to the outer world it is an allied entity. Consider then that Great Britain, the British empire, is a nation with separate parts. Our republic has its thirty-eight states. It is for external purposes a single nation. In estimating our commerce we treat the trade between the states as internal traffic, and we never include in our foreign commerce anything but the traffic with other peoples.

This point is important because it is true, as the Earl of Dunraven asserts:[1] " Our [the British] only

---

[1] *MacMillan's Magazine*, January, 1884, p. 251.

chance of increasing or maintaining our trade lies in the development of our colonies." That conviction prompts the suggestion, that "the mother country and the colonies might be drawn closer together by the abandonment of free trade and the formation of an imperial zollverein, or Greater Britain customs-union." John Morley considers the project, and deems it impracticable. It is so, but without any such union we can see the relations of colonial trade to the home country.

No fairness exists in treating Britain for certain purposes as a congeries of colonies and possessions, and for other purposes as a united empire. When the separate German states collected customs duties from each other, complaint was loud and fierce of the restrictions upon commerce. If our states were to set up custom houses upon their boundaries, a radical limitation would be placed upon traffic. Yet by such a device we could multiply manifold the figures by which our commerce would be stated. For that domestic traffic is far larger in volume and in value than the entire commerce of Britain as it is displayed in official returns.

WHAT IS BRITISH COMMERCE?

Now Britain is held up before our eyes as the model to be followed, for free trade has no ground to stand upon except the example of that single power. Yet the colonies collect duties, and protective duties too, upon the commerce of each other and of the mother country. In spite of all the burdens which India has brought upon the empire, even India, until 1882, collected customs duties upon British cotton manufactures, and such free trade apostles as Professor Fawcett justified the practice by reason of the poverty of India and the pressure of its financial burdens. The home islands are glad to receive from the colonies everything which they can send free of duty, for they need food and raw materials. But upon tea England collects heavy duties, and tea is one of the products of British India. The imports from the British possessions in India were, in 1882, £39,921,127, nearly one tenth of the entire imports from all lands, foreign and British.

Consider this fact, then. Britain collects at home duties on such a product of its Indian possessions. The colonies protect themselves against each other and against the home islands in their various manufactures. Is this the feast of free trade to which this country has been so zealously invited?

Aside from the commerce of these parts of Greater Britain, of the united British empire, what is the commercial supremacy to which our envy is directed? You will find in the "Statistical Abstract of the United Kingdom" that the commerce of England is reported with the British possessions and with foreign countries. Very clearly in any comparison which we are to make between that country and our own, we must take simply its foreign trade to compare with our foreign trade. Nobody even claims that, measuring our domestic traffic as well as our foreign trade, Britain comes anywhere near us in volume or value. But in the endeavor to depreciate our commerce, the figures are always cited of British commerce, including exports to the outlying possessions and colonies of the empire, and imports from them.

Take, however, the commerce of Britain with foreign countries, and we shall see what it is that has been bought by centuries of war and by all the efforts of diplomacy. Now in 1882, the total imports of Britain from foreign countries were £313,588,711, or $1,567,943,555.[1] The exports to foreign countries of British and Irish products were £156,646,727, or $783,203,635.[2]

In 1880 the imports of Germany were $680,544,000, and the exports were $731,064,000. These figures are less than those of the United States on both sides of the column.[3]

In 1881, which is the latest year for which official figures are at hand, France imported for home consumption 4,946,448,000 francs, or $989,289,600, while in the preceding year the figures were just over $1,000,000,000. The exports of France were in the

---

[1] *Statistical Abstract for the United Kingdom.* Thirtieth Number, p. 37.

[2] *Ib.* p. 67.

[3] The *Almanach de Gotha* for 1883 gives the following returns of German commerce, in marks:—

	1879.	1880.
Imports	3,773,200,000	2,835,600,000
Exports	2,775,700,000	3,046,100,000

same year 3,612,442,000 francs, or $722,488,400. This commerce like that of Britain is based on centuries of war and ages of diplomacy.

Notice that the imports of Britain are almost one third greater than those of France, but its exports are less than ten per cent. in excess of those of its immediate neighbor.

Observe that the imports of the United States in 1883 were $723,180,914; in 1882, $733,239,732, and in 1881 they were $833,925,947. Our exports were in 1882, $724,639,574, and in 1883 they were $804,223,632.

Thus the imports of Britain are larger than ours as those of France are; the imports of Germany are less than ours. But our exports, which are the true measure of a country's wealth and growth, already exceed those of either France or Germany. The excess of Britain over us in exports, excluding the trade with its own possessions, was in 1882 less than £12,000,000 or $60,000,000, and in 1883 our exports were greater than the British exports by $21,000,000.

But the assertion of British power in Turkey and Egypt has been quite as expensive as any cost of administration could possibly prove. Both of these countries are dependent upon Britain in such a degree that their trade is under British control. It is practically a real part of British commerce, as completely as that between England and Ireland. For any just comparison Turkey and Egypt should be treated as British possessions in an estimate of foreign commerce. Upon this basis British imports from foreign lands were, in 1882, $1,504,804,580, and the exports thereto were $738,838,405. In other words the true foreign exports of actual Britain were, in 1882, something more than our own, and less by $65,385,227 than were our exports in 1883.

If we accept the entire volume of commerce of Britain, including all of its traffic with its colonies and possessions, we have no reason to change our revenue system to follow in its footsteps. For our increase in both exports and imports has been far more rapid. In the period since the close of the Rebellion, we have developed in our commerce with strides with which Britain has not kept pace. At the same rate of increase, before another decade has passed our exports will exceed those for which the old country has paid so high a price, and our imports will be quite as large as discretion will justify. For in this interval of eighteen years, we have gained in exports over twenty times as rapidly as our great rival.[1]

With foreign countries the exports of Britain since 1865 have increased by £47,038,275, and this is less than one fourth of the exports to the same countries in that year. To the British possessions the exports have in the same period grown by £40,790,863, which is an increase of four fifths. This trade is really domestic traffic, and is far less than the development of commerce, for example, between our East-

---

[1] See ante, p. 231.

ern and Western states. British example, like our own, demonstrates that it is the market which is bound to us by national ties, by ligaments of state, in which we trade most freely. The questions of revenue charges affect traffic in much less degree than other considerations which lie at the foundations of states and determine the relations of peoples. The share of British commerce which grows most rapidly, and that even advances much more slowly than our foreign trade, is that with the colonies and dependencies.

WAR AND COMMERCE.

British experience does not differ from that of other nations. It has been cited simply because it is most fresh, and bears most directly upon the comparisons which are invited by the attempt to transfer the British revenue system to this republic. Commerce is the modern expression for national power in the minds of many persons. It has always been so. Mastery on the sea, strength of ships, from the days of the triremes to those of the iron-clad steamships, have been only the counterpart to armies, and have been measured as instruments for conquest and for the maintenance of prizes won in war. The aggrandizement of nations has been the aim of those who sought trade in far distant lands, and force has been the dependence of most nations in their quest. War has served to extend commerce, and commerce has brought on war. Even into great religious conflicts the element of mercantile profit has entered. The crusaders saw the treasures of the East, and lusted after them only less than after the holy sepulchre. The shores of the Mediterranean are covered with the wreck of states which aimed to control the trade of the nations, and to use it as an instrument for extending their military power. Upon that historic sea Carthage and Venice rehearsed the tragedies which Spain and Holland and France and England afterwards performed on the broader stage of the great Atlantic for the control of the New World. Human greed has impelled to unceasing strife, and ambition has both used this gnawing hunger for treasure and been used by it.

Our studies do not permit the full elucidation of the impressive lesson that those nations have been enduring, and that foreign commerce has stood the changes of time for the longest period, just in the degree that home production has been most diversified and most extensive. The career of Venice was brilliant while its manufactures were most prosperous, and even Florence flourished in its grandeur of art in largest degree when its woolens were in most favor at home, and its mechanics contributed most to its wealth. It was the variety of the fabrics of Holland, the skill of its workmen, and the enterprise of its manufacturers, which, more than the ships of Van Tromp and De Ruyter, rendered its policy and ambitions dangerous to England. The brief supremacy of Spain is hardly an exception. Ferdinand and Isabella listened to the appeals of the representative of a commercial city, and started in a career which won glory, and opened an abyss into which the national prosperity was hurled.

In the ages of violence the countries of agriculture and of domestic production were the countries in which governments endured for long periods. The story of the shepherd kings is the story of comparative length of dynasties. The pyramids stand to proclaim how a nation may endure for centuries, relying upon its own industry and developing its own resources. The chronology of China puzzles antiquarians and historians, and serves to show how a nation may thrive and maintain millions of inhabitants and confront all the dangers of centuries. Not to Egypt and not to China do we look for the model to be adopted. But neither is it well for us to rush along the paths which have led so many nations through a brief career of show and greed to sudden ruin or early decay.

Without the century-battles for mastery, France and England would have divided the trade of the New World. France fought and lost. Was the contest, grand as it was, worth the pains of defeat and the burdens which it has entailed? England fought and won, only to lose the brightest jewel of its crown. Did its armed controversy for the New World bring to it rewards adequate for the hazards and the sacrifices?

Is the commerce of Asia worth what Britain has already paid for it, in its armies and navies and diplomatic expenditures, — for its strife with Bonaparte, for its armed attitude towards all of Europe as well as Asia, for its hostility towards Russia, for the Crimean War, for the Berlin Conference? Is India paying for its cost to-day? Is Turkey, which is simply a defense for India, not a burden which is growing almost too heavy to bear? Is Egypt, with its bloodshed and its dangers, just the field in which British Christianity bears its most perfect flower? The policy of centuries cannot be changed at will. Britain cannot give up India, cannot abandon Turkey, dares not withdraw from Egypt, cannot even cease its interference in China. France finds it necessary to keep up its aggressions in Tonquin.

Until now commerce has been carried to unwilling peoples at the point of the bayonet and the mouths of Paixhan and Armstrong guns. British commerce is the resultant of centuries of the maintenance of the policy copied from every preceding power which has held the mastery of the seas. Whatever else it is, it is not the consummation of free trade. It is simply the echo of the drum-beat which Webster represented as following the sun around the world. It is the crystallization of the smoke of cannon. It is the modern phase of conquest by arms.

If we were able, do we want foreign commerce at such a price? If we were able, do we wish to maintain armies strong enough to penetrate to the heart of Asia, to the valleys of Africa? If we were able, do we want to reach out for the Soudan, and send forces to fight the false prophet in his deserts? If we were able, do we care to build and support navies competent to cover all seas; to stand off the harbors of Peru to hasten its overthrow; to bombard Alexandria, to hold the Suez Canal; to look on while France compels China to yield up Anam and Tonquin; to watch and wait for every opportunity to thrust our wares wherever disaster creates want, and violence supplants industry?

This is really a question of revenue. You will find no trouble with any surplus if you adopt this policy. You can multiply the expenses of your government so that imposts will run up to the standard of the years of the Rebellion. Do not deceive yourselves. Foreign commerce presupposes a large navy, and will bring with it a costly army. If you seek to force your products on countries which do not seek for them, you must not only degrade the wages and the character of your workingmen, to reduce prices, but you must pursue the traditional policy by which alone in the past nations have held control of foreign markets. You must be strong enough to defend your competition in Asia and Africa. You must have ships to convoy your merchantmen when hostilities threaten. You must compete with Britain in its diplomatic force and display in Constantinople and Pekin, in Rio Janeiro, and at the mouth of the Congo and the Zambesi.

Unless the policy had been already adopted, unless the burdens had been already assumed, unless the practices of centuries had become inwrought into every fibre of national action, no people in the world would to-day pay such a price for foreign commerce. The foremost thinkers of England are asking whether India and its trade are worth the price which they cost. In spite of all the outlay, in spite of the strife and the stress, the trident of the ocean must pass with the power which production will bestow. We could not secure foreign commerce if we wanted to, by parodying the career of Britain. The centuries have advanced in their march. We are to win, if at all, in the future, and not in the past, and by the methods of the future, and not by those which are rusty and weak with age.

The world comes to us for food because we produce it abundantly. Our agricultural implements are sent to far-off lands because of their excellence. Our clocks and watches keep time on every degree of latitude, because they testify to the best skill of our artisans. Our cotton and our leather are bought because no one else can furnish equal quality so cheaply. Our sheetings and our calicoes crowd those of Lancashire in Manchester itself, and win superior favor in far Eastern markets, upon their own merits. Our cutlery challenges Sheffield at its best, because it proves the taste and ingenuity of our mechanics. To what McCulloch calls the cuckoo-cry of free trade, that we must leave commerce alone, the loud demand of American industry is that government must keep its hands off of production.

Make and you will sell. Multiply your productions and the world will come to you to buy. Spare the money which armies and navies cost, and leave it to fructify in the pockets of the people, and you will provide the conditions of the cheapest because the most efficient industry, the most varied because the best rewarded production, and you will also establish the most attractive markets in which to buy and to sell that civilization has ever offered. The search for the gold which lies at the foot of the rainbow of foreign commerce has ceased to be even amusing. The quest has been the ruin of nations enough.

STATE INTERFERENCE.

The demand that government shall keep its hands off the individual does not relate to commerce alone. British policy does not leave commerce to itself. It seeks by every effort to extend trade everywhere. The traditions which sustained wars of centuries, which reached out for the New World, which grasped India, which took hold of the islands of the Southern Seas, have driven Britain to bleed and suffer in Egypt and to enter the heart of Africa; still to make a pet of foreign trade, still to carry British fabrics with all the influence of navies and armies, and all the arts of diplomacy. Against them, it is the American policy to array only the powers of peace, only the genius of our inventors, only the skill of our artisans, only the enterprise of our traders, only the overflowing tides of our varied production.

The history of the world proves that there is no free trade, and no commerce ever received more of government favor and patronage than that of the country which misuses the title. Our own experience as a nation proves that the path in which our glory is to be won, our wealth assured, is that of free production.

Two voices reach us from Britain which command our attention, concerning the relations of government to the people. One voice rises out of the contests of practical politics, — it is that of George J. Goschen, a leader in Parliament, conspicuous in finance, and connected in many ways with the administration of local as well as national affairs. The other voice rises out of the retirement of one of the most studious and original of modern thinkers, Herbert Spencer. Both of these voices warn the United Kingdom of the advance of government into the intimacy of individual life, into the relations of men with each other. Mr. Goschen spoke at Edinburgh recently, and illustrated how the government is interfering in education, in trade and manufacture, in the hours of labor, the treatment of workmen, the building of ships, and notably in the new laws relating to land contracts. Mr. Goschen points out the tendency to hold government morally responsible for the existing evils in society, and to look to it for remedies. He sees in all this movement the danger of sapping the old English love of personal liberty, and he points out the inevitable increase of taxation and of the concentration of power. John Bright complained that such measures have the same effect as the increase of the tariffs of foreign countries.[1] The sum of Mr. Goschen's conclusions is that "the time has gone by when the cry of *laissez faire* (hands off, do not meddle) was respected," and that "liberty has been made to yield to the claims of morality." The whole theory upon which even the shadow of free trade has been based has broken down.

Herbert Spencer in his latest essay, entitled "The New Toryism,"[2] and continued in his startling description of "The Coming Slavery,"[3] exposes the whole drift of modern legislation in Britain, by the sweeping declaration: "Either directly or indirectly, and in most cases both at once, the citizen is at each stage of this compulsory legislation deprived in one or other way of some liberty which he previously had." Accordingly he finds that "most of those who now pass as Liberals are Tories of a new type." The efforts to use Parliament to remove grievances, to correct the evils of irresponsible authority, and in due course to check the abuses which flowed from parliamentary action, have trained the British people to seek through Parliament the cure of evils outside of the sphere of politics. The central fact again is

---

[1] Speech in Manchester, September 13, 1877.

[2] *Contemporary Review* and *Popular Science Monthly* for February, 1884.

[3] In the same magazines for April, 1884.

that the plea that British policy springs out of the principle of freedom for the individual, is contradicted by every page of the statute-books in recent years, and by the whole drift of popular thought.

These two notable voices serve to herald the entire movement of parties and leaders in Britain, perhaps also in Europe. For the plans devised for the relief of the London poor, in their terrible distresses, whether proposed by Tories or Liberals, appeal to the state for radical action. The entire factory code testifies to abuses which demand the full force of the government to correct. Mr. Gladstone's whole ground of argument and of legislation with reference to Irish affairs accepts the responsibility of the government for the poverty of the tenants and for the burdens under which they are staggering, and he bravely sets himself about relieving the accumulated evils of the island. If in Irish affairs the Tories indict the premier for socialistic tendencies, in the purification of the slums of the capital city they run before him in sacrifice of the traditional rights of property, and in schemes for using the state as the grand almoner of permanent charities.

The lesson for us is that the exclusively commercial policy of Britain has brought the realm face to face with the gravest problems which can confront a nation. Every one of them points to heavier expenditure, and to consequent increase of government charges. Suppose it were true that commerce is free, is not interference in all domestic affairs too high a price to pay for the nominal advantage? Can we not well afford to let our revenue system rest on the solid rock on which our practice has placed it, and devote our attention yet awhile to favoring production without meddling in any degree with personal liberty? Better freedom throughout the land for every occupation and every person, than the pretense of non-interference at a few sea-ports.

CHAPTER XII.

CONCLUSION.

Fallacy of Free Trade. — Fact of Freedom of Industry. — State Interference most Beneficent when exerted in Behalf of Industry. — Freedom most Fruitful in Production. — Free Will most Active in the United States. — Low Wages the Bequest of Ancient Serfdom. — They increase with Population. — They advance with Liberty. — Extent of Territory does not compel High Wages. — Destruction of Caste. — Soldiers. — Clergymen. — Lawyers. — Doctors. — Salaries and Earnings. — Science and Industry. — Pay of Skilled Mechanics. — Rewards of Production. — Advantages of such Rewards. — Professor Seeley's Declaration. — Our Continental Position. — Our Diversified Production will develop Commerce. — Our Flag will return to the Ocean to stay. — Mr. Gladstone's Prediction of our Commercial Supremacy the Echo of our Home Industries.

AGAINST the fallacy of free trade stands the fact of the freedom of industry. Here is the vital point of the discussion which we have been pursuing. This is the complete justification of the American system of revenue. In whichever way you turn you must accept the demonstrations of history.

If you tolerate state interference with industry at any point, it renders its best service in fostering production at home. If you magnify industrial freedom, that freedom is nowhere so important, nowhere bears such ripe and nutritious fruit as in removing every restraint, every burden from the production of a nation. Thus we have demonstrated the truth of Professor Seeley's declaration that this republic " is the state in which free will is most active and alive in every individual,"[1] in labor and trade as well as in society and politics.

WAGES AND FREEDOM.

Very radical is this other consideration. Low wages are not caused by density of population, by the strife for a livelihood to-day. They are the bequest of the ancient serfdom, they have grown out of the caste which has prevailed everywhere in the Old World. The pay for labor has been lowest where despotism has been most arrogant and caste most exclusive. Show me the standard of wages which have been paid on farm and in shop, and I can tell you the type of the government, by era and by country. You have been told of the grinding tyranny of Oriental countries. There wages have been infinitesimal, and, as in Egypt, the ruler enforced unlimited demands for personal service. In Europe in the Middle Ages the mechanic received the most nominal salary, — half a franc a day. In England in Elizabeth's time, Hume tells us, labor was well paid at eight pence a day. It is not the crush of numbers, not the present stress of necessity alone, which is responsible for the low wages in the Old World. On the contrary, with the growth of population labor receives

[1] *Expansion of England.*

better pay and higher consideration. With the advance of personal liberty the pay of the producers in every class has become higher.

The improvement of the material condition of peoples has kept even pace with their gain in political institutions. With the breaking down of the monarchy in France the people everywhere secured a larger share in the rewards of production. You can follow the march of wages in the progress of the British constitution. Through the continental nations constitutional liberty has either immediately preceded or at once followed considerable amelioration in the condition of the industrial population.

Wages have been high in America, in the British colonies only in less degree than in the United States; they have attained a similar standard in Australia, not simply because of the unbroken soil and broad expanse of territory, but because the spirit of independence inspired the early settlers, and has ruled with unchallenged sway. But the expanse of millions of square miles, untried by the plow, has not created an industrial class on the Congo or the Niger, or in Zululand, or at the foot of the Andes, or on the banks of the Amazon. For freedom has not set up its altars there. Even on the banks of the Nile, where power has ruled with as great grandeur as anywhere on earth, where population can go and trade, can reach quickly and cheaply, there is no industry, there is no civilization. Mere acres under whatever sun and sky will not create wealth. You must be free from caste; you must offer adequate rewards to manhood.

OCCUPATIONS.

Civilization, which has stricken down caste, has lifted up the laborer. Science has adopted him as its ally and heir. With his hand on the valve of the locomotive the engineer holds traffic subject to his will. At the telegraph instrument the operator takes part in the councils of capital and of statecraft. The master of the machinery, in factory or press-room, ceases to be a servant, and increases his personal value by every horse-power which he controls.

Thus it results that the tournament of the world has changed its fields and its weapons. Men no longer strive with lance for a lady's favors. They struggle with matter to change its forms and add to its value. He who can render industry more varied or more efficient, who can turn any element or gift of nature to novel use, is the winner of the prize.

The world has not outgrown its demand for soldiers, and perhaps it never may. But they are not now the only favorites of fortune and of mankind. Society will not dispense with professional men, although they do not stand so far above the level as in generations ago. We will call upon lawyers when we get into strife over property, and they are necessary to the social structure which protects the person. While sickness comes doctors will maintain their calling. So long as there is a soul which longs for immortality clergymen will be welcome in home and pulpit.

But with expanding industries, with developing science, new professions have gained favor. Commerce has its spheres in which high training and strong intellects are needed and are well rewarded. So has the varied mechanism of this age. In the professions, hundreds are starving in this country, in the foolish pride of a decayed caste. In the walks of production wealth invites every man who will bring brains and industry, which will win skill. The salaries which are, on the average, highest in this country to-day, are those of skilled mechanics, and especially those who are competent to administer large establishments. Add experience and judgment to science and trained skill, and furnace and factory, mine and mill, enterprise in varied forms, will proffer compensation dependent only upon ability and fidelity.

The demand for professional men, under the old classification, is limited; that for skilled labor in its manifold forms is widening far beyond the supply. Inquiry as broad as I have been able to conduct has forced upon me the conclusion that, of all who enter the three learned professions, including college graduates with all of their advantages, not one half, in this country, earn an average of one thousand dollars a year from their professions.

Figures more in detail can be obtained with reference to clergymen than to the other professions. A gentleman who is carefully studying the subject reports that only one hundred and eighty ministers in this country receive a salary as high as $5,000 a year; a very few are paid a larger sum. In the Episcopal Church, out of 3,559 ministers, 2,090 receive $1,000 or more. In the Presbyterian Church North, out of 5,218 ministers, 3,100 attain that standard. In every other denomination reported, the number receiving so high a salary is far less than one half. A table on the next page presents instructive details.

Among physicians, pretty diligent inquiry justifies the estimate that not one in a hundred receives from his profession as much as $8,000 a year; not four in a hundred can count upon $5,000 annually; not seven in a hundred will earn $4,000; perhaps one fifth will receive $2,500. If a total of one third be set down at $2,000 and upwards, the figures will be liberal. Then the earnings descend rapidly. One fifth will earn less than $1,500 a year. The next one fifth will strive for $1,000 a year. In every hundred this will leave over one fourth to keep body and soul together at $600, $500, or often less, as the full returns for education and service.

Among lawyers great prizes are nominally more numerous; but the number of those who starve, or eke out an existence by outside operations, is also greater. In a considerable number of estimates, only five in a hundred overrun $5,000 a year from legal

SALARIES OF MINISTERS IN THE UNITED STATES.

Denominations.	Ministers.	Churches.	Members.	Salaries of Ministers.					Average Salary.
				$5,000 +	$4,000 +	$3,000 +	$2,000 +	$1,000 +	
Baptists	17,827	27,913	2,474,771						$450
Congregationalists	3,795	4,016	385,113	26	80	100	430	1,200	600
Disciples of Christ	3,330	4,240	846,300						300
Episcopal	3,559	2,033	304,300	40	50	100	400	1,500	600
Lutheran	3,660	6,327	800,189						600
Methodist, North	13,116	18,741	1,691,072						550
Methodist, South	6,876	16,465	849,717						425
Presbyterian, Cumberland	1,439	2,591	113,760						400
Presbyterian, North	6,218	6,868	690,696	50	75	325	650	2,000	600
Presbyterian, South	1,070	2,040	120,028		10	15	60	160	430
Presbyterian, United	707	839	85,448						450
Presbyterian, Reformed	107	119	10,492						600
Reformed (Dutch)	560	616	80,166						600
Reformed (German)	707	1,432	160,678						550
United Brethren	2,220	4,463	160,517						430
Catholics	8,471	6,866	6,377,330[1]						425 Monsignor Capel says not $500.

[1] Entire Roman Catholic population.

business. Perhaps five more will receive $3,000 a year. Another five will earn $2,500 annually. If the annual earnings of one fourth are set at $2,000 and upwards the estimate will err on the side of liberality. One tenth, in addition, receive $1,500 a year. No calculation can bring the number getting $1,000 a year from their profession to one half of those on the rolls as in active practice. One fourth do not earn $500 annually from legal business.

The number of lawyers and doctors, as well as clergymen, who, after pursuing a college course, fail to earn more than from four to six hundred dollars a year, can hardly be less than one fourth of the entire enlistment. To not one third of the total number in these professions is a steady income assured equal to $2,000 a year. Outside of the largest cities, not one twentieth ever acquire a settled income of as much as $5,000 a year from their professions.

On the other hand, a good mechanic, who has health, cannot well fail to earn as much as $600 a year, — $750 is a common rate, — and special skill commands, in almost any vocation, from $800 to $1,250. It may safely be stated that by far more persons earn from $1,200 to $1,500 a year in mechanical occupations than in the professions. The parallel can be carried farther. As overseers and superintendents skilled men are in constant demand at salaries ranging from $2,000 to $3,000 a year, and the places are many which will return such salary steadily. In the grades of still greater compensation, manufactures in their various forms offer prizes more numerous and on a more liberal scale than can be obtained in the professions. The only exception, in these days, is not to be found in the pulpit or in medicine and not in regular law practice, but with the few persons who enlist in the service of the largest operators in stocks and railroads. This is not legal practice; it is service, almost menial, to speculators and jobbers, who seek, often, to set aside law and trample on justice.

ADVANTAGES OF SUCH REWARDS.

These liberal earnings in actual production afford opportunity for study and for all of the comforts which civilization provides. They permit the extension of every convenience and accomplishment to one's family; they tend to liberalize society and to adorn it. Wealth offers privileges, and it imposes obligations. The distinction of our country is that its prizes are offered not simply to the professions, but in larger and more general measure to the producers. Where education is allied with experience, it has many advantages in the competition. But many a man mistakes, and assumes that education, especially a college course, will prove a substitute for that training which only time and toil can bring.

The demand is for skilled labor, with brains and education behind it. Let it be far from me to warn out of the professions any who are called to them. Let the clergyman prove his devotion by unselfishly entering a vocation where he may, even in poverty, serve God and man. The doctors will care for our bodies on such pay as they can get. The lawyers we may be sure will secure their own fees whether they win our cases or lose them. In the mean time the production, which has become the most prolific in the annals of our race, summons recruits to its service.

This is my response to the complaint that our revenue system keeps labor high in this country, and thus interferes with commerce. Our markets are already, both for buyer and seller among our people, the most desirable that can be attained. Our foreign trade is growing in every healthy direction, more rapidly than that of any rival. Above all, our production exceeds that of any equal number of persons known to history. The consequence is that the rewards of industry are steadily greater here than anywhere else. You know that the Greek word poet signifies a maker, not simply the framer of verses, but one who makes in any sphere. In a sense which Athens never reached, the American people are poets, for they make things rare and marvelous as well as useful. This is the triumph which has been won by the maintenance of the highest rates of wages ever paid for labor in any land at any time.

These high rewards for labor must draw increasing numbers into the ranks of production, into factory and mill, to forge and engine. Natural ability and energy will win prizes for those who with every disadvantage strive without ceasing. Our education is not responsible for the failure of graduates to enter the spheres where fortune and social power invite them. The personal mistake of individuals crowds the professions, and leaves the first places in manufactures to aliens, or to those who have not received the lessons of science and of history. Remember that out of the ranks of the Union army came generals who rendered valuable service and attained to deathless honor. But after all, the chiefs who were the foremost in battle, and to the end carried the nation to victory, were educated soldiers. Labor has no Annapolis or West Point. The field of fortune in production stands wide open for whoever will ally brain and education with manual labor and persistent industry.

This is the full flower of the American system of revenue. It offers the highest prizes of life to the American mechanic and producer, — the prizes of wealth, and everything which wealth can secure. It has already broadened the arena of honorable occupation far beyond the professions, and has broken down even the semblance of caste which attached to them. Professor Seeley's declaration crystallizes the sum: " There is more happiness in the United States, and of a less demoralizing kind, than in any other country." Better that happiness than foreign commerce, purchased by sacrificing it. Foreign trade will come when we get a good ready. We are preparing for it by every addition to our industry, by every invention, by every improvement in production, by every achievement of science. In the mean time, if the choice is forced to that, better, far better American homes, with schools and churches and freedom, than foreign markets bought by degrading our labor and playing the parrot to any rival, by war and costly diplomacy.

Professor Seeley declares of Britain that "a maritime vocation was that to which she was called by nature herself."[1] She is insular; we are continental. Nature has called this republic to a task distinctively its own. It is that of extending and diversifying human production, of training men, of elevating all the homes of our producers.

Upon this diversified production foreign commerce must be developed. With agriculture so productive, with manufactures so masterful, with mining industries outstripping the world, we must be able to win a share of the carrying trade. We will on the sea, as on land, conquer the balance caused by high wages.

I remember well sitting on the slope of Vesuvius, and beholding on the blue waters far below an American ship-of-war, from which the Stars and Stripes were floating under the blue Italian skies. The hope came to me that again our flag shall return to the seas, for trade and for all the missions of peace. Nor do I doubt that it will return. It will be impelled upon the broad currents of our industrial pros-

[1] Page 126.

perity. Perhaps the improvements in the making of steel will afford the form of vessel which, like our wooden clippers of the days before the war, will rival in cheapness and speed all competitors. Perhaps capitalists will be willing to accept lower dividends than they are earning now in railroads and telegraphs. Perhaps Britain will drift into a great naval war, and will lose her commercial power as she gained it. In some way, and in due time, I know our flag will return to the ocean, and will win for us our full share of all the prizes of foreign trade. With unparalleled production to sustain and defend it, with a continent facing two oceans for ports, and for every resource, when the American flag shall recover its place on the great deep, it will go there to stay. Mr. Gladstone's prediction of our coming commercial supremacy is the echo of all our home industries.

INDEX.

ABOLITION of all customs, 315.
Accumulation of wealth, 210.
Acharnians of Aristophanes, 76.
Acland, Sir Thomas, on failure of food supply in England, 252.
Adams, John Quincy, report, 103.
Adjustment of duties, 321.
Admissions about free trade, 330; concerning immigration, 225; of Professor Cunningham, 330; admission of Sir Thomas Brassey, 232.
Advance in wages in Britain and on the continent, 305.
Advantages of high wages, 265, 307, 373.
Adverse balance of trade dangerous, 218.
Aggrandisement of nations, 354.
Aggregate of imposts, 248.
Agricultural theory of economy, 326.
Agriculture, 33, 90, 97, 98, 167, 181, 190; and imposts, 130, 139, 157, 166; and manufactures, 168, 183, 186, 192; and national life 355; increase of, since 1850, 191; persons engaged in, 174; product of, in 1880, 187; Say on, 186.
Alleged over-production, 180.
Alternatives of protection, 308.
American colonies and England, 58.
American colonists against any taxes, 83.
   confederation, 84.
   development, allies in, 264.
   flag on the ocean, 341, 376, 377.
   imposts, incidence of, 101, 150, 319.
   labor, efficiency of, 304.
   manufactures, Brougham's proposal to stifle, 59, 98; French commissioners on, 299; growth of, 194, 263; superiority of certain, 290.
   methods and results, 82.
   people, condition of, 264, 266, 302, 307.
   policy of peace, 360.
   production, German commissioners on, 299.
   results, 82, 307, 374.
   revenue legislation favors production, 313; not complex, 86; the earliest, 86.
   shipping, 341, 377.
   statesmen and the tariff, 85.
   system, flower of, 375; justification of, 365; taxes, wealth, and waste, 319.

American tariff experience, 313.
   tariff of 1789, 83; of 1790, 89; of 1791, 89; of 1812, 94; of 1816, 96, 97; of 1818, 99; of 1819, 99; of 1824, 99; of 1828, 101; of 1836, 107; of 1841, 107; of 1842, 108, 124, 125; of 1846, 111, 124, 126; of 1857, 112, 124, 126; of 1860, 115; of 1861, 117; of 1862, 117; of 1864, 117; of 1865, 117; of 1867, 117; of 1870, 117; of 1872, 118; of 1878, 118; of 1883, 118, 120.
   war loans, 214.
Argentine Confederation, 70.
Aristophanes and Athenian revenue, 34; and protection, 76.
Aristotle favors protection, 36.
Armies necessary to commerce, 353.
Asia, cost of its commerce, 356.
Assyrian revenues, 31.
Athena and Poseidon, 77.
Athens and its methods, 34, 35, 76; chooses industry before commerce, 77.
Attica and its revenues, 34.
Attitude of the nations on trade, 219.
Auctions and imposts, 145, 151, 184.
Augustus Cæsar, 37, 38.
Australia and protection, 73, 313; taxes imports from Batavia and from Britain, 314.
Austria, 43, 49, 75, 313.
Austria-Hungary, 67, 70, 71.
Authority, argument from, 80.

Bacon, Lord, views of, on government, 21.
Balance of trade, adverse, dangerous, 218; against Britain, 223; against France, 227; and the United States, 227; Blanqui on, 219; no mystery, 208.
Banker of the world, 225.
Bankruptcy of an individual, 211.
Barter the beginning of commerce, 205; commerce broader than, 203.
Batavia, products taxed in Australia, 314.
Bavaria, 70, 71.
Beecher, Henry Ward, against all indirect taxation, 316.
Belgium, 64, 68, 70.
Benevolences of Henry the Eighth, 57.
Bessemer rails, 152.

Bismarck and his policy, 49, 324; on the development of the United States, 197.
Blanqui and Charles the Fifth, 47; complains of the spread of protection, 79; on balance of trade, 219; on gold and silver, 217; on the effect of protective duties, 192.
Books and merchandise, 150.
Boots and shoes, 262.
Bounty to foreign competitors, 247.
Brassey, admission of Sir Thomas, 232.
Brazil, 70, trade with, 239; trade with Great Britain, 240.
Bright, John, on burdens on British workingmen, 318; on state interference, 362; on wages, 271; on wars of Britain, 343.
Britain. See GREAT BRITAIN.
British budget for 1882, 61.
    capital in the United States, 224.
    carrying trade, 224, 331, 376.
    colonies, 58, 66, 73, 313, 314, 348, 350.
    commerce, conquest by arms, 357; not free trade, 357, 360; price of, 343, 354.
    conservatives against free trade, 333.
    free trade, cuckoo cry of, 359.
    markets passing out of British control, 253.
    policy protective until 1846, 60
    possessions, 58, 73, 350.
    production, 304.
    products taxed in Australia, 314.
    property owners, complaints of, 337.
    revenue, 60, 61.
    revenue system, 251; assailed at home, 61; burdens home production, 317; does not even promote commerce, 229; favors commerce, 58; injustice of, 315.
    tariff, 61.
    taxation, "Quarterly Review" on, 337.
    trade with the United States, 238, 241.
    wars, John Bright on, 343.
    workmen, complaints of, 336.
Brooklyn Revenue Reform Club, 316.
Brooks, Rev. Stopford, on the degradation of London, 294.
Brougham's proposal to stifle American manufactures, 59, 98.
Buchanan, James, 99.
Buckle on foreign trade, 220
Building a state, 168.
Bureau sciences, 308.
Burke on revenue, 173.
Business risk, imports a, 142, 153, 157.
Business of statesmen, 310; of everybody, 312.
Business plants, taxes on, 139.
Buy where you can, 236.

Cæsar, Augustus, 37, 88.

Cairnes, Professor, declares political economy an applied science, 309.
Calhoun, John C., for nullification, 104; for protection, 97; influence on the tariff, 124, influence on Clay's compromise, 105; on incidental protection, 108, 328.
Canada, 70, 73, 313.
Capital and imposts, 142, 151, 157, 332.
    in trade, 211.
    to labor, ratio of, 275.
Capitation tax, 31, 37, 51, 133.
Carey, Henry C., on diversity of industry, 178.
Carlyle, Thomas, 198, 346.
Carrying trade, 176, 208, 210, 341; of Britain, 224, 341, 376.
Carthage and commerce, 355; and its revenue, 32.
Caste made wages low, 366.
Causes of the development of the United States, 204.
Change in British sentiment, 336.
Charges by our coastwise fleet, 286; paid by merchants, 28, 30, 49.
Charity Organization Society in England on cost of living, 294.
Charity begins at home, 221.
Charles the Fifth, 47.
Checks to free trade, 165, 203.
Children of operatives, 302.
China, cost of trade of, 347, 357; duration of, 356; trade with Britain, 240; trade with the United States, 239.
Chinese revenue, 39, 66.
City douanes, 51, 53.
Civilization and labor, 368.
Civitate Dei, 21.
Classes and imposts, 158; spring from force, 20.
Class taxes, 35, 36, 48.
Clay, Henry, 97, 99, 102, 104, 105, 124.
Clay's compromise, 104, 105, 107, 110, 112, 125.
Clergymen and their salaries, 370.
Clothing in the United States and abroad, 295, 297.
Cobden Club favors abolishing all customs and excise, 315; reports protection not dead, 315.
Cobden, Richard, admits British revenue is derived unduly from the poor, 318; his prediction not fulfilled, 80, 318; his treaty with France, 54.
Coffee, 68, 102, 118-120, 148, 157.
Colbert, raises French customs, 52, 326.
Collecting revenue, cost of, 64, 93.
Colonial trade, not foreign commerce, 349; growth of, 353.
Colonies, American, 83.
    British, 58, 348; protective duties collected in, 314, 350.
    Dutch, 63; Phœnician, 33.
Commerce and diplomacy, 356.
    and industry, contests between, 339.
    and peace, 255.
    and production, 165, 168, 377.

INDEX. 381

Commerce and revenue, 246.
    and the national government, 84.
    and wages, 358, 374.
    and war, 94, 176, 255, 343, 346, 354, 357, 358.
    Asiatic, 356.
    barter, the beginning of, 205.
    British, 357, 360; the price of, 343, 354.
    broader than barter, 203; complex and continuous, 235; confers value, 208; conflict for, 343; development by diversified production, 376.
    English, how gained, 343.
    importance of, 163.
    national, the sum of individual trade, 204.
    natural collector of imposts, 327; navies necessary to, 358; not production, 166; not secured by change of revenue, 341; obstructed by imposts, 165.
    of the United States, 227.
    persons engaged in, 174; profits of, 221, 245; quest of, ruinous rivalries of, 36, 165; should pay its share of the revenue, 131; treaties of, 34, 54; two profits in, 245; Tyrian, 33; Venetian, 42, 355.
    rivalries, 36, 341.
Commercial school, 157.
    rivalries, 36, 341.
    supremacy of the United States, 233, 377.
    treaties, 34, 54.
Commissioners for customs in the colonies, 83.
Commodities, equation of, 151; prices of, 287, 292, 296.
Comparisons with Britain, 231, 351; why made, 230.
Competition and customs duties, 149, 156, 160, 322, 329.
Complaints of British workmen, 336; of British property owners, 337; of the tax-gatherer, 199.
Concentration of power, 362.
Conclusion, 365.
Confederacy, Southern, forbids encouragement to industry, 125.
Confederation, the American, 84.
Conflict for commerce, 343.
Conservatives in Britain against free trade, 338.
Constitution, Madison on the, 86.
Constitutions, 19.
Consular reports on wages. 272, 274.
Consumer and imposts, 146, 166.
Consumption, effects of imposts on, 146; of coffee, 148; of salt, 148; of sugar, 147; of tea. 147; relation of, 146, 170, 172.
Contents. table of, 5.
Contest between commerce and industry, 339.
Continental Congress and duties, 86.

Contrast between the United States and Britain, 229.
Convention at Harrisburg, 1827, 100.
Corporations taxed, 68, 71, 123, 130.
Cost of collecting revenue, 64, 93, 162; of living, 274, 292, 294, 296, 297; of maintaining markets, 250.
Cotton manufactures, 269, 322; increase of, 323.
    mills, efficiency in, 304; wages in Cheshire and in New York, 272.
Cottons, duties on, 92, 97, 100, 103, 104, 111, 112, 116.
Crises, industrial, 182.
Cromwell and protection, 75, 78.
Crusades and oriental treasures, 355.
Cunningham's, Professor, growth of industry and commerce of England, 330.
Custom Houses, Ruskin on, 79.
Customs duties, 26, 37, 40, 51, 57, 60, 61, 66, 71, 86, 90; abolition of all, 315; cheapness of collection of, 163; and competition, 149, 156, 160, 322, 329; distributed, 153; fall in part on foreign producer, 155; incidence of, 149, 153; limited to the frontier, 200; might have been collected in America, 83; not inquisitorial, 301; once for all, 200; proceeds of American, 89, 110, 118, 121, 122; voluntary payments of, 210.
Customs Union of Great Britain, 349.

Dallas, Alexander J., report as Secretary of Treasury, 96.
Dallas, George M., vice-president, carries tariff of 1846, 111.
Dawes, Henry L., 118.
Debates on the tariff, 97, 99, 101, 103, 105, 109, 110, 113, 115, 117.
Debts in trade, 211.
Demand for skilled men, 369.
Demands for change in Britain, 336.
Denmark, 70, 71.
Diplomacy and commerce, 356.
    of Britain, 347.
Direct tax at Athens, 35; of 1791, 93; of 1813, 108; of 1862, 121.
    imposts on London and the Jews, 66.
    taxation advocated by Secretary Oliver Wolcott, 93.
    taxes, 137, 142, 144, 316.
Disasters resulting from exclusive industries, 181.
Discriminating duties, 86, 95.
Distress relieved by the tariff, 112.
Distribution, 170; of imports, 221.
Diversified production will develop commerce, 376.
Diversity of industry, 178, 331, 376.
Divine right, 18.
Divisions of time in our revenue, 123.
Dodge, Professor J. R., Letter from, on products of agriculture, 187; statistics of, 189.

Domestic imposts and foreign commodities, 250.
    trade and shipping, 341.
    trade gives two profits here, 245.
Douanes, city, 51, 53.
Droits, 132.
Duration of nations, 355.
Duties, 71, 132; adjustment of, 321; *ad valorem*, 88, 110; discriminatiug, 88, 95; export, 29, 34, 40, 66; on leather, 92, 112; on sugar, 68, 91-93, 112, 119; solely for income, 103, 109; specific, 87, 99, 109, 110, 116; wages and prices, 264. See also CUSTOMS DUTIES; RATES OF DUTIES.

Earliest American revenue legislation, 85.
    commercial treaties, 34.
Earnings aud imposts, 158, 161; earnings in trade, 212; of professional men, 369, 370.
Economist, Senior on sphere of the, 310.
Economists, genuine, 310, 327.
Economy, agricultural theory of, 326.
Education and industry, 373.
Efficiency of labor, effect of, on exports, 232; greater in the United States, 304; the impetus to commerce, 304.
Egypt, cost of trade of, 347, 352; revenues of, 28, 39, 70, 71, 75; part of British possessions, 352.
Election of 1840, 107.
Elizabeth, Queen, and commerce, and wars for trade, 346.
Emigration, Professor Fawcett on, 280.
Employment aud population, 174; stability of employment, 330.
Employments in the United States, 174.
England and American colonies, 58.
    and France, wars of, 345, 356.
    and industrial crises, 182.
    expansion of, 345; failure of food supply in, 252; fair trade in, 61, 315, 336; growth of tobacco prohibited in, 60; how her commerce has been gained, 343; protection in, 59, 79, 315, 338; revenue of, 55; war with Holland, 346, 355.
English navy founded, 346.
English restrictions on American colonies, 58.
Equality in condition, 300.
Equation of commodities, 181; of exports and imports, 209.
    of sales and purchases, 236.
    of taxes, 250.
    of wages and prices, 267, 300.
Equal rights, 18.
Equilibrium in purchasing power, 301.
Europe, protection in, 73, 313; wages in, 100, 270-272, 274, 305, 367.
Everybody's business, 312.
Evidence on wages before Tariff Commission, 275.
Evolution of nations, 22.
Exaggeration in Germany, 325.

Exchange, 16, 166, 215; its two sides, 245.
Excise of 1791, 92.
Exclusive industries, disasters from, 181.
Expansion of England, 345.
Expenses of living classified, 293.
Experience of maukind, 25, 81, 311.
Export duties, 29, 34, 40, 66.
Exports and imports, equation of, 209.
    of France, 351; of Germany, 351; of Great Britain, 223, 229, 231, 253, 351; of gold aud silver, 217; of the United States, 174, 229, 231, 352.

Fact of freedom of industry, 365.
Fair trade in England, 61, 315, 336.
Fallacies about markets, 235.
Family outlay, 292, 296.
Famiue in Ireland, 251; in lands of a single crop, 181.
Farmers and the tariff, 90, 97, 98, 110, 139, 244; debts and credits of, 206, 212, 213; of the revenue, 35, 38, 39, 53, 58, 64.
Farms, imposts ou, 157, 247.
Fawcett, Professor, admits spread of protection, 80.
    against retaliatory duties, 62.
    on famine in Ireland, 251.
    on emigration, 280.
    on protection in India, 314.
Fees, 34, 71.
Fillmore, Millard, reports tariff of 1842, 108, 124.
Final payment of imposts, 132, 160.
Financial reform in England, 62, 316.
    tasks increased by free trade, 114.
Finished commodities, imposts on, 320.
First American tariff, 85, 88.
Flag, American, on the ocean, 341, 376, 377.
Florence, 451; commerce of, 44; revenue of, 43.
Flower of the American system, 375.
Fluctuations in importations, 95.
    in revenue under low duties, 110.
Food and its cost, 295, 297.
Food supply, failure in England, 252.
Force bill of 1832, 104.
Foreign balances of the United States, how adjusted, 215.
    commerce, rainbow of, 360.
    commodities and domestic imposts, 250.
    competition checked by protective duties, 322.
    debt, how paid, 225.
    exchanges, J. S. Mill on, 216.
    goods, prohibition on, 29, 32.
    markets, creating, 239; and protective duties, 341.
    trade, and home labor, 250, 374; and tariff, 226, 233; Buckle on, 220; gains on, 223. McCulloch on, 244; of Great Britain, 351; to be secured through extension of domestic industry, 340, 376;

INDEX. 383

trade will be restored to the United States, 377.
Forms of trade for individuals and nations the same, 206, 212.
France, 51, 68, 70, 71, 74; and England, wars of, 345, 355; balance of trade against, 227; Cobden's treaty with, 54; exports of, 351; imports of, 351; octroi duty in, 53, 72; patents in, 52, 60; protection in, 52, 54, 78; tobacco monopoly in, 54; workingmen in, 54.
Franklin on taxing the colonies, 83.
Free cities, 69.
   homes or free ports, 364.
   labor most fruitful, 172.
   list and dutiable goods, 123.
   markets impossible, 250.
   production or free trade, 204, 339.
   trade and labor, 330, opposition of British Conservatives to, 338; checks to, 165, 203; compels special industries, 330; cuckoo cry of British, 359; increases financial tasks, 114; movement against, in Holland, 64; McCulloch on, 359; not proved by history, 361; of Great Britain, 349.
   will, most active in the United States, 366.
Free-trade countries, 73.
Freedom and imposts, 137, 164; for homes, 164, 354; industrial, asserted by protective duties, 341; most beneficent in production, 365; of industry, 365; of labor, 172; of production, 165, 203, 365; the gift of nature, 19.
Freight charges and general prices, 285.
French commerce, 226.
   commissioners on American manufactures, 299.
   tariff schedules, 55.
   workingmen and imposts, 54.
Friction of imposts, 144, 161; should be as light as possible, 163.
Frontier, duties collected only on the, 200.

Gains on foreign trade, 223.
Gallatin, Albert, denounces excise, 92; secretary of the treasury, 91, 94; reports a surplus, 94.
Genuine economists, 310, 327.
George, Henry, on land taxes, 142; on poverty and progress, 142.
German commissioners on American production, 299.
Germany, 47, 49, 70, 71, 74, 313, 324, 325; exports of, 351; imports of, 351; protection in, 49; raw materials in, 230.
Ghent, treaty of, 95, 150.
Gibbon on Roman methods, 37, 38, 78.
Gifts, 30, 39.
Gladstone, W. E., and British manufactures, 253; declares the United States the wealthiest nation, 196; "Kin beyond Sea," 196, 233; predicts commercial supremacy of the United States,

233, 377; urges extension of state interference, 363.
Gold and silver, Blanqui on, 217; exports of, 217.
Gold driven from the country, 114.
Goschen, George J., on state interference, 361.
Government, and the people, 361; must interfere, 203; origin of, 17; Otis (James) on, 19; restraints of, 21: title of, to authority, 19; views on, of Grotius, Hobbes, Locke, Rousseau, and Herbert Spencer, 17, 18; views on, of Plato, Sir Thomas More, and Lord Bacon, 21.
Government charges in the United States, France, and Great Britain, 275.
   charges and general prices, 286.
   interference in Britain, 330.
   revenue, 25.
Grain, tax on, 28, 30, 31, 56.
Granger, Francis, of New York, 112.
Great Britain, 55, 68, 70, 71, 74, 79; and the Continent, 305; contrast between United States and, 229; balance of trade against, 223; collects duties on its domestic trade, 350; customs union of, 349; diplomacy of, 347; exports of, 223, 229, 231, 253, 351; imports of, 229, 231, 253, 359, 351; increase of debt and taxation in, 337; iron and steel in, 193; manufactures of, 253; private enterprise, waning in, 331; savings banks in, 281: Seeley on maritime vocation of, 376: supremacy of, 343, 349; trade with China, 240; true foreign commerce of, 352; wages in, 100, 270-272, 274, 305, 367.
See also BRITAIN; BRITISH; ENGLAND.
Great Charter and customs on merchants, 56.
Greece, 34, 70, 71.
Greeley, Horace, on early American statesmen, 85.
Grotius on social compact, 17.
Growth of American manufactures, 194, 268; of colonial trade, 353; of commerce of the United States and Britain, 230; of industries under the tariff, 334; of population in the United States, 331.

Hamburg enters the Zollverein, 50; revenue of, 69.
Hamilton, Alexander, and first tariff. 87, 124: first report from the treasury, 89; report on manufactures, 89.
Happiness in the United States, 266.
Harrisburg. Convention at, in 1827, 100.
Harvests, Malthus on, 179.
Hayne, Robert T., of South Carolina, 102.
Hebrew revenue, 30.
Henry VIII., benevolences of, 57.
History proves there is no free trade, 361.
Hobbes on government, 18.
Holland and England, 346, 355; colonies of, 63; manufactures of, 365; move-

ment against free trade in, 64; revenue of, 62, 71, 74.
Home and foreign markets, 244.
    labor and foreign trade, 250, 374.
        markets, Sidgwick on advantages of, 329.
            production, prices determined by, 247.
Homes, 177, 265, 302; and markets, 376; freedom for, 164, 364.
Humanity and revenue, 221.
Hungary, 49.

Immigrants enter manufactures, 279.
Immigration, admission concerning, 225; extent of, 227, 278; testimony about wages and cost of living, 281; to United States, money value of, 227.
Importations, fluctuations in, 95.
Imported goods, undervaluation of, 154, 250.
Imports and domestic imposts, 250; and exports, equation of, 209, distribution of, 221; of France, 351; of Germany, 351; of Great Britain, 229, 241, 253, 351; of Great Britain, from India, 350; of the United States, 89, 95, 98, 174, 229, 231, 352.
Imposts, aggregate of, 248; and agriculture, 130, 138, 157, 166; and auctions, 145, 151, 184; become an element in cost, 139, 143, 150, 160; and capital, 142, 151, 157, 332; and classes, 158; and earnings, 158, 161; and personal liberty, 198, 201; and services, 136; and sacrifices, 136; consumer and, 146, 166; effect of on consumption, 146; effect of, on consumption in 1866, 122; effect of repeal of, 146; final payment of, 132, 160; friction of, 144, 161, 163; incidence of, 101, 132; law of incidence of, 157; in the United States in 1880, 129; multiplication of, 140, 142, 148, 157, 166, 248, 319; natural collector of, 327; obstruct commerce, 165; on farms, 157, 247; on finished commodities, 320; on personal property, incidence of, 142; on production, 247; on salt, 38, 53, 67, 68, 70, 92, 102, 106, 161; reason for, 138; restrain production, 165; should favor freedom, 164, 166; should not be felt, 1 3; terror in, 163.
Incidence of American imposts, 101, 150, 319; of customs duties, 149, 153; of imposts, 101, 132; of imposts, law of, 157; of imposts on occupations, 143; of imposts on personal property, 142; of income tax, 143; of land tax, 139, 157, 158; of licenses, 143; of taxes on movables, 142, 159, 161; of taxes on necessary articles, 144; of taxes on persons, 144; on wealth and waste, 319.
Incidental protection impracticable, 328.
Income tax, 35, 37, 48, 52, 68, 123, 143, 161; friction of, 161; incidence of, 143.

Increase of agriculture since 1850, 192; of debt and taxation in Britain, 337; of production, 192, 195; of wealth, 195.
Indebtedness of farmers creates panic, 213; of nations, 218.
Independence, national, 177.
India and its revenue, 31, 69, 74; and protection, 74, 314; cost of trade of, 345, 357, 359; struggle for, 347.
Indirect taxes, 137, 316.
Individual rights, 19.
Industrial activity and progress, 267.
    crises, 182.
    freedom, 464.
    theorists, 326.
Industries, growth of, under the tariff, 334; protected, 260.
Industry and commerce, contest between, 339; and education, 373; and science, 868, 373; before commerce in Athens, 77; diversity of, 178, 331, 376; freedom of, 365.
Ingham, Samuel D., of Pennsylvania, 98.
Injustice of British revenue system, 315.
Interference of the state, 360, 365.
Internal and external taxes, 83.
Internal taxes, 48, 52, 92, 144, 157, 199; incidence of, 142, 157; of 1791, in the United States, 92; abolished, 93; of 1813, in the United States, 108; abolished, 108; of 1862, in the United States, 121, 122, 199.
Introduction, 15.
Ireland, famine in, 251; manufactures of, suppressed, 60.
Iron and steel in Britain, 193; in the United States, 192, 268.
Iron, duties on, 92, 97, 100, 108, 112; 116, 117; how to make cheap, 256; manufacture of, 320; mills, wages in, 270; prices of various articles, 288, 296.
Italian republics, 41; spared labor in taxation, 43.
Italy, 70.

Jackson, Andrew 101, 102, 104.
Japan, 70, 74, 313.
Judicious tariff, 101.
Justification of the American system, 365.

"Kin beyond Sea," 196, 233.
Kings as traders, 28, 30, 32, 57.

Labor, American, efficiency of, 304; and capital, ratio between, 275; and civilization, 368; and revenue systems, 307, 330; and wealth, 158, 167; before exchange, 174; effect of efficiency of, on exports, 232; freedom of, 172; in commodities, 248; restrictions on, harmful, 172, 203; skilled, prohibition on, 36, 42, 58, 75; underlies human prosperity, 327.
Land, prices of, 266; property in, 142.

INDEX. 385

Land tax, 28, 30, 31, 36, 38, 40, 48, 51, 55, 62, 67, 71, 130, 138, 142, 157, 161, 166, 247; causes complaint, 139; friction of, 161; Henry George on, 142; incidence of, 138, 157, 158; multiplied more than any other, 140, 142, 159, 166, 247; must be paid in a lump, 159.
Law in the last analysis, 22.
Lawyers and their earnings, 370.
Leather, duties on, 92, 112; prices of, 289.
Legacies and successions tax, invented by Augustus, 38; collected, 69, 123.
Legislation, American, shows eighty years of protection to fifteen of free trade, 126; before 1812, 90; from 1812 to 1832, 105; from 1832 to 1842, 107; from 1857 to 1883, 118; from nullification to compromise, 102; from nullification to secession, 114; of mankind, 81; restrictive, 361; should be adequate, 329; should be deliberate, 328; should be intelligent, 329.
Liberty and wages, 366, 367; infringed, 198.
Licenses, incidence of, 143.
Life, national, 23, 134.
Liquor taxes, 67, 89, 92, 102, 106, 111, 112, 123, 137, 144.
List, Frederick, 84, 309.
Liverpool, wholesale prices in New York and, 288.
Living, cost of, 274, 292-294, 296.
Living expenses, 292, 293.
Loans, 57, 60, 214.
Local taxes, 72, 129, 247; enter into cost of commodities, 247.
Locke, declares labor the only source of wealth, 167; on government, 17, 19; on incidence of all taxes on land, 137.
London and its degradation, 294.
"Spectator" on restoration of protection, 338.
Lotteries taxed, 69.
Lowndes, William, reports tariff of 1816, 97.

Madison, James, on the Constitution, 86; on the tariff, 86, 124.
Making things the beginning of riches, 168.
Mallary, Rollin C., of Vermont, reports tariff of 1828, 101.
Malthus on fine harvests, 179.
Mankind, experience of, 25, 81, 311.
Manufactures, agriculture and, 163, 183, 186, 192; Brougham's proposal to stifle American, 59, 98; cotton, 269, 322; development of, 180, 182, 190, 192, 239, 299; importance of, 167; French commissioners on American, 299; increase of, since 1850, 194; influence of, on land, 189; monopoly in, 334; of Great Britain, 253; persons engaged in the United States, 174; product of, in 1810, 91; in 1830, 107; in 1850, 194; in 1860, 194; in 1870, 194; in 1880, 187, 194; royal, 33; taxed, 28, 40, 123.

Markets and homes, 376; and imposts, 246; and political ties, 354; cost of maintaining, 250; creating foreign, 239; fallacies about, 235; foreign and home, 244; must we buy in the cheapest and sell in the dearest? 236; sacrifices for, 59, 98, 150, 152; shall labor or trade support them? 250; the best, 237, 255, 263, 360.
McCulloch on foreign trade, 244; on free trade, 359.
McDuffie, George, of South Carolina, 101, 102, 104, 111, 113.
Matches, repeal of stamp on, 146.
Mechanics and their wages, 372.
Megara and Athens, 36.
Mercantile theorists, 167, 326.
Merchants pay charges, 28, 30, 49.
Merritt, Consul-General E. A., report of, 272, 292.
Mexico, 70.
Military service, 72.
Mill, J. S., on foreign exchanges, 216; on wages, 300.
Mines, 28, 33, 34, 39.
Mining industries in United States and other nations, 195.
Ministers and their salaries, 370, 371.
Modern nations, sources of their revenue, 66, 71; and protection, 73, 81.
practices abroad and at home, 66.
Moiety laws repealed, 120.
Money, purchasing power of, 301.
Monopolies, 54, 58, 67; by patents, 335; in manufactures, 334.
Montesquieu on poll-tax, 162.
More, Sir Thomas, views on government, 21.
Morrill, Justin S., 113, 115-117.
Morrill tariff, 115.
Movables, incidence of taxes on, 142, 159, 161.
Multiplication of imposts, 140, 142, 143, 157, 166, 248, 319.

National commerce, the sum of individual trade, 206.
duration and production, 355.
government to levy taxes and regulate commerce, 84.
independence, 177.
life, 23, 134; agriculture and, 356.
Nations, aggrandizement of, 354; duration of, 355; elements of, 22; evolution of, 22; have distinct characters, 23; how divided relative to protection, 73; indebtedness of, 218; necessary, 23, 25; their authority cited, 73, 81.
Navies necessary to commerce, 358.
Navy, maintained to support trade, 347; of England founded, 346.
Necessary articles, incidence of taxes on, 144.
Netherlands, revenue of, 62, 70, 71, 74.
New England and the tariff, 101, 103.
New industries make fresh prizes, 180, 190.

New World, struggles for, 58, 345.
New York, wholesale prices in Liverpool and, 288.
Non-interference at seaports, 364.
Norway, 70.
No tariff at all, 315, 316.
Nullification, 104; to compromise, 102, 124.

Obstacles to commerce, imposts, 165, 203; to the Union, 84.
Occupations, persons employed in various, 174.
Occupation taxes, 38, 40, 48, 69, 123, 143; incidence of, 143.
Ocean, American flag on the, 341, 376, 377.
Ocean trade, how recovered, 377; must follow production, 360.
Octroi of France, 53, 72.
Old World methods, 26.
Opposition to any tariff at all, 315.
Order from conflict, 20.
Origin of government, 17; of protection, 75.
Otis, James, on government, 19.
Our greatest revenues, 122.
Overproduction, 180.

Panics, 113, 118.
Passenger fares and general prices, 283.
Patentes in France, 52, 53, 69.
Patents confer monopoly, 335.
Patriotism, 134.
Peabody Trust, report on wages, 274.
Peace, American policy of, 360; and commerce, 255.
Peculiar sources of revenue, 69.
Peloponnesian war, 36.
People and the government, 361.
Peppercorn financiers, William Pitt on, 178.
Period from the revolution to the war of 1812, 90; from 1812 to nullification, 105; between nullification and secession, 114; of the civil war, 118.
Persia, 32, 75.
Personal liberty and imposts, 198, 201.
    property, incidence of imposts on, 142.
    service, 28, 33, 35, 72.
Persons, tax on, 35, 38, 48, 56, 130, 144; natural to servitude, 162.
Phœnician colonies, 33.
    commerce, 32.
    revenue, 32.
Physicians and their earnings, 370.
Physiocratic school, 326.
Pig-iron, development of, 192; in the United States and Britain, 193.
Pitt, William, for customs duties in the colonies, 83; on peppercorn financiers, 178; seeks in Germany to conquer America, 346; taxation no part of governing power, 83.
Place to sell and to buy, 235.
Plato's Republic, 21, 168.
Poets are makers, 374.

Political economy an applied science, 309; Professor Cairnes on, 309; defined, 15; everybody's business, 312; is it a science, 24, 309; must promote production, 166; schools of, 326; sphere of, 16, 312; Sidgwick's, 80, 181; Stewart's, 60.
    science, mission of, 311.
    ties and markets, 354.
Poll-tax. See CAPITATION TAX, and PERSONS, TAX ON.
Population and employment, 174; and wages, 366; growth of, in United States, 331.
Porter, Robert P., on wages, 270.
Portugal, 70.
Poseidon, Athena and, 77.
Poverty and progress, 142.
Poverty in London, 294.
Power, concentration of, 362.
Preface, 3.
Price of British commerce, 343, 354.
Prices, determined by home production, 247; equation of wages and, 267, 300; lowered by the tariff, 339; of commodities, 287, 292, 296; of land, 266; of leather, 289; retail, in New York State and rural Britain, 296.
Private enterprise, waning in Britain, 331.
Privileges by patents, 335.
Prizes offered to producers, 368, 373.
Problem of revenue, 314.
Production, 16, 165, 179; and commerce, 165, 168, 377; and national duration, 355; and revenue, 246, 328; and tariff, 192; and trade, question between, 204; and wages, 374; British, 304; freedom of, 165, 203, 365; importance of, 168; imposts on, 247; increase of, 192, 195; ocean trade must follow, 360; persons engaged in, 174; restrained by imposts, 165; sacrificed to commerce in Britain, 254; stimulated by protective duties, 161, 194; the condition of commerce, 250.
Productive supremacy of the United States, 233, 359.
Professional men and their earnings, 369, 370.
Profits of commerce, 221, 245.
" Progress and Poverty," by Henry George, 142.
Prohibition on foreign goods, 29, 32; on skilled labor, 36, 42, 58, 75.
Property in land, 142.
Prosecutions in Prussia, 49.
Protected industries, 260.
Protection and modern nations, 73, 81; alternatives of, 308; at Athens, 76; begins in the United States with the Constitution, 86; Cromwell and, 75, 78; favored by Aristotle, 36; favored by Calhoun, 97; German commissioners on American, 299; in all Europe, 73, 313; in Australia, 73, 313; in Austria, 49, 74; in British colonies, 73,

313 ; in England, 59, 79, 315, 338 ; in France, 52, 54, 78 ; in Germany, 49 ; in India, 74, 314 ; in Japan, 74, 313 ; in Rome, 78 ; of industries, 260 ; origin, 75 ; practiced by Julius Cæsar, 47, 78 ; prohibited by Constitution of Southern Confederacy, 124 ; "Spectator" on restoration of, 338 ; spread of, 80 ; stimulates production, 161, 194.

Protective duties, and a foreign market, 341 ; and the carrying trade, 341 ; assert industrial freedom, 341 ; Blanqui on the effect of, 192 ; collected in British colonies, 314, 350 ; enlist idle capital and labor, 332 ; may fall on foreign producer, 155 ; should be adequate, 329 ; should be changed only for reason, 323 ; should be moderate to be permanent, 324 ; should favor American labor, 323 ; should offset internal taxes, 250, 322 ; stimulate production, 161, 194 ; system interferes with commerce, 341 ; will check undue foreign competition and excessive prices, 322.

Prussia, its revenue, 48, 63, 70, 71.
  prosecutions in, 49.
Public lands, 28, 30, 31, 33, 34, 36, 40, 51, 67, 71 ; of the United States, 67, 94.
Purchases and sales, equation of, 236.
Purchasing power of money, 301.

"Quarterly Review" on British taxation, 337.
Quesnay and his school, 167, 326.
Question between production and trade, 204.

Railroad charges, 283, 285.
Railroads, their testimony about wages and prices, 283 ; taxed, 68, 71, 123, 130.
Rails, Bessemer, 152.
Rainbow of foreign commerce, 360.
Rates of duties in 1789, 88 : from 1791 to 1809, 91 ; to 1812, 94 ; from 1812 to 1815, 95 ; 1816 to 1817, 98 ; from 1824 to 1827, 100 : in 1828, 101 ; from 1831 to 1842, 107 ; 1844, 108 ; from 1846 to 1856, 112 ; in tariff of 1857, 131 ; in tariff of 1861, 116 ; lowest and highest under several tariffs, 126.
Ratio of labor to capital, in the United States, France, and Britain, 275 ; of various items of expenses of living, 293, 296 ; of wages to prices, 265.
Raw materials, 32, 90, 111, 140, 256, 320 ; in Germany, 260.
Recent revenue legislation protective, 74.
Reform, English financial, 62, 316.
Relations of government to the people, 361.
Rent, share of, in cost of living, 293, 297.
Repeal of imposts, effect of, 146.
Republic, Plato's, 21, 163.
Restoration of American shipping, 341, 377.

Restraints on production, 165 ; restrictions imposed by England on American colonies, 58 ; on commerce, 36, 165 ; on labor, harmful, 172, 203 ; on trade, 203.
Restrictive legislation, 361.
Retail prices in New York State and rural Britain, 296.
Retaliatory duties, Professor Fawcett against, 62.
Revenue and commerce, 246 ; and humanity, 220 ; and production, 246, 328 ; Burke on, 173 ; cost of collection, 64 ; farmers of, 35, 38, 39, 53, 58, 64 ; fluctuations of, under low duties, 110 ; must favor production, 204 ; of Assyria, 31 ; of Attica, 34 ; of Carthage, 32 ; of China, 39, 66 ; of Egypt, 28, 39. 71, 75 ; of England, 55 ; of Florence, 43, 451 ; of Great Britain, 60, 61 ; of Hamburg, 69 ; Hebrew, 30 ; of India, 31, 69, 74 ; of modern nations, 66, 71 ; of Prussia, 32, 48, 68, 71 ; of Rome, 36, 78 ; of Spain, 62, 67, 71 ; peculiar sources of, 69 ; problem of, 314 ; standard, 103, 109 ; uniformity of laws of, 25, 81 ; voluntary payments of, 137, 200.
  legislation, earliest American, 85 ; American, favors production, 313.
  systems and labor, 307, 330.
Revolutionary period, 90.
Revolution started from revenue, 83.
Rights at sea, 94 ; individual, 19.
Rivalries of commerce, 36, 341.
Roman methods, Gibbon on, 37, 38, 78.
Rome and its revenue, 36, 78.
Rousseau on social contract, 18.
Royal manufactures, 33.
Ruskin on custom houses, 79.
Russia, 70 ; and its methods, 63, 71, 75.

Sacrifices and imposts, 136.
Salaries of clergymen, 370.
Sales and purchases, equation of, 236 ; tax on, 123.
Salt, consumption of, 148 ; imposts on, 38, 53, 67, 68, 70. 92. 102, 106, 161.
Savings banks in the United States and Britain, 281.
Say and agriculture, 186 ; nations pay for products with products, 216 ; on sphere of political economy, 312.
Schools of political economy, 326.
Science and industry, 368, 373 ; of revenue, 309.
Sciences of administration, 308.
Sea, rights at, 94.
Seaports, non-interference at, 364.
Secession, 104, 113, 115, 116, 124.
Seeley, Professor, expansion of England, 345 ; on free will in the United States, 366 ; on happiness in the Unit-

ed States, 266, 477; on maritime vocation of Britain, 376.
Selling in order to buy, 205, 246.
Sell where you must, 236, 246.
Semper ab omnibus ubique, 81.
Senior on sphere of the economist, 310.
Serfdom bequeathed low wages, 366.
Service, personal, 28, 33, 35, 72.
Services and imposts, 136; in trade, 211.
Shaw, Consul A. D., on wages, 272.
Sherman, John, 115, 116, 124.
Shipping and domestic trade, 341; restoration of American, 341, 377.
Shipping, first American charges on, 88.
Sidgwick, Henry, on advantages of home markets, 329; on free trade and labor, 330; on underproduction, 181; political economy, 80, 181; protective duties may fall on foreign producer, 155.
Silk, duties on, 31, 99, 102.
Silks American, production of, 155, 269; fall in prices of, 156; surplus of, 152; undervaluation of, 154.
Silver and gold, Blanqui on, 217.
Sismondi and consumption, 170.
Skilled labor, prohibition on, 36, 42, 58, 75.
    mechanics and their earnings, 372.
    men, demand for, 369.
Slavery, 102, 103, 105, 125, 200.
Slums of London, 294.
Smith, Adam, 167, 186, 326.
Socialistic tendencies, 363.
Social compact unknown to history, 18.
Society a necessity, 17.
Solomon's House of Lord Bacon, 21.
Solomon's importations and trade, 30, 75.
South Carolina, 102-104, 107, 112.
Southern Confederacy destroys our commerce, 342; its constitution prohibits protection, 125.
    leaders, 101-103, 105, 107, 113, 115, 124.
Spain and its revenue, 62, 67, 70, 71.
Spanish war and foreign trade, 346, 355.
Specializing industries under free trade, 330.
Specific duties, 87, 99, 109, 110, 116.
"Spectator" on restoration of protection, 338.
Spencer, Herbert, on state interference, 362.
    on the state, 18.
Spoils and tributes, 28, 31, 34, 39.
Stability needed, 324.
    of employment, 330.
Stamp tax in the colonies, 83.
Stamps, 68, 69, 71, 123; on matches, repeal of, 146.
State, sphere of the, 21, 134, 361.
State interference, 360-363, 365; increases taxation, 363; renders its best service in fostering production, 365.
State taxes, 72, 248.

Statesmen, American, and the tariff, 85.
    business of, 310.
Statistics of wages, 270.
Stevens, Thaddeus, 115, 117.
Stewart's "Political Economy," 60.
Stuarts and taxation, 57.
Sugar, consumption of, 147; duties on, 68, 91-93, 112, 119.
Sumner, Professor William G., before Tariff Commission, 186, 310.
Superiority of certain American manufactures, 290.
Supremacy of Great Britain, 343, 349; of the United States, 233, 359, 377.
Surplus, at Athens, 35; commodities, 59, 98, 145, 150, 152, 184; in treasury, 94, 102, 108.
Sweden, 70.
Switzerland, 70.
Systems of revenue, choice between American and British, 339.

Table of revenue of modern nations, 71; of salary of ministers, 371.
Tariff and foreign trade, 226, 233; and production, 192; British, 61; debate on, 97, 99, 101, 103, 105, 109, 110, 113, 115, 117; distress relieved by, 112; experience, American, 313; for revenue, 103, 108, 109; influence of Calhoun on, 124; judicious, 101; legislation not complex, 86; Madison on the, 86, 124; prices lowered by, 339.
Tariff Commission, 186, 275, 310; and wages, 275.
Tariffs. See AMERICAN TARIFFS.
Task of the United States, 376.
Taxation and Stuarts, 57; indirect, 316; no part of governing power, 83; of corporations, 68, 71, 123, 130, 162; of manufactures, 28, 40, 123; of States and local divisions, 67, 129, 248; "Quarterly Review" on British, 337; state interference increases, 363.
Taxes, American colonists against, 83; class, 35, 36, 48; direct, 137, 142, 144, 316; equation of, 250; incidence of, 142, 157; indirect, 137, 316; internal, 48, 52, 92, 144, 157, 199; on business plants, 139; on farms, 139; on movables, incidence of, 142, 159, 161; on necessary articles, 144; on occupations, 38, 40, 48, 69, 123, 143; on personal property, 142; on sales, 123; on tenements, 139; State, 72, 248.
Tax-gatherer, the agent of restraint, 198; complaints of the, 199.
Tea, 68, 88, 91, 92, 102, 117-120, 147, 148, 157, 317, 350.
Telegraphs taxed, 68, 71, 123.
Tenements, taxes on, 139.
Terror in imposts, 163.
Testimony, before the Tariff Commission on wages, 275; of Chancellor Bismarck, 196; of French and German commissions, 299; of the nations, 73.
Theorists, mercantile, 167, 326.

INDEX. 389

Time, divisions of, in our revenue, 123.
Tobacco, growth prohibited in England, 60; monopoly in France, 54; tax, 67, 70, 93, 112, 122, 123, 144, 161.
Tonnage dues, 89.
Trade, adverse balance of, dangerous, 218; and production, 204; and war, 345; attitude of the nations on, 219; restrictions on, 203; services in, 211.
Traders, kings as, 23, 30, 32, 57.
Transportation, 168, 219.
Treasury, surplus in, 94, 102, 108.
Treaties of commerce, 34, 54.
Treaty of Ghent, 95, 150.
Tributes and spoils, 23, 31, 34, 39.
True foreign commerce of Britain, 352.
Turgot proposes a single impost, 52.
Turkey, 70; cost of trade of, 347, 357; part of British possessions, 352.
Two profits in commerce, 245.
Tyrian commerce, 33.

Underproduction, 181.
Undervaluation of imported goods, 154, 250.
Uniformity of the laws of revenue, 25, 81.
United States, abolition of internal taxes, 92, 93, 108; and Great Britain contrasted, 229; balance of trade and, 227; Bismarck on development of, 197; British capital in, 224; British trade with, 238, 241; causes of their development, 264; commerce of, 227; commercial supremacy of, 233, 377; declared by Gladstone the wealthiest nation, 196; development of pig-iron in, 193; employments in, 174; exports of, 174, 229, 231, 352; foreign balances of, how adjusted, 215; growth of population in, 331; happiness in, 266; has a task, 23, 376; imports of, 89, 95, 98, 174, 229, 231, 352; imposts in, in 1880, 129; iron and steel in, 192, 268; mining industries in, 195; money value of immigration to, 227; persons engaged in manufactures in, 174; productive supremacy of, 233, 359; public lands of, 67, 94; savings banks in, 281; Seeley on free will in, 366; trade with China, 239; wages in, 110, 270, 272, 274, 305, 372; wealth of, 195; workingmen in, 265.
Utopia, 21.

Venetian commerce, 42, 355.
Venice and its manufactures, 355; and its revenues, 41; and protection, 46.
Virtue has a sphere in revenue, 173.

Vital point in the discussion, 365.
Voluntary payments of revenue, 187, 200.

Wages, advantages of high, 265, 307, 373; and commerce, 358, 374; and liberty, 366, 367; and population, 366; and prices, equation of, 267, 300; and production, 374; and revenue systems, 307; benefits of high, 265, 307, 373; consular reports on, 272, 274; effect of caste on, 366; evidence on, before Tariff Commission, 275; in Britain and in Europe, 100, 270-272, 274, 305, 367; in the United States, 110, 270, 272, 274, 305, 372; John Bright on, 271; J. S. Mill on, 300; low, bequeathed by serfdom, 366; of mechanics, 372; Report of Peabody Trust on, 274; Robert P. Porter on, 270; statistics of, 270; tend upward, 303, 320; the type of government, 366.
Walker, Robert J., Secretary of the Treasury, report, 109, 124, 125.
War and commerce, 94, 176, 255, 345, 346, 354, 357, 358; and trade, 345; loans, 214; how adjusted, 215; of 1812, 59, 94, 341, 347; Peloponnesian, 36.
War revenues, culmination of, 117, 122.
Wars for America and India, 58, 78; for commerce, Peloponnesian, 36; Spanish succession, 78; with France, 78, 345, 355; with Holland, 79, 346, 355; with China, 40, 347, 357.
Washington signs the first tariff, 85.
Waste and wealth taxed, 319.
Wealth, accumulation of, 210; and labor, 158, 167; increase of, 195; of the United States and other nations, 195.
Wealthiest of all nations, 196.
Webster, Daniel, 97, 99, 101, 124; for protective duties, 101, 105, 110.
Wholesale prices in New York and Liverpool, 288.
Wool and woolens, duties on, 92, 97, 99-101, 112. 116, 119.
Wool, growth of production of, 258, 268; how to get it most cheaply, 256; prices of, 258; Silas Wright on, 101.
Woolen mills, wages in Scotland and New York, 272.
Workingmen against the British system, 336; in France, 54; in United States, 265.
Wright, Silas, on wool, 101; on tariff of 1842, 108.

Zollverein, 50, 66, 69.

www.ingramcontent.com/pod-product-compliance
Lightning Source LLC
Chambersburg PA
CBHW032021220426
43664CB00006B/326